'A welcome and very helpful guide to Hume's masterpiece, *A Treatise of Human Nature*. Students will find it both accessible and engaging, and even scholars of Hume's *Treatise* will profit from reading Kail's book.'
Miren Boehm, *University of Wisconsin-Milwaukee, USA*

The Routledge Guidebook to Hume's *A Treatise of Human Nature*

David Hume is widely acknowledged as the greatest philosopher to have written in the English language. His 1739/40 *A Treatise of Human Nature* is commonly regarded as his masterpiece. It is a profound work of great ambition, seeking to reorient philosophy by establishing a 'science of human nature'.

Following the structure of the original work closely, *The Routledge Guidebook to Hume's A Treatise of Human Nature* provides a clear and accessible introduction to its key themes, and explores:

- the lasting philosophical significance of the work
- the context of Hume's philosophy
- the character of Hume's theory of human nature
- the two central themes of scepticism and naturalism
- the unity of the three original volumes.

Written for readers approaching Hume's seminal work for the first time, this guidebook includes a helpful overview of the text, chapter summaries and further reading throughout. It is an essential introduction for undergraduate students studying the history of modern philosophy, and all those who wish to engage more deeply with this classic work.

P. J. E. Kail is Official Fellow and Tutor in Philosophy at St Peter's College, and an Associate Professor in the Faculty of Philosophy, University of Oxford, UK. He is the author of, among other things, *Projection and Realism in Hume's Philosophy* (2007), *Berkeley's A Treatise Concerning the Principles of Knowledge* (2014), and *Simply Nietzsche* (2019).

THE ROUTLEDGE GUIDES TO THE GREAT BOOKS

The *Routledge Guides to the Great Books* provide ideal introductions to the texts which have shaped Western Civilization. The Guidebooks explore the arguments and ideas contained in the most influential works from some of the most brilliant thinkers who have ever lived, from Aristotle to Marx and Newton to Wollstonecraft. Each Guidebook opens with a short introduction to the author of the great book and the context within which they were working and concludes with an examination of the lasting significance of the book. The *Routledge Guides to the Great Books* will therefore provide students everywhere with complete introductions to the most significant books of all time.

James's Principles of Psychology
David E Leary

Berkeley's Three Dialogues
Stefan Storrie

Smith's Wealth of Nations
Maria Pia Paganelli

Paine's Rights of Man
Frances A. Chiu

Moore's Principia Ethica
Susana Nuccetelli

Nietzsche's Thus Spoke Zarathustra
Matthew Meyer

Hume's A Treatise of Human Nature
P. J. E. Kail

For more information about this series, please visit:
https://www.routledge.com/The-Routledge-Guides-to-the-Great-Books/book-series/RGGB

The Routledge Guidebook to Hume's *A Treatise of Human Nature*

P. J. E.
Kail

LONDON AND NEW YORK

First published 2025
by Routledge
4 Park Square, Milton Park, Abingdon, Oxon OX14 4RN

and by Routledge
605 Third Avenue, New York, NY 10158

Routledge is an imprint of the Taylor & Francis Group, an informa business

© 2025 P. J. E. Kail

The right of P. J. E. Kail to be identified as author of this work has been asserted by them in accordance with sections 77 and 78 of the Copyright, Designs and Patents Act 1988.

All rights reserved. No part of this book may be reprinted or reproduced or utilised in any form or by any electronic, mechanical, or other means, now known or hereafter invented, including photocopying and recording, or in any information storage or retrieval system, without permission in writing from the publishers.

Trademark notice: Product or corporate names may be trademarks or registered trademarks, and are used only for identification and explanation without intent to infringe.

British Library Cataloguing-in-Publication Data
A catalogue record for this book is available from the British Library

Library of Congress Cataloging-in-Publication Data
Names: Kail, P. J. E. (Peter J. E.), author.
Title: The Routledge guidebook to Hume's A treatise of human nature / P.J.E. Kail.
Description: Abingdon, Oxon; New York, NY: Routledge, 2025. | Includes bibliographical references and index.
Identifiers: LCCN 2024050544 (print) | LCCN 2024050545 (ebook) | ISBN 9781138943445 (hardback) | ISBN 9781138943551 (paperback) | ISBN 9781315667874 (ebook)
Subjects: LCSH: Hume, David, 1711–1776. Treatise of human nature. | Knowledge, Theory of.
Classification: LCC B1489 .K35 2025 (print) | LCC B1489 (ebook) | DDC 128—dc23/eng/20250103
LC record available at https://lccn.loc.gov/2024050544
LC ebook record available at https://lccn.loc.gov/2024050545

ISBN: 978-1-138-94344-5 (hbk)
ISBN: 978-1-138-94355-1 (pbk)
ISBN: 978-1-315-66787-4 (ebk)

DOI: 10.4324/9781315667874

Typeset in Times New Roman
by codeMantra

For Teddy and Steph

Contents

Preface and Acknowledgments ... xi
Abbreviations and Citations to Primary Literature ... xii

Introduction ... 1

1 Of Ideas, Their Origin, Composition, Connexion, Abstraction, Etc. ... 23

2 Of the Ideas of Space and Time ... 44

3 Of Knowledge and Probability ... 55

4 Of the Sceptical and Other Systems of Philosophy ... 99

5 Of Pride and Humility, Love and Hatred ... 133

6 Of the Will and Direct Passions ... 152

7 Of Virtue and Vice in General ... 177

| 8 | **Of Justice and Injustice** | **188** |
| 9 | **Of the Other Virtues and Vices** | **205** |

Bibliography of Secondary Literature — 223
Index — 231

Preface and Acknowledgments

There are countless persons from whom I have learned and with whom I have discussed Hume and I am grateful to each and every one. I would like, however, to single out my graduate students who are now friends and from whom I have learned so much and not just about philosophy. They are Kevin Busch, Christopher Fowles, Haruko Inoue, Alessio Vaccari, and Gabe Watts. I am also grateful for the comments from the anonymous readers for Routledge, and I have followed their advice in most things.

I am grateful for fine editorial assistance from Emily Daly, funded by the John O'Connor Research Fund.

ABBREVIATIONS AND CITATIONS TO PRIMARY LITERATURE

References to Hume's texts are parenthetical, according to the conventions below. All italics in quotations are original unless otherwise noted.

A Treatise of Human Nature: T, followed by Book, Part, Section, and paragraph numbers in the Clarendon Edition, ed. D. Fate Norton & M. J. Norton (Oxford: Clarendon Press, 2007). References to the *Abstract*, in the same volume, are marked *Abstract*, followed by paragraph number, and to the *Appendix*, T App., followed by paragraph number. References to the introduction are T Intro., followed by paragraph number.

A Letter from A Gentleman to his Friend in Edinburgh: LG, followed by paragraph number, in the Norton & Norton edition of the *Treatise* above.

An Enquiry Concerning Human Understanding: EHU, followed by Section and paragraph number in the Clarendon edition, ed. T. Beauchamp (Oxford: Clarendon Press, 1998).

Dialogues Concerning Natural Religion: DNR, followed by Part and paragraph number in the Cambridge edition, ed. D. Coleman (Cambridge: Cambridge University Press, 2007).

A Dissertation on the Passions: D, followed by Section and paragraph number cited from *A Dissertation on the Passions and the Natural History of Religion*, ed. T. Beauchamp (Oxford: Clarendon Press, 2007).

An Enquiry Concerning the Principles of Morals: EPM, followed by Section and paragraph number in the Clarendon edition, ed. T. Beauchamp (Oxford: Clarendon Press, 1998). The Appendices are referred to by AP, number, and paragraph number. *A Dialogue*, in the same volume is cited as *A Dialogue*, followed by paragraph number.

The Letters of David Hume: HL, followed by volume and page number, ed. J. Y. T. Greig (Oxford: Oxford University Press, 1932), 2 volumes.

Essays: Moral, Political, and Literary: EMPL, followed by page number, ed. E. F. Miller (Indianapolis: Liberty Press, 1985).

OTHER PRIMARY TEXTS

Bayle, P., *Historical and Critical Dictionary: Selections*, ed. R. Popkin (Indianapolis: Hackett, 1991).

Burke, E., *A Philosophical Enquiry into the Origin of our Ideas of the Sublime and Beautiful* (Cambridge: Cambridge Library Collection, 2014).

Clarke, S., *A Discourse Concerning the Unchangeable Obligations of Natural Religion, and the Truth and Certainty of the Christian Religion* 5th edn (London: Knapton, 1719).

Hobbes, T., *Leviathan*, ed. C. Brooke (London: Penguin, 2017).

Hutcheson, F., *An Inquiry into the Original of Our Ideas of Beauty and Virtue* ed. W. Leidhold (Indianapolis: Liberty Press, 2004).

Hutcheson, F., *An Essay on the Nature and the Conduct of the Passions, with Illustrations on the Moral Sense*, ed. A. Garrett (Indianapolis: Liberty Press, 2002).

Leibniz, G. W., *The Monadology,* ed. N. Rescher (London: Routledge, 1992).

Leibniz, G. W., *New Essays on Human Understanding,* ed. P. Remnant and J. Bennett, (Cambridge: Cambridge University Press, 1996).

Locke, J., *An Essay Concerning Human Understanding,* ed. P. H. Nidditch (Oxford: Clarendon Press, 1975).

Malebranche, N., *The Search After Truth*, ed. T. M. Lennon and P. J. Olscamp (Cambridge: Cambridge University Press, 1997).

Malebranche, N., *Treatise on Ethics*, ed. C. Walton (Dordrecht: Kluwer, 1993).

Newton, I., *Philosophical Writings*, ed. A. Janiak (rev. edn) (Cambridge: Cambridge University Press, 2014).

Stewart, D., 1829, *An Account of the Life of Adam Smith*. In *Collected Works*, Vol. 7. (Cambridge: Hilliard and Brown, 1829).

INTRODUCTION

A BRIEF BIOGRAPHY

David Hume was born in Edinburgh on 26 April 1711.[1] His father, Joseph, died when Hume was very young, so he was raised by his mother, Katherine, together with his elder brother, also named Joseph, and his sister, also named Katherine. His name was originally spelled 'Home', but he changed it in 1734 to avoid the English habit of mispronouncing it. The family estate, Ninewells in Berwickshire, was destined to go to his elder brother, so David had to think of a way to make his fortune. He went up to Edinburgh University, then called the College of Edinburgh, in 1721 to study law. It was a subject for which he showed little enthusiasm, saying in 'My Own Life', his autobiography written late in his life, that he 'found an insurmountable aversion to every thing but the pursuits of philosophy and general learning'.[2]

Leaving without taking a degree, as was common at the time, Hume spent a few months working in Bristol before leaving for France. In a letter to an unknown physician dated 1734, Hume reports two things. First, that at the age of 18 he had discovered 'a new Scene of Thought', one which had 'transported [him] beyond Measure, & made [him], with an Ardour natural to young men, throw up every other Pleasure or Business to apply entirely to it'.[3] We do not know what this 'new Scene of Thought' might be, but presumably it fed into the content of the *Treatise*. Second, the intense philosophical study into which Hume threw himself began to affect his health in various ways, both physically and mentally. He consulted another doctor who declared that Hume was suffering from the 'Disease of the Learned'. His health varied as he tried different remedies such as moderating his study, 'anti-hysteric pills', drinking a pint of red wine a day, and riding. Nevertheless, he was never quite free from his 'distemper' and concomitant physical symptoms, and, breaking from his studies and his 'inflam'd imaginations', he resolved to 'consider seriously how [he] should proceed in [his] Philosophical Enquires'.[4] As we shall see, Hume dramatises the effect of intense philosophical study towards the end of Book One of the *Treatise* and it is highly probable that his own experience is reflected there.

It was in France that Hume composed the bulk of the *Treatise*. He lived modestly in La Flèche, in Anjou, which is situated near the Jesuit college where Descartes was educated. In 1737 he went to London to find a publisher. He was not successful immediately and spent about a year editing his work before securing the services of John Noon, who published Books One and Two of the *Treatise* in January 1739. Book Three was published separately by Thomas Longman in 1740. Hume expressed disappointment in its reception, writing in 'My Own Life' that the work '*fell dead born from the press*; without reaching such a distinction as even to excite a Murmur among the Zealots'.[5]

This is somewhat of an exaggeration, but we will discuss this and the *Treatise* as a book in more detail in the next section. Hume continued to write and publish, despite his disappointment, though this time he wrote in essay form, publishing *Essays, Moral and Political* in 1741. This was a rather more successful endeavour. Perhaps emboldened by this success, Hume applied for, but failed to secure, the Chair of Ethics and Pneumatical Philosophy at Edinburgh in 1745. His failure was a legacy of the *Treatise*. Although it was published anonymously, a common practice during the period, it was well known that Hume was its author, and what's more, its contents were held to be dangerous to religion. A pamphlet circulated against Hume, and he attempted to discharge the accusations levelled against him by publishing a reply titled, *A Letter from a Gentleman to his Friend in Edinburgh*. All of this was to no avail.

After a brief tenure as a tutor to the Marquess of Annandale, Hume became secretary to General St Clair, and spent further time in France. Hume was still writing, recasting much of the material from Book One of the *Treatise*, under the initial title *Philosophical Essays in Human Understanding*, which later became *An Enquiry Concerning Human Understanding*. In 1751 he published *An Enquiry Concerning the Principles of Morals*, and in 1752 *Political Discourses*. He was also working on the *Four Dissertations*, which was published in 1757, and *Dialogues Concerning Natural Religion*, a work that would be published posthumously. After another failed attempt to get a university chair, this time at Glasgow, he became Keeper of the Advocates Library in Edinburgh, a position he held until 1757. This provided him with the opportunity to research and write his very successful six-volume *History of England*.

In 1763 Hume became the private secretary to the British Ambassador in Paris. There he was the darling of French society, striking up something of a relationship with the Comtesse de Boufflers, and mixing with Diderot and other *philosophes*. Among them was Jean-Jacques Rousseau, who had been expelled from Switzerland, and whom Hume invited to accompany him to England. Sadly, the two soon fell out, Rousseau accusing Hume of plotting against him. Hume returned to Edinburgh and, eventually, to a new house in New Town since the kitchen in his old house was, he tells Sir Gilbert Elliot, 'too small to display [his] great Talent for Cookery, the Science to which [he] intend[s] to addict the remaining Years of [his] Life'.[6] (He claimed his beef and cabbage to be a 'charming dish', and that 'nobody excels' him in his old mutton and claret.) There he lived his remaining years with his sister until his death in 1776.

THE *TREATISE*

The full title of the *Treatise* is *A Treatise of Human Nature: Being an Attempt to Introduce the Experimental Method of Reasoning into Moral Subjects*. It comprises an introduction and three books, one on the understanding, one on the passions, and one on morals. The first two books were published in 1739. 'Of morals' was published in 1740, a volume that contained an appendix to Book One in which Hume makes some corrections since 'some of [his] expressions have not been so well chosen' (T App. 1), and in which he confesses a problem with his account of personal identity.

Hume claimed that the *Treatise* fell 'dead-born from the press', but, as already noted, this is somewhat of an exaggeration. There were reviews, the first in late 1739, but none was particularly good, seeing in the work a deeply sceptical tone and principles dangerous to religion. These charges were repeated in the pamphlet attacking Hume when he was trying for the chair in Edinburgh, and they are not altogether groundless, as we shall see. About ten years later, Hume wrote in a letter that the 'Heat of Youth & Invention [caused him] to publish too precipitately',[7] and even in 1740 he confessed to 'some Impatience for a second Edition principally on Account of Alterations [he] intend[s] to make in [his] Performance', suggesting that he was guilty of 'a very Great Temerity to publish at [his] Years so many Noveltys in so delicate a Part of Philosophy'.[8] His disappointment with the reception of the *Treatise* led him to publish anonymously *An Abstract of a Book Lately Published; Entituled A Treatise of Human Nature, &c.*, his own review of Books One and Two. Often appended to modern editions of the *Treatise*, it provides a useful summary of, and entryway into, Books One and Two, but did not bolster the reputation of the book.

Nevertheless, the *Treatise* continued to be read during Hume's lifetime (and, obviously, beyond) but its association with Hume continued to be problematic for him. We have already noted how it was used against Hume when he tried for the Edinburgh chair, but the work continued to attract criticism after his failure to get the chair, much of which seems fundamentally misplaced. Critics included Thomas Reid and James Beattie, both of whom were professors in Scottish universities, the latter of whom published a particularly vituperative, and bestselling, attack on Hume's philosophy in 1770. Less than a year before his death, Hume instructed his publisher to append an advertisement to his collected works as a 'compleat Answer to Dr. Reid and that bigotted silly Fellow, Beattie'.[9] There, Hume asks that the later writings (*An Enquiry Concerning Human Understanding, An Enquiry Concerning the*

Principles of Morals and the 'Dissertation on the Passions') be taken as 'containing his philosophical sentiments and principles'. He writes that most of his thoughts and reasonings contained in these works:

> ...were published in a work in three volumes, called A *Treatise of Human Nature*: A work which the Author had projected before he left College, and which he wrote and published not long after. But not finding it successful, he was sensible of his error in going to the press too early, and cast the whole anew in the following pieces, where some negligences in his former reasoning and more in the expression, are corrected. Yet several writers, who have honoured the Author's Philosophy with answers, have taken care to direct all their batteries against that juvenile work which the author never acknowledged, and have affected to triumph in any advantages, which they imagined, they had obtained over it: A practice very contrary to all the rules of candour and fair-dealing, and a strong instance of those polemical artifaces, which a bigotted Zeal thinks himself authorized to employ.[10]

Most commentators, however, disregard this advertisement and see the *Treatise* as Hume's masterpiece. The tone of the advertisement is unlike Hume's normal moderate prose, suggesting an impatience with the polemical and rhetorical responses garnered by the *Treatise*. What Hume tells us about the *Treatise* is that he was young when he composed it, that it is the manner of its presentation rather than its content that he regrets, and that it is highly original (it contains 'so many Noveltys in so delicate a Part of Philosophy').

We might add to this the fact that the *Treatise* is a highly ambitious work. In the *Treatise,* Hume is trying to offer a science of human nature. Not only is this project of interest in its own right, but such a science serves as a foundation for all other sciences. ''Tis evident', he writes, 'that all the sciences, have a relation, greater or less, to human nature', and even '*Mathematics, Natural Philosophy,* and *Natural Religion,* are in some measure dependent on the science of MAN' (T Intro. 4). What is needed to put these on a sound footing is knowledge of the subjects 'whose connexion with human nature is more close and intimate' (T Intro. 5). Hume mentions four such subjects: logic, morals, criticism, and politics. Two of these are explicitly considered in the *Treatise*, logic and morals. Although Hume alludes to a volume on criticism in the advertisement to the first two books, it seems he did not even start writing it. The same is true with the topic of politics, although Book Three, 'Of morals', includes some discussion of political matters. Logic is the subject of Book One, 'Of the understanding'; in the introduction to the *Treatise*, Hume tells us that the 'sole aim of logic is to explain the principles and operations of our reasoning faculty, and the nature of ideas' (T Intro. 5). What of the passions, the subject matter of Book Two? Whilst Hume tells us that Book Three is 'in some measure independent of the other two books' (advertisement to Book Three), Books One and Two 'make a compleat chain of reasoning by themselves' (advertisement to Books One and Two). As we shall see, the fundamental mechanisms operative in the explanations offered in Book One are also operative in Book Two which, at least in part, explains why together those books make 'a compleat chain of reasoning'.

Whilst I focus on the *Treatise* I shall sometimes make some references to the two *Enquiries* and the 'Dissertation on the Passions', as well as other works. The relationship between these works is a delicate one, and beyond the scope of the present book. Where I do make such references it is done in such a way that is consistent with thinking that the aims of these works might be different from that of the *Treatise*.[11]

THE *TREATISE*: THREE ASPECTS OF ITS PHILOSOPHY

We have seen that Hume mentions the novelty of the *Treatise*. Indeed, he thought that the work was singularly novel. Writing to Henry Home, Lord Kames, Hume says that his 'principles are so remote from all the vulgar sentiments on the subject, that were they to take place, they would produce almost a total alteration in philosophy: and you know, revolutions of this kind are not easily brought about'.[12] The sheer revolutionary character of his philosophy is one factor in its poor reception, and its tendency to be misunderstood. The style, too, may have been a contributory factor, since, and especially in Book One, it can be arch and self-conscious.

Readers of the *Treatise* have also tended to emphasise one of three aspects of the work, leading to very different views on what the centre of gravity of the work might be; in this section I shall offer some very broad-brushed sketches of these aspects. The immediate reception of his work saw a destructive *scepticism* as its main lesson. A central charge levelled against Hume in the pamphlet circulated when he was trying for the Edinburgh chair was one of 'universal scepticism'. Here, Hume reports in *A Letter from a Gentleman*, he is accused of doubting 'of every Thing (his own Existence excepted) and maintains the Folly of pretending to believe any Thing with Certainty' (LG 14). Reid and Beattie, both of whom Hume viewed as great irritants, saw his philosophy as deeply sceptical, which for Reid showed the absurdity of Hume's starting points. T. H. Green, the idealist philosopher who edited an edition of Hume's works in the nineteenth century, wrote that Hume adopted a 'method, which began with professing to explain knowledge, showed knowledge to be impossible'.[13] In the twentieth century, Hume's reputation for being a sceptic was at the forefront of discussions of the problem of induction, since it was believed that Hume held that experience provides no reasons for beliefs about that which we presently do not perceive. According to Bertrand Russell:

> Hume's philosophy...represents the bankruptcy of eighteenth-century reasonableness...[H]e arrives [by thoroughly pushing this conception] at the disastrous conclusion that from experience and observation there is nothing to be learned. There is no such thing as a rational belief.[14]

Staying briefly in the twentieth century, there is another theme running through key parts of the *Treatise* which was of great prominence for large parts of that century. For the sake of a label, let us call this the *conceptual* aspect, or conceptual empiricism. Hume is customarily called an *empiricist*, and, at a broad level of characterisation, we can say that an empiricist philosopher holds that all knowledge rests on sense experience. At this broad level, Hume is certainly an empiricist, but what was found important in Hume is a thesis about the relationship between thought, or concepts, linguistic meaning, and experience. Hume holds that words acquire a meaning by expressing *ideas*, and that all ideas are ultimately traceable to impressions, or experience. If we cannot trace some supposed idea to a suitable experience, then, Hume holds, there is no such idea and so the word that is alleged to express that idea lacks a meaning. The spirit of this claim appealed to positivist philosophers of the twentieth century, who sought to dissolve metaphysical debates by seeking a criterion of cognitive significance. The aim was to work out what claims were genuinely meaningful, and what claims were literally nonsensical by determining what renders claims meaningful or not. The thrust of this (admittedly unsuccessful) project followed the spirit of Hume by trying to frame the criterion in terms of the possible object of sense experience. Thus, as one commentator puts it, 'in effect', Hume's 'theory of meaning constitutes a criterion of cognitive significance indistinguishable from one of the positivists' earliest attempts to frame a principle of verifiability [namely, that any claim should be verifiable by experience]'.[15]

Hume certainly holds that meaning is related to experience, and we shall see how this plays out in the course of this book. But this aspect of his philosophy plays a relatively small role in the debate about the overall centre of gravity of the *Treatise*. The view of Hume as a destructive sceptic has far greater prominence in the general view of the *Treatise*. And this brings us to another aspect of the work, which goes under the general term of Hume's *naturalism*. Partly in reaction to sceptical readings like that of Green, Norman Kemp Smith published a pair of articles in 1905 in which he argued that Hume's aim was not sceptical but was to offer a new theory of human nature.[16] Kemp Smith does not deny that there are sceptical aspects to the *Treatise*, but he views them instead as subservient to this positive aim. Kemp Smith later consolidated these thoughts in a highly influential book published in 1941.[17] Although very few of the details of Kemp Smith's readings are now accepted, this general attitude to understanding Hume's project has a major place in Hume scholarship.[18] What naturalism might mean, however, and how it is expressed in Hume's philosophy, is a difficult question, not to mention how it might relate to the sceptical aspects of his philosophy. In the next section we shall approach how Hume's 'naturalism' should be understood, and then turn to its relation to scepticism.

NATURALISMS

Many very diverse philosophers, from Aristotle to Spinoza, from Wittgenstein to Quine, have been called 'naturalists', and, given this diversity, the label is not in itself very illuminating. Furthermore, like most 'isms' there are very different senses of 'naturalism'. Here we will focus on two.[19]

The first sense of naturalism is *methodological*. Methodological naturalism is, very roughly, the view that philosophical questions are best approached with the methods of the sciences. That this is Hume's approach is evident from the *Treatise's* subtitle and his introduction to the work. The *Treatise* is an 'attempt to introduce the experimental method of reasoning into moral subjects'. The term 'moral subjects' covers not merely what we think of as moral philosophy today, but any subject that is not the object of the then nascent natural sciences. As noted, Hume is offering an account of human nature, and human nature manifests itself in various ways, including, but not restricted to, psychology, morality, politics, art, and economics. The attempt to introduce the experimental method of reasoning for Hume involves the idea that the science of human nature 'must be laid on experience and observation' (T Intro, 4). Let us look at the context of this claim in a little more detail.

Hume compares the length of time between Francis Bacon's introduction of empirical methods to human subjects and his own attempt with the period between the received beginning of ancient Greek philosophy to one of its most famous figures, that of Socrates, insinuating the significance that he attributes to the *Treatise*. But, more relevant to our concerns, Hume notes the achievements of natural philosophy in Britain, and in particular, those of Sir Issac Newton. Newton's conception of the methods of science feeds into Hume's methodological naturalism. It is difficult to overestimate Newton's towering significance during the period, and Hume's name is often associated with Newton's. Hume himself writes of his own principles of association that they constitute 'a kind of ATTRACTION, which in the mental world will be found to have as extraordinary effects as in the natural' (T 1.1.4.6), a remark which some commentators, including Kemp Smith, see as evidence that Hume models his key principles on Newton's findings in physics. We shall see presently that this is not the case, and we should also note that, given Newton's huge prominence during this period, appeals to Newtonian themes in philosophy were a commonplace.[20] That being said, the following remark by Hume connects him quite nicely with Newton's attitude to science. Hume writes:

> to me it seems evident, that the essence of the mind being equally unknown to us with that of external bodies, it must be equally impossible to form any notion of its powers and qualities otherwise than from careful and exact experiments, and the observation of those particular effects, which result from its different circumstances and situations. (T Intro. 8)

The relevance of this remark lies in the fact that Newton's methodology developed partly in response to the work of Descartes. Descartes argued that it was possible to know the essence of external bodies and held that in virtue of our having a non-sensory form of representation, the intellect, we are able to grasp *a priori* (that is, without experience) the essence of matter or 'external bodies' as pure extension. Newton read Descartes' research on light and began to realise that his interpretation of empirical results was being distorted by his conception of material substance as pure extension. Partly in response to this, Newton coined his famous dictum, *hypotheses non fingo* ('I frame no hypotheses'), a key sense of which is the rejection of any *a priori* conception of the essence of material substance. Instead, on Newton's view, we should only consider experience and experiments to arrive at fundamental principles, and then generalise on that basis. Thus, in the *Opticks* Newton writes:

> As in mathematics, so in natural philosophy, the investigation of difficult things by the method of analysis ought ever to precede the method of composition. This analysis consists in making experiments and observations, and drawing general conclusions from them by induction, and admitting no objections against the conclusions but such as are taken from experiment or other certain truths. For hypotheses are not to be regarded in experimental philosophy...By this way of analysis we may proceed from compounds to ingredients and from motions to the forces producing them, and in general from effects to their causes and from particular causes to more general ones till the argument end in the most general.[21]

This shift away from a conception of science as involving *a priori* metaphysical foundations to empirical generalisations was one that took a while to be accepted. For example, the French Cartesian philosopher, Nicolas Malebranche, claimed that Newton was an 'excellent'[22] experimentalist but a 'poor physicist'[23] because of his failure to provide *a priori* metaphysical foundations for science. Hume, however, follows Newton in rejecting such *a priori* starting points. In the *Abstract* he writes of a 'great vogue' in recent Britain for a 'new kind of philosophy':

> If, in examining several phenomena, we find that they resolve themselves into one common principle, and trace this principle into another, we shall at last arrive at those few simple principles, on which all the rest depend. And tho' we can never arrive at the ultimate principles, 'tis a satisfaction to go as far as our faculties will allow us.
>
> (*Abstract* 2)

Concerning the methodology of his own science of human nature, he 'proposes to anatomise human nature in a regular manner, and promises to draw no conclusions but where he is authorised by experience. He talks with contempt of hypotheses' (*Abstract* 2).

Hume's methodological naturalism thus follows Newton by identifying some fundamental principles by experience, using these principles to explain various phenomena, and rejecting any pretensions to an *a priori* science. We 'cannot go beyond experience' (T Intro. 8) and 'establish any principles which are not founded on that authority' (T Intro. 10).

We shall discuss some of these principles presently whilst we consider our second sense of 'naturalism'. Naturalism can be construed as an ontological doctrine, the claim that only the natural exists. But that claim is vacuous if we have no conception of what the 'natural' is. If we define the natural as 'all that there is' then the claim is trivial. To give the notion some more bite, one might argue that the natural is what is recognised in scientific explanation. On this conception, ontological naturalism is the claim that only that which is recognised by the sciences exists. Hume, however, does not explicitly take this approach.

Perhaps this is not surprising since his focus is on human nature rather than on nature *per se*. But there is a different ontological stance that connects with naturalism, encapsulated by the slogan that human beings are part of nature. This may seem to raise the question again of what the relevant sense of nature is, but we can forestall this worry in the following way. Hume's contemporaries are guided by a contrast, explicit and implicit, between the nature and powers of human beings and the nature and powers of the rest of animal creation. This difference is conceived to be not one of degree or of mere complexity but a difference in *kind*, a difference which had many complex dimensions, including the immortality of the soul, freedom, sin, consciousness, reason, and the Christian biblical claim that human beings were given dominion over all the animals.[24]

This last point connects to perhaps the most important point of contrast. As Denis Des Chene puts it, during this period the:

> concept *animal* is charged not only with designating a class of creatures...but also with supplying a contrast to the human. In Christian anthropology, the animal represents material nature in the most perfect condition it can attain without the intervention of spiritual nature.[25]

The Christian interpretation of human nature is one which makes for a difference in kind between human beings and the rest of animal nature, an aspect of the doctrine that humans, unlike animals, are made in the image of God. The sense in which we are made in the image of God, and hence different in kind, is expressed in different ways, including the ways noted above.[26] What is significant for our purposes is that Hume seeks to explain human nature *only* in terms that were deemed to be operative in animals. In this respect, human beings are understood to be part of nature, inasmuch as any difference between humans and the rest of the animals does not mark a difference in kind, and so humanity is naturalised. Moreover, this is not merely an academic matter since this difference in kind is inextricably linked to a particularly Christian interpretation of the nature of humanity.

This brings us to something that needs to be addressed, namely Hume's notoriety in the area of religion. We noted above that the contents of the *Treatise* were thought to be dangerous for religion, and, although Hume denied being an atheist, his reputation as one persisted throughout his lifetime and beyond. His *Dialogues Concerning Natural Religion* and 'Of miracles' (originally intended for the *Treatise but* published in the First *Enquiry*) question the cogency of 'natural' religion, namely any religion founded on argument, and his account of the psychology of religion is one that makes God redundant in the explanation of religious belief. As we shall see, his conception of virtue, and his account of morality in general, is far from congenial to Christianity. Hume is artful in his presentation of these criticisms, but it is not too difficult to see him, a man who lost his faith in his early years, as deeply sceptical of the Christian conception of the world. Indeed, some commentators have claimed that the *Treatise* itself is part of Hume's irreligious campaign, and this is not an implausible thesis. What the naturalisation project contributes to this idea is a view of human nature that does not warrant the view that humans are different in kind from the rest of nature.[27]

Hume does not trumpet this naturalisation project at the outset of the *Treatise*. Nevertheless, we can get a flavour of it by considering some passages from Leibniz which serve nicely as an introduction to the alleged differences between humans and animals on the topic of reason. Now, it is important to note that I am not claiming that Hume is engaging directly with Leibniz. Instead, Leibniz nicely illustrates a position that was widely held. So, for example, Thomas Hobbes, a philosopher very different from Leibniz, nevertheless distinguishes animals from humans on the topic of reason in a similar way, as I shall briefly illustrate below. But consider first this passage:

> Memory provides a kind of connectedness to souls which resembles reason but must be distinguished from it. For we see that animals which have a perception of something that strikes them and of which they have previously had a similar perception expect...that which have been conjoined in that previous perception, and are thus led to sensations similar to those they have had before. For example, when one shows a stick to dogs, they recall the pain that it caused them and whine and run off.[28]

The kind of 'connectedness' Leibniz refers to here is what Hume will call the 'association of ideas', and it is a phenomenon noted by philosophers throughout the period, including Hobbes, Spinoza, Locke, Berkeley, Malebranche, and many others. Roughly, experience produces habits of moving from one thought or idea to another without reflection. Quite often, such habits are explained by how the brain is affected by repeated experience, but the key point is that such patterns of thinking are habitual and not caused by conscious reflection. Furthermore, as Leibniz says, this phenomenon is that which explains animal inference. The dog has come to associate the stick with pain, and so when it perceives the stick it comes to think of pain. Such a movement of thought resembles reason inasmuch as it is the movement from what is presently perceived to what is yet to be perceived, and so it can be called an inference. Why it is *not* reason, is, broadly speaking, because when the dog draws the inference, he does not do so because he is aware of something that connects the stick with the pain. That is, he does not have in mind something that counts as a reason in favour of thinking that pain will occur. He just sees the stick and the idea of pain immediately springs to mind.

Experience, and the produced habits, then enter into the explanation of behaviour. Thus, in section 27 of the *Monadology*, Leibniz writes of a 'forceful impression' which 'strikes and moves' the animal. As we shall see, Hume talks of impressions and ideas, and of the former being more forceful and vivid than the latter. In the next section, Leibniz notes that humans 'function like beasts' because they too often draw inferences by association only. When, however, we reason, the nature of our inference is different from association. Leibniz puts this most clearly in his *New Essays on Human Understanding*:

> Beasts pass from one imagining to another by means of a link between them which they have previously experienced. For instance, when his master picks up a stick the dog anticipates being beaten.... This could be called 'inference' or 'reasoning' in a very broad sense. But I prefer to keep to accepted usage, reserving these words for men and restricting them to the knowledge of some *reason* for perceptions' being linked together. Mere sensations cannot provide this: all they do is to cause one naturally to expect once more the same linking that has been observed previously.[29]

This again suggests what we said above, namely that reason, as opposed to association, involves inferences made in light of some knowledge of a connection between things.

What we shall see, and particularly in Chapter Three, is that Hume argues that a picture like the one presented by Leibniz is impossible, that our reason is no different in kind than the mechanism underlying animal inference. And as I mentioned above, Hobbes, a very different philosopher, shares in this view. Association for Hobbes is the 'trayne of imagination'. The imagination is nothing but 'decaying sense', namely a 'more obscure' image of a sensory impression. The repeated impact of connected sensory experience leaves a 'trayne of imagination', whereby one idea or image is connected with another, leaving unreflective habits of inference. Roughly where A and B have been associated through sense experience, the thought or idea of B will occur to one when one thinks of A. This 'trayne of the imagination' issues in what he calls 'prudence', which is a 'Prœsumption of the

Future, contracted from the Experience of time Past'. But prudence, declares Hobbes, is not 'what distinguisheth man from beast'. Reason acquired, by the invention of language, marks the distinction. Language allows us definitions, which move us from mere 'knowledge of Fact', provided by sense and memory, to 'knowledge of Consequences, and the dependence of one fact upon another', which ultimately resolves itself to knowledge of cause.[30] Most humans operate solely on the level of prudence or association, which is fine for practical purposes: 'ignorance of causes' writes Hobbes, does not take 'men farre out of the way'.[31] But it is not reason.

As I mentioned, Hume does not announce his naturalisation project at the beginning of the *Treatise*. Instead, he introduces a set of materials, which are widely used in explanations of animal cognition, impressions, ideas, and the association of ideas. He will then go on to use the central notion of the association of ideas (which we know now to be modelled on animal cognition, and not, as Kemp Smith claimed, Newtonian attraction) to explain human cognition in a way that does not see our nature as different in kind from other animals. Of course, there is a good deal more complexity to the human animal, and, we shall see, how Hume explains these differences. Later in the *Treatise*, Hume drops in an explicit statement of his naturalisation project, writing, almost as an afterthought, that the 'whole sensitive creation...[e]very thing is conducted by springs and principles, which are not peculiar to man, or any one species of animals' (T 2.2.12.1).

SCEPTICISM

What, then, of Hume's scepticism? It is undeniable that there are sceptical aspects to Hume's *Treatise*, but it is difficult to say much in advance of discussing the particular arguments. So, we will have to wait to look at these sceptical aspects in their context. Nevertheless, we can make a few very general remarks here.

First, as noted, Hume attempts to understand human nature as no different in kind from animal nature, and this relates to a long-standing trope from ancient Pyrrhonian scepticism, which was later yoked to Christianity. It is one with descriptive and evaluative dimensions. The descriptive dimension is that there appears to be no difference in kind between animals and humans, cognitively speaking (and, indeed, in some areas non-human animals exceed humans). The 'appears' is important here, since the sceptics are consistent and do not assert that it is true that there is no difference, only that it seems so. The evaluative aspect is that, in showing that it appears that there is no cognitive difference, we prick the pretention that humans are somehow morally superior. A version of this attitude is expressed in the influential writings of Michel de Montaigne, where scepticism and Christianity make a heady combination, and we can see Hume reacting to this sceptical trope in 'Of the Dignity or Meanness of Human Nature', an essay written very soon after he finished the *Treatise*.[32] There, Hume discusses two views of human nature, one of which 'exalt[s] our species to the skies, and represent[s] man as a kind of human demigod, who derives his origin from heaven, and retains evident marks of his lineage and descent', and one which 'insist[s] upon the blind sides of human nature, and can discover nothing, except vanity, in which man surpasses the other animals, whom he affects so much to despise'.[33] For Hume, these two extremes rest on the idea that in 'forming our notions of human nature, we are apt to make a comparison between men and animals, the only creatures endowed with thought that fall under our senses',[34] and those who are optimistic about human nature tend to stress our cognitive superiority. The sceptical trope, however, denigrates human nature by forming 'a new and secret comparison between man and beings of the most perfect wisdom',[35] arguing that we fall short and that the difference between us and animals is rather narrower than the optimistic view. For Montaigne, the conclusion of this two-way comparison is to stress the extent that we should be utterly humble. Hume however takes the animal comparison to suggest not that we are god-like creatures of a different kind but, rather, sophisticated animals.

This aspect of Hume's philosophy is related to scepticism inasmuch as the comparison between animal and human cognition was a favoured sceptical trope, but Hume's own naturalism is not a form of scepticism. Hence, the relation here is somewhat tangential. However, there is a further, and more direct, point about scepticism which is important to note here. It concerns a distinction which, although it is one that Hume only draws explicitly in *An Enquiry Concerning Human Understanding*, is applicable to the *Treatise*. The distinction is between *antecedent* and *consequent* scepticism (EHU 12.3–4).

By 'antecedent scepticism' Hume means a scepticism antecedent to any theory or empirical investigation. Here, he has in mind the project of Descartes' *Meditations* which involved Descartes first subjecting his cognitive faculties to the strongest sceptical doubts in order to arrive at something which survives all sceptical scrutiny, thereby allowing him to build a new epistemology and metaphysics. Hume rejects Descartes' view as an impossible aspiration but allows for a moderate form of this idea, which involves being impartial, free from prejudice, and starting from evident principles when beginning any investigation. This, however, is hardly a form of scepticism at all.

Scepticism consequent 'to science and enquiry' Hume discusses at greater length. Here empirical investigation into our faculties renders problematic what we previously took for granted. He illustrates how such scepticism might arise in the case of our belief in the external world, and in the case of reason itself, and we shall see versions of how this scepticism works later in this book. The key point to note here is that it is scepticism born of an enquiry into our faculties. But this cuts across another distinction of Hume's which we should take note of, namely that between excessive or Pyrrhonian scepticism, and mitigated or Academic scepticism. This distinction is an allusion to two schools of ancient scepticism, though Hume's own use of the terms does not map accurately onto the doctrines of the ancient schools.[36] Consequent scepticism would be excessive in showing the 'absolute fallaciousness' (EHU 12.5) of our mental faculties. When he discusses the external world and reason in the context it might seem that he is suggesting that consequent scepticism leads to excessive scepticism. That is to say, a scepticism that evaluates beliefs as entirely lacking in epistemic support. But his attitude towards excessive scepticism is not one of endorsement. He holds that excessive scepticism yields conclusions that cannot have any serious hold on our beliefs and so are impotent, practically speaking. The paradoxical conclusions do not affect our nature and the 'more powerful principles of our nature' and sceptical principles 'vanish like smoke' (EHU 12.21). 'Nature', he famously writes, 'is always too strong for principle' (EHU 12.23).

This might read as if Hume's settled attitude to scepticism is simply that sceptical conclusions are psychologically unbelievable, but that nevertheless those conclusions are sound. He therefore holds that scepticism is the correct position rationally speaking, but, fortunately, psychologically impossible. There are readings of Hume that have him adopting this position, broadly speaking.[37] We shall, however, pursue a different response in Chapter Four. Hume himself goes on to identify two species of mitigated scepticism and seems to endorse a generally mitigated scepticism, which itself 'may be the result of' excessive scepticism (EHU 12.24).

The first result, and species of mitigated scepticism, is its corrective to dogmatism, the inclination among many to 'haughtiness and obstinacy' in belief:

> [A] small tincture of PYRRHONISM might abate their pride, by shewing them, that the few advantages, which they may have attained over their fellows, are but inconsiderable, if compared with the universal perplexity and confusion, which is inherent in human nature. In general, there is a degree of doubt, and caution, and modesty, which, in all kinds of scrutiny and decision, ought for ever accompany a just reasoner'.
>
> (EHU 12.24)

The second species of mitigated scepticism, which itself is a form of consequent scepticism, is a recognition of the limitations of our faculties. We come to learn that our minds cannot extend beyond experience and that philosophical decisions are 'nothing but the reflections of common life, methodized and corrected' (EHU 12.25). In the introduction to the *Treatise*, Hume had already alluded to this feature of his philosophy, writing that when 'we see that we have arriv'd at the utmost extent of human reason, we sit down contented; tho' we be perfectly satisfy'd in the main of our ignorance, and perceive that we can give no reason for our most general and most refin'd principles, besides our experience of their reality' (T Intro. 9). Hence, Hume thinks, empirical investigation into our faculties reveals their limits.

SUMMARY

We shall be following the structure of the *Treatise* in this book. In Chapter One, Hume's account of ideas, and their relation to experience, is introduced, as is his distinction between feeling and thinking. It further discusses his account of the association of ideas, and its naturalistic background, and his account of abstract ideas. In Chapter Two, Hume's views of space and time are introduced. Chapter Three discusses, among other things, Hume's account of causal inference, his account of belief, and his novel approach to the topic of causation. Chapter Four discusses Part Four of Book One, 'Of the sceptical, and other systems of philosophy', which is perhaps the most complicated part of the *Treatise*. There Hume discusses a range of different topics, including the external world and the self. At the same time, however, he exposes, in a self-conscious way, deep difficulties that emerge from highly reflective thought.

Chapter Five begins the discussion of Book Two, 'Of the passions', by looking at Hume's indirect passions of pride and humility, love and hate. In Chapter Six, we examine Hume's treatment of freewill, his discussion of motivation, and the direct passions in general. Chapter Seven introduces Hume's moral epistemology, and also provides some context to his views. Chapter Eight turns to Hume's account of the 'artificial virtues', and in particular his account of justice. Finally, Chapter Nine discusses Hume's account of the 'natural virtues'.

NOTES

1 Hume refers to this birthdate as 'old style'. The calendar changed in the eighteenth century from the Julian to the Gregorian calendar, so his April

birthdate is according to the Julian calendar. The date in the Gregorian calendar is 7 May 1711.
2   References to 'My Own Life' from Hume's Letters, HL, I, p. 13.
3   HL, I, pp. 13–14.
4   HL, I, p. 16.
5   HL, I, p.2.
6   HL, II, p.208.
7   HL, I, p.158.
8   HL, I, p.38.
9   HL, II, p.301.
10 The advertisement is appended to the modern Clarendon edition of *An Enquiry Concerning Human Understanding.*
11 For discussion, see Stewart (2005) and Harris (2015), Chapter Four.
12 HL, I, p.26.
13 Green, T. H., 'General Introduction', *The Philosophical Works of David Hume*, Vol. 1, ed. T. H. Green & T. H. Grose (London: Longmans, Green and Co., 1874), p.2.
14 Russell (1979), p.645.
15 Rosenberg (1993), p.66.
16 Smith (1905a & b).
17 Smith (1941).
18 Barry Stroud's book (1977) also played a major role in the promotion of naturalist approaches.
19 We will discuss a third sense of naturalism when we discuss Hume's account of causation in Chapter Three.
20 An old, but still excellent, discussion of this topic is Barfoot (1990).
21 Newton, *Opticks*, Query 31.
22 Malebranche, *The Search After Truth*, p.689.
23 Letter to Berrand (1707), quoted in Hankins (1967), p.197. Malebranche himself offered a science of human nature and argued that it should be held in 'higher regard' than the other sciences (*The Search After Truth*, p.xli). He also regards it as only an 'experimental' science since, as opposed to a true *a priori* science, we cannot know the essence of the mind.
24 For some sense of this complexity one can consult the artful entry on Rorarius in Pierre Bayle's *Dictionary*.
25 Des Chene (2006), p.216.
26 For an illuminating discussion of how the image of God doctrine permeated the philosophy of the period, and how it relates to Hume, see Craig (1987).
27 See Craig (1987), and Russell (2008).
28 *Monadology* section 26.
29 Leibniz, New Essays on Human Understanding, p.143.
30 Hobbes, *Leviathan*, p.115.
31 Hobbes, *Leviathan*, p.116
32 For further discussion see Kail (2012).

33 EMPL, pp.80–81.
34 EMPL, p.82.
35 EMPL, pp.82–82.
36 For a complete reading of Hume that centres itself on this discussion, see Fosl (2020).
37 See e.g. Fogelin (1985).

1
OF IDEAS, THEIR ORIGIN, COMPOSITION, CONNEXION, ABSTRACTION, ETC.

INTRODUCTION

Part One of Book One of the *Treatise* introduces the fundamental building blocks of Hume's theory of cognition, and the aim of this chapter is to do the same, but in a way which renders explicit that which remains only implicit in Hume's own presentation. T 1.1 is a rather short part of the *Treatise* and proceeds in a manner that appears to be more of a set of announcements than the carefully laid groundwork for a new science of mind. But Hume's brevity here is not surprising: much of the material he presents in this part would have been familiar to his readers. Here, I briefly introduce some key aspects of Hume's account, and some of its background.

PERCEPTIONS, THE COPY PRINCIPLE, AND REPRESENTATION

'All the perceptions of the human mind', Hume writes, 'resolve themselves into two distinct kinds, which I shall call

IMPRESSIONS and IDEAS' (T 1.1.1.1). We shall return to the distinction between impressions and ideas in the next section, but both are kinds of perceptions. But what is a 'perception'?

First, perceptions are 'what is before the mind', i.e. the things that we are immediately conscious of. When I smell, see, or touch, there is something of which I am conscious. Furthermore, what I am immediately conscious of are sensory qualities, colours, tastes, smells, etc. Through our eyes, we perceive colours and shapes, through our noses, we perceive smells etc. Having such things 'before the mind' is, in the first instance, being conscious of them. What we have 'before the mind' are smells, shapes, colours, etc., and it is these sensory qualities which constitute perceptions, the things which we are immediately conscious of.

Matters, however, are more complicated than this simple picture has it. Although I have introduced the concept of 'perception' in terms of the common-sense notion of the five senses, there are other sources of perceptions. There are emotions, like anger, fear, etc. and these too are perceptions. T.1.1.2, 'Division of the subject', distinguishes between perceptions of *sensation* and perceptions of *reflection*. The former perceptions are those which we sense directly, 'the kind [that] arises in the soul originally, from unknown causes' (T 1.1.2.1), whereas the latter are, very roughly, emotions that arise in reaction to what we immediately perceive and think about. I perceive or think of something, a spider, say, and my perceiving or thinking about the spider produces a new, internal impression, in this case fear. Fear is a perception because it is something that is felt or experienced, albeit something felt or experienced internally.

We will return to reflective perceptions when we look at Hume's theory of the passions, while in this part, we will mostly concentrate on perceptions of sensation. However, there is an important reason why I have drawn attention to this distinction. Hume conceives minds as populated by items that are fundamentally *qualitative* in nature. Sky blue has a characteristic appearance, which distinguishes it from brick red, and the feeling of a toothache is different from the feeling of anxiety in the pit of one's stomach. If we take the senses to include what we feel internally, everything that enters our mind is something we sense, be it a colour, taste, toothache, or an emotion. What makes a perception the perception it is, is a matter of its peculiar feeling or sensory character. When Hume is referring to perceptions, he is referring precisely to the peculiar feeling or sensory character which makes the perception the perception that it is.

Hume distinguishes between *simple* and *complex* perceptions. Our experience is typically a composite of different sensory qualities: before my eyes there is an array of coloured shapes, each differing in more or less dramatic ways. In other words, what I experience is a *complex* of different qualities. These complexes can, nevertheless, be distinguished into the simple qualities that enter into their composition. Simple perceptions are those which 'admit of no distinction or separation', whereas complex perceptions may 'be distinguish'd into parts' (T 1.1.1.2). This distinction is more complicated than it might seem at first sight, but the intuitive idea seems plain enough. Suppose I am perceiving a cat. I experience a complex of shapes, colours, scents, and noises, and I am able to distinguish the different parts or elements of that composite, the different shades of ginger, the shape of the tail as opposed to the shape of the paw, and the different meows. At a first approximation, the simple perceptions are those which I can imagine independently from others: I can imagine a particular meow without imagining anything else.

Hume treats perceptions as *objects* or *things* rather than mere representations *of* things (though they can be, and often are, representations as well). This requires some explanation. Imagine that I have a vivid hallucination of a cat in front of me. I have a perception *as of* a cat, but since there is no cat there, I do not genuinely perceive a cat. To perceive something requires the existence of the thing which is experienced (it is a 'factive' notion), whereas to have a perception *as of* a cat does not. There is nothing that is *perceived* but a perceptual state that *represents* something that might not exist. Hume's perceptions are the items that we perceive, rather than merely perceptions or representations of something else. What is 'before the mind' is something composed of sensations or feelings.

Does this mean that perceptions do not represent? No, it does not. Hume mentions two kinds of perceptions—*impressions* and *ideas*—which he holds to be the distinction 'betwixt feeling and thinking' (T 1.1.1.1). Impressions are the perceptions which constitute what we experience through the senses, including the 'inner' senses, and ideas are the perceptions that constitute thoughts *about* what we sense. I experience a sound, and I can also *think* about the sound after I hear it. But for Hume, experiencing the sound—having an impression—and thinking of the sound—having an idea of it—differs only in the fact that the idea is 'fainter' or less 'lively' than the impression. My idea is itself a perception, just like the impression, except it is 'fainter'. Now, we will come to what 'fainter' and 'less lively' might mean presently, but our question is about whether perceptions can be representations. How do these 'faint' perceptions end up being representations?

The key to this is Hume's 'first principle of human nature' (T 1.1.1.12), which has become known as the 'Copy Principle', and which states that 'all our simple ideas in their first appearance are deriv'd from simple impressions, which are correspondent to them, and which they exactly represent' (T 1.1.1.7). The first thing to note is that simple ideas are caused by simple impressions. The second thing is that simple ideas *resemble* their causes. There is, Hume says, 'a great resemblance betwixt our impressions and ideas, in every other particular, except their degree of force and vivacity' (T 1.1.1.3). Simple impressions cause simple ideas, which exactly resemble those impressions, and hence simple ideas are *copies* of those simple impressions. It is this combination of causation and resemblance that constitutes the core of Hume's account of representation. A simple idea is an idea *of* a simple impression in virtue of being a copy of that impression.

That all our ideas are derived from sense experience is one reason why it is appropriate to label Hume as an *empiricist*. More precisely, it makes him a *concept* empiricist. Our capacity to think involves the possession of simple ideas, or fundamental *concepts*, which constitute the elements or constituents of thought. The elements or constituents are derived from, and represent, what is given in experience. We shall briefly mention some of the ramifications of this claim presently, but note first that the Copy Principle concerns only simple perceptions. We are able to recombine simple ideas to form complex ideas that represent things of which we have no impression. Even though I have never seen a pink cat with eight legs and three ears, I have had impressions, and hence ideas, of all the elements that go into the idea of such a fantastical beast. Thus, I can have complex ideas without corresponding complex impressions. Second, he allows that at least some of our complex ideas do not 'exactly' (T 1.1.1.4) resemble their objects. To use Hume's example, my idea of Paris does not faithfully resemble each and every element that was presented to me in my experience when I was there. Nevertheless, the implication is that my idea resembles Paris sufficiently to represent it.

The Copy Principle is the core of Hume's account of mental representation. Of course, there are other kinds of representation, like how a red cross can stand for medical aid or how '30' on a sign next to a road can represent a speed limit, but here Hume offers an account of how the mind represents the world. It is an account that is notoriously brief, and notoriously problematic. Simple ideas are caused by, and resemble, the correspondent simple impressions. But resemblance is neither necessary nor sufficient for representation. It is not sufficient because two things can resemble each other—say, two pound coins—without one being a representation of the other. Nor is it necessary: the word 'cat' represents cats, but it does not resemble them. The claim that simple ideas are *caused* by simple impressions might get us further, and a lot of contemporary philosophy tries to understand mental representation in terms of causal relationships, but it is fair to say that Hume's account is exceedingly underdeveloped.[1] Nevertheless, it is naturalistic in the sense that Hume does not take the representational powers of the mind as given, as philosophers such as Descartes had, but offers the beginning of an explanation of representation in terms of resemblance and causation.[2]

Hume also holds that what we can think or represent is not only explained by experience but is *constrained* by it. He puts this point in the *Enquiry Concerning Human Understanding* thus: 'all our ideas are nothing but copies of our impressions, or, in other words...it is impossible for us to *think* of any thing, which we have not antecedently *felt*, either by our external or internal senses' (EHU 7.4). As we already noted, Hume's account of complex thoughts allows that we can have ideas of complex entities of which we have had no impression, like the pink cat described above. However, here Hume is insisting that the basic or simple constituents of thought are derived from impressions, and that if there is no relevant simple impression there is no simple idea. This, in turn, is linked to his claim about how words get meaning. Words are meaningful by being appropriately related to ideas, but there can be words for which there is no relevant idea. Those words lack a meaning. In order to determine what that idea is, or, indeed, whether there is an idea associated with the relevant word, Hume seeks to find the relevant impression. He thinks that some key philosophical theses are, in fact, meaningless in this sense, and attempts to expose certain philosophical terms as meaningless by showing how no relevant impression is possible.

An early example of this tactic of Hume's comes in T 1.1.6, where Hume first discusses the philosophical notions of substance and mode.[3] The twin notions of substance and mode have a long and complicated history in philosophy, and we shall look at them in a little more detail later in this book, but for present purposes the following sketch will suffice. A substance is something that is an independent existence whereas a mode is something the existence of which depends on substance. For John Locke, a fellow empiricist, all we can know are the properties or modes that our senses reveal, while the nature of substance—that upon which the observable properties of things depend—is something unknowable. We know, as it were, the 'surface' properties of material objects, but not the nature of the substance upon which those properties depend. But the substance—the thing, whatever it is, that observable properties depend on, is something that we never have an impression or experience of. For Hume, because we have no impression of such a thing, we 'have no idea of substance' (T 1.1.6.1) in that sense. The only sense we can give to the term 'substance' is the collection of the observable qualities, rather than the unobservable 'thing' that is supposed to 'own' those qualities. The other sense of 'substance'—which philosophers intend—is meaningless.

What the implications are of some terms being 'meaningless' will be explored later when we come to the details of Hume's applications of the Copy Principle. However, having laid down his first general principle, Hume immediately admits an exception to it, claiming that under certain, very specific, circumstances, it is possible to form a simple idea without a prior simple impression of it. He asks us to imagine someone who has experienced every particular shade of blue except for one, and allows that such a person could, as it were, 'fill the gap' and imagine—form the idea of—the missing shade of blue. This 'instance', says Hume, is 'so particular and singular' that it does not 'alter our general maxim' (T 1.1.1.10). Hume is probably right that this instance is a special case. Colour is such that different shades are so related to each other by resemblance that it is possible to extrapolate from a number of examples to others on the basis of that resemblance.[4] As we shall see, Hume will use the Copy Principle to argue that for some key topics such as causal power and the self, we do not have the ideas we think we have, and so it might be thought that because he allows one counter-example, other ideas he argues against by using the Copy Principle are themselves counter-examples. But the 'singular' character of the missing shade of blue blunts that objection. Rather than go into the details of the singular nature of the missing shade of blue, what is more important is to consider just *why* Hume mentions it here. The most plausible explanation is that Hume is showing his naturalistic credentials. The claim that all simple ideas are derived from antecedent impressions is a generalisation that is *empirical*, one based on, and justified by, observation and experience. As such, it conforms to Aristotle's observation that what happens in nature is 'always, or for the most part'. The fact that our minds copy ideas from impressions is a fact about the nature of the mind—which, like anything else in nature, occurs always, or for the most part.

THE DIFFERENCE BETWEEN FEELING AND THINKING

There is something intuitive about the picture sketched so far. There is sensory input into our mind, which in turn is used to represent the world. Our capacity to think is explained by causal processes, a matter of sensory input yielding cognitive output. We first *feel* which then enables us to *think*. So, our senses (including our 'inner' senses) are our fundamental points of contact with the world, and it is in virtue of these fundamental points of contact that we are able to think of the world at all. Our thinking reflects or mirrors what we experience since our ideas are copies or images of experiences. Since all ideas are images, and, as we shall see, our mental life is governed by these images and their relations, the most fundamental faculty of the mind is the *imagination*.

This picture commits Hume to a priority claim, namely that impressions occur prior to ideas, at least when it comes to simple perceptions. Hume holds this to be an empirical claim, that is, one based on observation. We 'find by constant experience, that the simple impressions always take the precedence of their correspondent ideas, but never appear in the contrary order' (T 1.1.1.7). But in order to know that impressions precede ideas we need to tell which perceptions are impressions and which are ideas. Hume tells us that everyone will 'readily perceive the difference betwixt feeling and thinking' (T 1.1.1.1). Certainly, we do have an intuitive grasp of when we are perceiving something and when we are merely thinking about it. But Hume also tells us that the difference between feeling and thinking consists in impressions differing from ideas in their degree of 'force', 'liveliness', or 'vivacity'. Impressions are more forceful, lively, and vivacious than ideas. This, however, has perplexed commentators because it seems that, however we understand force, liveliness, or vivacity, these never serve to mark the distinction between feeling and thinking. We can always imagine cases where what we are thinking is more forceful, lively, and vivacious than what we are perceiving. Let us explore this a little further.

Suppose we take 'liveliness' and 'vivacity' to mean some kind of pictorial property of sensory experience, a kind of brightness or saturation. Look, for example, out the window on a sunny day and then close your eyes and try to imagine what you have just seen. You might be able to picture the scene in your imagination, but it won't have the same saturation or brightness of your visual experience. So, impressions have liveliness so construed, and thoughts do not, or at least not to the same degree. But this would be a hopeless way to capture the distinction 'betwixt feeling and thinking', since counterexamples are easy to concoct. I am lying in bed in a dark room, a room so dark that the only thing I can see is the faint outline of the curtains, but, at the same time, I am vividly imagining a sunny afternoon on holiday. It seems easy to concede that my thought—my imagination—is more lively in the relevant sense than what I am perceiving. So perhaps instead, rather than taking the distinction between impressions and ideas to be a pictorial one, the terms 'force' and 'violence' suggest that the difference between impressions and ideas should be understood in terms of their respective causal effects. Impressions 'strike the mind' in that they affect thought and behaviour far more than mere thought. The mere thought of a truck heading in my direction does not affect me in anything like the way my perceiving the truck heading in my direction as I absent-mindedly stroll out into the road does. Thoughts of course do affect our behaviour, but the suggestion here is that sensory experience has a more immediate and powerful effect on the mind than mere thought. But, again, it is easy to generate counterexamples. I can be sat quietly in my office reading a book, and all of a sudden, I remember that I have left the oven on, causing me to dash home to switch it off. The *thought* that I have left the oven on strikes with more force than what I am presently perceiving. Commentators thus tend to think that Hume's attempt to draw the distinction between feeling and thinking on the basis of force and vivacity is hopeless.

We shall revisit force and vivacity when we come to discuss Hume's theory of belief, but it is easy to see why commentators are sceptical of their use in drawing the distinction between feeling and thinking. However, there is a different way of reading what Hume is telling us here that does not render it hopeless. One could instead say that impressions—instances of feelings—have external causes, and that being lively or forceful generally *indicates* that a perception is an impression rather than an idea. Impressions would be impressions because they have external causes, and that is what constitutes them as such, but *typically* they are more lively and more forceful than mere thoughts. Perceptions being more lively and more forceful is an *indicative* criterion of being an impression, rather than a *constitutive* one.

Why should we think this? Aside from the fact that the term 'impression' suggests it, Hume tells us so at the beginning of Book Two of the *Treatise*, where he writes that 'impressions of sensation are such as without any antecedent perceptions arise in the soul, from the constitution of the body, [such as bodily pain],...or from the application of objects to the external organs' (T 2.1.1.1). He goes on as follows:

> 'Tis certain, that the mind and its perceptions, must begin somewhere; and that since the impressions precede their correspondent ideas, there must be some impressions, which without any introduction make their appearance in the soul. As these depend upon natural and physical causes, the examination of them wou'd lead me too far from my present subject, into the sciences of anatomy and natural philosophy.
>
> (T 2.1.1.2)

Indeed, it was a pretty standard position about sensation at the time, namely that such impressions were the result of physical causes in the brain, of which ideas were faint copies. Ephraim Chambers' *Cyclopedia*, a popular reference work first published in 1728, tells us that the imagination is the faculty of the soul 'whereby it conceives, and forms ideas of things, by impressions made on the fibres of the brain, by sensation'.[5]

That impressions have external causes is perfectly consistent with there sometimes being impressions that are not as forceful or lively as ideas. As Hume himself says:

> ...in sleep, in a fever, in madness, or in any violent emotions of soul, our ideas may approach to our impressions: As on the other hand it sometimes happens, that our impressions are so faint and low, that we cannot distinguish them from our ideas.
>
> (T 1.1.1.1)

If an impression was treated as a perception with an external cause, and the distinction between ideas and impressions simply a matter of force and vivacity, then the second sentence of this quotation would not make sense. If impressions were 'so faint and low', then it would be the case that they *are* ideas—not merely that we could not distinguish them from ideas. But compare this to a passage from Nicolas Malebranche's *The Search After Truth*, a work which Hume was extremely familiar with. It sometimes

> ...happens that persons whose animal spirits are highly agitated by fasting, vigils, a high fever, or some violent passion have the internal fibres of their brain set in motion as forcefully as by external objects. Because of this such people *sense* what they should only *imagine*, and they think they see objects before their eyes, which are only in their imaginations. This shows with regard to what occurs in the body, the senses and the imagination differ only in degree.[6]

Here Malebranche is explicit about the brain and the body and their relation to perception. But this raises a question. If Hume thinks that the difference between impressions and ideas is a matter of the former having external causes, why does he not allude to the brain trace account right at the beginning of the *Treatise*?

Hume's answer is in one of the quotations above, namely that establishing such an account 'wou'd lead [him] too far from my present subject, into the sciences of anatomy and natural philosophy'. Impressions have some external cause, but it is not the aim of the *Treatise* to determine the precise nature of such a cause. This is why in a footnote (T 1.1.1.1n) Hume says that he is using the term 'impression' for the 'perceptions themselves' rather than the 'manner' by which they are impressed in the soul. He steers clear of the details of the mechanism, though we shall see in the next chapter that there is one place where Hume feels the need to draw explicitly on the brain.

Commentators tend to think, however, that he does not explicitly appeal to external causes because he cannot. They think that Hume is a sceptic about the external world, indeed, to such an extent that he does not believe in such a thing. Hence the difference between feeling and thinking must be constituted by force and vivacity alone. But things are far more complicated than that, and Hume's sceptical attitude to the external world cannot be assumed at the outset of the *Treatise*. We shall see later that Hume's discussion of the external world does not upset what is said here.

RELATIONS: THE PRINCIPLES OF ASSOCIATION

As noted, ideas are *images*, which are stored in the *imagination*. We can think of the imagination as a faculty that stores and manipulates ideas, and, as such, the imagination is the basis for all mental activity by relating ideas in the imagination. How, then, are ideas related?

Hume distinguishes two kinds of relation, *philosophical* and *natural* (T 1.1.3). Philosophical relations are those relations in which things stand to one another and which we can discover by considering and comparing those things. We will return to these relations when we discuss Hume's account of knowledge and probability in Chapter Three. Our present concern is with the natural relations. What are these? These are the relations which determine how ideas are connected in our imagination, whereby, without conscious reflection, we pass from one thought or idea to another. Hume thinks that there are three natural relations, or principles of association, that guide such connections. When ideas *resemble* each other, they tend to combine in the imagination, when ideas are *contiguous* they also tend to combine in the imagination, and when ideas are related by *cause* and *effect*, they also tend to be related in the imagination. Here is an example of the natural relation of resemblance: if I see someone who looks like my brother, the idea of my brother suddenly springs to mind. In the case of contiguity, consider the following. Suppose that I pass a room and that each time I pass it, I see a particular person sitting in that room. When I pass that room again, my mind immediately turns to the thought of that particular person. Finally, there is cause and effect. Steam causes scalding, and if I have experienced steam causing scalding, when the idea of steam comes to mind it is often followed by the idea of scalding.

It is difficult to overstate the importance of these three principles of association to Hume's *Treatise* philosophy. In the *Abstract*, Hume tells us that it is easy to:

> conceive of what vast consequences these principles must be in the science of human nature, if we consider, that so far as regards the

mind, these are the only links that bind the universe together, or connect us with any person or object exterior to ourselves.

(*Abstract* 35)

The 'vast consequences' are that Hume thinks that all human mental life—all thinking—is explained solely in terms of these principles. And yet for something so central to his account and from which flow 'vast consequences', he spends only seven short paragraphs introducing them, and the reader might find what he says too compressed to be fully intelligible. So why is he so brief? Well, again in the *Abstract*, Hume tells us that his claim to 'so glorious a name as that of *an inventor*,' tis the use he makes of the principle of the association of ideas, which enters into most of his philosophy' (*Abstract* 35). As this suggests, Hume did not invent the principles of association, but put them to new uses. Hume is quick in presenting the principles of association because he expects his readers to already be familiar with similar doctrines. It is illuminating to take a brief look at their background.

The phenomenon of association of ideas was a commonplace in the period (even if it is not always called 'association'), and can be found in authors such as Descartes, Hobbes, Spinoza, Malebranche, Leibniz, Locke, Hutcheson and many, many others. The key point is that we have dispositions to think—to move from one idea to another—that (a) are not the product of conscious reflection and (b) are produced by the impact of our experience of the world on our minds, which, for most philosophers of that time, includes our bodies and our brains. For Hobbes, for example, the imagination is nothing but 'decaying sense', where, just as for Hume, fainter images of sense impressions are stored.[7] Such repeated experience leaves a 'trayne of the imagination', the disposition to move from one idea to another. Furthermore, and importantly, it is this phenomenon which guides non-human animals. Although it was accepted that *some* of our thinking is determined by association, it was thought that all non-human thinking—of inferring one idea from another—is determined by association. Thus, Leibniz tells us that the

> ...thought sequences of beasts are only a shadow of reasoning, that is, they are nothing but a connection in the imagination—a passage from one image to another; for when a new situation appears similar to its predecessor, it is expected to have the same concomitant features as before.[8]

And Malebranche, explicitly appealing to the brain, writes that:

> ...beasts, though without a soul...can, in their way, recall the things that have made an impression in their brain, and [so it is easy to conceive] that they are capable of acquiring habits.[9]

This view of the nature of animal inference overlaps with a widespread, but not universally accepted thesis, that animals are merely machines. As Malebranche succinctly puts it, 'the principle of a dog's life is not very different from the motion of a watch'.[10] This gives us a clue as to why associative relations are thought to be 'natural'. The mechanisms that govern the association of ideas are not different in kind from the mechanisms that govern the rest of the natural world. This often connected to a neurophysiology involving 'animal spirits', of which Malebranche offers the most systematic presentation, but which makes its presence felt elsewhere. Thus, for example, John Locke discusses association in his *Essay Concerning Human Understanding*, and, whilst he is generally chary about appealing to neurophysiology—he will not 'meddle with the physical consideration of the mind',[11]—he nevertheless tells us that the phenomenon of association seems 'to be but trains of motion in the animal spirits'.[12]

Hume expects his readers to be familiar with association, hence his brevity, and like Locke, does not 'meddle with the physical consideration of the mind'. (Or, at least, he does not generally do so, but, as we shall see in a moment, he makes an exception when it comes to the associative relation of resemblance.) Instead, he takes the principles of association to be observable phenomena, the existence of which was widely accepted by philosophers. No wonder, then, that he felt he could afford to be so brief in introducing them. However, their significance for Hume's philosophy is great, but not readily apparent at the beginning of the *Treatise*.

As I indicated above, association was understood to be the mechanism which governed animal thought, and, given that humans are themselves embodied creatures, we, too, are prone to such habits of thought. Leibniz puts matters like this:

> Men function like beasts insofar as the connections among their perceptions come about only on the basis of memory...For example, when we expect it to be day tomorrow, we are behaving as empiricist, because until now it has always happened thus.[13]

However, for Leibniz and all of Hume's contemporaries, there are a number of significant differences between humans and animals, and the key one for our concerns is that among the faculties of the human mind is the distinct one of *reason*, which is different in kind from the mechanisms of association. What is novel and indeed revolutionary in Hume is that he is going to attempt to explain *all* human thinking, including reasoning, in associative terms. As he puts it in Book Two, '[e]very thing is conducted by springs and principles, which are not peculiar to man, or any one species of animals' (T 2.2.12.1). This is nothing but a statement of the version of substantive naturalism discussed in the introduction to this book.

The natural relations, then, are general principles which philosophers thought to be no different in kind to the mechanisms that operate in the natural world, and which explain the thought—and hence behaviour—of animals. A key aim of Hume's project is to explain human thought and behaviour in their terms. We also noted that, although association—like the distinction between impressions and ideas—is often explained in terms of the brain, Hume does not make any such appeal. Their causes are 'mostly unknown', and he treats them as '*original* qualities of human nature, which [he] pretend[s] not to explain' (T 1.1.4.6). But this is misleading, because a little later he makes an explicit appeal to the brain in connection with mistakes that originate from associative principles, especially that of resemblance. For such mistakes, he says that although he has not thus far appealed to the idea of brains and animal spirits, he 'must here have recourse to it' (T 1.2.5.20). The account he offers is pretty much the same as that which Malebranche offers, and, in outline, it is as follows. Repeated experience leaves channels or canals on the tissue of the brain, and so when a channel is activated, the relevant idea is produced. The mind is 'endow'd with the power of exciting any idea it pleases' and this is a matter of animal spirits running through those channels. However, sometimes these animal spirits run down the wrong path—they fall 'into the contiguous traces' (T 1.2.5.20)—and so the wrong idea is produced.

What are we to make of this? The key take away is, I think, that the principles of association which Hume uses should be understood as squarely in a naturalistic view of the world, whereby they are mechanical principles that are assumed to be part of the natural world. As such, there is a mechanical underpinning to thinking or a psychophysiology to be developed, but Hume does not see it as his role to develop it. The real significance of Hume's naturalisation of the mind programme will come into focus in Chapter Three of this book.

ABSTRACT IDEAS

Everything we perceive is particular. A particular shade of blue, a particular cat, or a particular pair of glasses. Nevertheless, we are capable of talking not only about this or that particular shade of blue, but of blueness, not of this or that particular cat, but of cats in general, and not of this or that pair of glasses, but of glasses in general. That is, we can talk about general kinds of things, rather than just particulars. How though is this possible, given that all of our ideas are derived from experience, and that we only ever experience particular things?

In T 1.1.7.1 Hume introduces this issue with a question concerning 'abstract or general ideas, whether they be general or particular in the mind's conception of them'. The background to this question is George Berkeley's critique of John Locke's theory of abstract ideas. Indeed, Hume calls Berkeley 'a great philosopher', and holds that his critique of Locke is 'one of the greatest and most valuable discoveries that has been made of late years' (T 1.1.7.1). Locke held that general talk is possible because we form general ideas by a process of abstraction from particulars. Hence the term 'abstract idea'.

It is in the very nature of this abstract idea to represent general things. Abstraction from particular ideas yields new ideas which represent, by its nature, blueness, or cats, rather than this or that particular instance of blue or this or that particular cat.[14] The general terms 'blue' and 'cat' have a meaning because they are related to abstract ideas which represent blueness or the kind cat.

Berkeley famously argues that such ideas are impossible. Suppose the putative idea is the idea of blueness. Blueness comes in many different shades. Could we have an idea that is blue but no particular shade of blue? Or could we have an idea that is an idea of every shade at once? We also talk about colours in general, but could an idea be colour but not of any particular colour or of all colours at once? Suppose, to change the example, the putative idea is the idea of cats. Some cats have tails, others do not, some are black, some are ginger, and some have fur and some do not. How can I have an idea of a cat that is an idea of something that both has and does not have a tail?

As I mentioned, Berkeley thinks such ideas are impossible, and there are two broad ways of understanding why he thinks so. One is that he thinks all ideas are mental images, and that it is impossible to form the relevant images. Suppose the idea of blueness is a blue image. It seems difficult, to say the least, to form an image that is not some *particular* shade of blue, and impossible to form an image that is at once light blue and dark blue. It is no good replying that you can imagine dark blue on the left and light blue on the right—that would be two different ideas, rather than a single idea that represents both dark and light blue. The point is that no single idea, or image, can be light blue and dark blue at once. Think now of the cat. How could one form an image of a cat that is all the colours that cats can be? Or an image of a cat that at once has fur and lacks fur, or that at once has a tail and does not have a tail? Alternatively, one may think that the image might be something that leaves out what is peculiar to particular cats, and keeps only what is common to cats. But then we are faced with trying to form an image of a cat with no particular colour and no particular number of tails.

However, there is another way to understand Berkeley's critique, which, as we shall see, is closer to Hume's position. Rather than arguing that abstract ideas require impossible mental images, his argument rests on the assumption that abstract ideas involve conceiving impossible objects. For example, a triangle that is at once scalene, isosceles, and equilateral. However, Berkeley holds, it is not possible to conceive—form an idea of—impossible objects. There could, to change the example, be nothing blue that is not a determinate shade of blue, nor could there be a colour that is no particular colour. Such things are impossible, and hence inconceivable. Hence there could be no abstract ideas as Locke conceives them.

If there are no abstract ideas, how then do general terms like 'cat' and 'blue' get their meaning? Berkeley's answer relates to Hume's original question, which was whether ideas for general terms 'be general or particular in the mind's conception of them'. Berkeley holds that *particular* ideas can be used 'to stand for' the relevant kind. Consider, for example, the red cross sign. This is used to signify medical assistance. There are plenty of particular red cross signs, individual pictures, dotted around the world. There is a convention of use that governs all these particular signs. There is no inherently general sign, just the *use* made of particular signs. Analogously, Berkeley thinks that when I converse about blueness or cats, I have in mind a particular idea which I use to 'stand for' blueness or cats.

Hume certainly agrees with Berkeley that there are no abstract ideas after the manner of Locke, and, what's more, on the grounds that such putative ideas are ideas of impossibilities. Thus:

> 'tis a principle generally receiv'd in philosophy, that everything in nature is individual, and that 'tis utterly absurd to suppose a triangle really existent, which has no precise proportion of sides and angles. If this therefore be absurd in *fact and reality*, it must also be absurd in idea; since nothing of which we can form a clear and distinct idea of is absurd and impossible.
>
> (T 1.1.7.6)

That is to say, there can be no triangles that are not either scalene, isosceles, or equilateral—i.e. triangles with 'precise proportion of...angles'—and so we cannot form an idea of such things.

Furthermore, since our ideas are derived from impressions, and all that is presented to the senses is 'determin'd in in its degrees both and quality and quantity', then there is no idea which has:

> no particular degree nor proportion. That is a contradiction in terms; and even implies the flattest of all contradictions, *viz.* that 'tis possible for the same thing both to be and not to be.
>
> (T 1.1.7.4)

Hume, then, sides with Berkeley, concluding that 'abstract ideas are therefore themselves individual, however they may become general in their representation' (T1.1.7.6). But Hume has something more to add. I said above that Berkeley states that we use some particular idea to 'stand for' the things of the relevant kind, but there is something lacking in his account, namely an explanation of *how* we come to do that. Locke's account of abstract terms attempted to explain how it is we come to use general terms by appealing to the creation of abstract ideas, whereas Berkeley argues that their meaning consists in our practice of using them to 'stand for' the relevant kinds. He might be right about that, but he lacks an explanation about how humans come to do so. What Hume adds is an explanation of how human beings come to use particular ideas to stand for their relevant kinds. The explanation rests on the principles of association, and, in particular, the associative relation of resemblance. If idea a resembles idea b, then when we have idea a, we automatically think of idea b. Our mind, however, does not stop there. If idea c resembles idea b, then idea c will also come to mind because it resembles idea b, and so on. This serves to explain how abstract terms acquire a meaning, together with an account of what our understanding of those terms consists in. The word 'red' brings to mind a particular idea of red, which then triggers a host of resembling ideas, giving the mind a grasp of the different particular instances of red. It doesn't mean that we get ideas of every particular determinate shade of red, but the train of ideas itself has causal effects, in as much as it causes the mind to acquire a further disposition or power to recall resembling instances, and subsequently the word brings this disposition to mind. The word 'not being able to revive the idea of all these individuals, only touches the soul, if I may be allowed to speak, and revives that custom which we have acquir'd by surveying them' (T 1.1.7.7). This disposition allows us to verify claims about general terms, and also falsify them. Thus, if someone claims that the angles of any triangle are always equilateral, then the disposition can bring to mind a counterexample, thus falsifying the claim. Again, Hume is showing his naturalistic credentials, in that he is giving a causal account of our capacity to use general terms.

SUMMARY

Commentators tend to see the central take-away lesson from the brief opening part of Book One of the *Treatise* as Hume's statement of empiricist credentials. All ideas—concepts—are ultimately derived from experience, and where a word is not appropriately connected with experience—where there is no corresponding impression—that word lacks a meaning. Fundamentally, all thought depends on experience. The rest of the *Treatise* will use this doctrine, enshrined in the Copy Principle, to expose various philosophical notions as meaningless and so bogus. It is undeniable that this is an aspect of Hume's procedure, and we will see many instances where Hume seeks to trace the origin of a given (putative) idea to its corresponding impression. But at least as important, if not more so, is Hume's associationism. As we noted, Hume is very brief in introducing it, but its significance runs deeper than its presentation suggests. Association governs animal thought, the nature of which is no different from the processes that govern the natural world. If this governs human nature, then human nature is no different in kind from the rest of the natural world.

NOTES

1 This is not to say that Hume does not have the resources to develop a more sophisticated account, which some commentators have done. See the Further Reading section.
2 We will return to the question of whether impressions can represent later in this book.

3 Hume has more to say about this traditional notion later in the *Treatise*, as we shall see.
4 For fuller discussions of the missing shade of blue, see e.g. David Pears (1990), pp.25–27, and Garrett (1997), pp. 50–23.
5 Entry on the imagination, 1728.
6 Malebranche, *The Search After Truth*, p.88. Hereafter SAT.
7 Hobbes, *Leviathan*, Part I, Sections 1–5.
8 Leibniz, New Essays on Human Understanding, Section 51.
9 SAT pp.109–110.
10 SAT p.661.
11 Locke, *Essay Concerning Human Understanding* Book 1, Chapter 1, Section 2. Hereafter ECHU.
12 ECHU 1.33.6.
13 Leibniz, *Monadology*, section 28.
14 It is not clear whether that is really Locke's view of abstract ideas, but it is how Berkeley understands it. For further discussion, see Kail (2014a), Chapter Three.

FURTHER READING

For a thorough survey of the question of Hume on mental representation, see Landy (2017). See also Garrett (1997), Chapters Two and Three, Garrett (2006), and Schafer (2013). On the distinction between impressions and ideas, it is still worth looking at Barry Stroud's classic discussion (1977), Chapter Two, and, more recently, Landy (2006). For a more historically grounded discussion of Hume's first principles, see Wright (2009), Chapter Two. For an incisive critique of Hume's characterisation of thought, see Fodor (2003).

2

OF THE IDEAS OF SPACE AND TIME

INTRODUCTION

Part Two of Book One of the *Treatise* is generally regarded as the least successful aspect of the whole work. Very little of what Hume has to say here made its way into the *Enquiry Concerning Human Understanding*, or any of his other writings. He did, nevertheless, maintain some interest in its topics. He drafted an essay on the metaphysical principles of geometry, which he had planned to include in the volume comprising the four extended essays known as the *Four Dissertations*. However, he abandoned it, writing in a letter to William Strahan that a conversation with Lord Stanhope, a skilled mathematician, convinced him that there was 'some defect in the argument or in its perspicuity'.[1] Nevertheless, Einstein would much later applaud Hume's views on time, seeing them as anticipating his own.[2] In this chapter, we shall highlight some of the main themes as well as those features which will inform the rest of the *Treatise*. In line with his naturalism, Hume is primarily focussed on explaining the origin of our ideas and space and time rather than trying to offer a metaphysical account

DOI: 10.4324/9781315667874-3

of space and time. In so doing he also evinces his scepticism. What we can determine about the world is restricted to the appearance of objects to the senses. Any attempt to move beyond such appearance 'will be full of scepticism and uncertainty' (T 1.2.5.26n12).

OF THE INFINITE DIVISIBILITY OF OUR IDEAS OF SPACE AND TIME, AND OF THE INFINITE INDIVISIBILITY OF SPACE AND TIME

Part Two does not start in the way one might expect. One might have expected that Hume would begin by illuminating our ideas of space and time by tracing them to the impressions from which they originate. He does later take this approach, but not where the part begins. Instead, he addresses whether the *ideas* of space and time are infinitely divisible, and then turns to the issue of whether space and time themselves are infinitely divisible (though, in fact, he really only discusses the notion of space here, construed as extension).

Hume's argument against the infinite divisibility of ideas begins with the claim that it is 'universally allow'd that the capacity of the mind is limited and can never attain a full and adequate conception of infinity' (T 1.2.1.2). He then exploits an assumption about ideas, namely that some perceptions, and hence ideas, are extended in two dimensions. My impression of, say, a red circle is something that has a visual extension and my idea of it, being an exact copy, is also extended. This is a consequence of Hume's conception of ideas, and their relation to experience, discussed in the previous chapter. My visual experience is extended and so my visual ideas, which are copies of experience, are extended. He then considers whether any such ideas are infinitely divisible and argues that none are. He writes that 'whatever is capable of being divided *in infinitum*, must consist in an infinite number of parts' (T 1.2.1.2), but this is an absurdity because anything comprising infinite parts, he thinks, must be infinitely extended. This contradicts the acknowledged limited nature of the mind. So, we must conclude that any finitely extended idea is constituted by non-extended parts that admit of no further divisibility.

We shall come to this last point presently, but we should pause to note a fallacy in the above argument. Hume is thinking that either parts are extended—and given infinite divisibility, such parts are extended—or that we reach some minimal non-extended points. When we conceive of dividing something we need not think of it as containing discrete parts of the same size: instead, these notional parts are a matter of *proportion*. So, we can imagine dividing something in half, and then in half again, and so on *ad infinitum* without thinking that this leads to absurdity. Hume, however, thinks such parts must be 'aliquot', i.e. parts with a fixed extension, rather merely being proportions.

Whatever we might think of Hume's arguments, his conclusion is that our extended ideas are constituted by extensionless coloured points. He illustrates this with an example. If one puts a spot of ink on a piece of paper, and moves it away, then 'at last you lose sight of it; 'tis plain, that the moment before it vanish'd the image or impression was perfectly indivisible' (T 1.2.1.4). Extended ideas are composed of minimally sensible points, otherwise known as *minima sensibilia*. These themselves are not extended but the 'disposition of [these] points' (T 1.2.3.5) constitutes any particular extension. Recall the spot of ink on a piece of paper. As the piece of paper recedes, the spot of ink gets smaller and smaller and then it vanishes. There is a minimum that anything perceptible can reach. Our ordinary extended ideas then are composed of these points, though we do not perceive them *as* points. The points are 'minute and so confounded with each other' (T 1.2.4.19) that we experience a continuous extension rather than a series of points. And, although Hume does not explicitly mention it at this early stage, visual ideas are not the only extended ideas. Extension is also grasped by touch, and he mentions the disposition of tangible points, a collection of different *minima sensibilia*. Fundamentally, our experience of extension is a matter of the extension of ideas, an extension composed of *minima sensibilia*.

What, then, of space and time themselves, rather than our *ideas* of space and time? This is the topic of T 1.2.2, and Hume begins with a general claim about 'adequate ideas':

> Wherever ideas are adequate representations of objects, the relations, contradictions and agreements of the ideas are all applicable to the objects...[and hence] whatever *appears* impossible and contradictory

upon the comparison of these ideas, must be *really* impossible and contradictory, without any farther excuse or evasion.

(T 1.2.2.1)

On the assumption that our ideas of extension are adequate representations, then it seems that, since those ideas are not infinitely divisible but are composed of indivisible and extensionless points, then space itself—extension—must be composed of indivisible and extensionless points. But before we conclude that Hume is making a claim about how the world in itself is—that is, the nature of the world external to our minds—we need to note something that Hume says later in Part Two. He writes that his 'intention never was to penetrate into the nature of body', and contents himself with 'knowing perfectly the manner in which objects affect [his] senses' (T 1.2.5.26). A passage from the *Appendix*, which he wanted inserted into Part Two at this point continues:

> As long as we confine our speculations to the *appearances* of objects to our senses, without entering into disquisitions concerning their real nature and operations, we are safe from all difficulties, and can never be embarrass'd by any question...If we carry our enquiry beyond the appearances of objects to the senses, I am afraid, that most of our conclusions will be full of scepticism and uncertainty.
>
> (T 1.2.5.26n12)

There is, then, a tension here. On the one hand, Hume seems to be telling us that if our ideas are adequate representations of objects,[3] then we can know something about the nature of space and extension itself. Since our ideas are composed of indivisible extensionless units, space itself must be so composed. Yet, on the other hand, he is telling us that we cannot know anything beyond the mere appearances of objects. How can we resolve this tension?

First, we need to consider what Hume means by 'adequate ideas'. He himself does not explain that notion, but the use of 'adequacy' by other philosophers of the period points to a conception of adequacy whereby adequate ideas reveal *everything* about the objects of those ideas. Spinoza and Locke, though both having rather different conceptions of ideas, nevertheless take adequacy to mean that such ideas involve complete knowledge of their objects.[4] We can see why Hume thinks that ideas are adequate representations of their objects, since they are exact copies of the objects that cause them. But those 'objects' are impressions or the 'appearances of objects'. There is, however, no reason to think that *impressions* themselves are adequate representations of external objects. Hume holds that we can have only an extremely limited conception of the world beyond our senses, and later in the *Treatise* reveals that he does not think that impressions are adequate representations:

> any conclusion we form concerning the connexion and repugnance of impressions, will not be known certainly to be applicable to objects.... As an object is suppos'd to be different from an impression, we cannot be sure, that the circumstance, upon which we found our reasoning, is common to both, supposing we form the reasoning upon the impression. 'Tis still possible, that the object may differ from it in that particular.
>
> (T 1.4.5.20)

What we should conclude then is that Hume's claims about space are claims not about the world external to our senses but simply about the world as it appears.

Before we turn to Hume's account of the origin of our ideas of space (and time), we should briefly note that his limitation of our conception of space to the appearances of objects informs his view of geometry. Geometry is a subject that seems *a priori* knowable, and, at the same time, describes the spatial world. However, for Hume, our ideas of space are drawn not from space itself but 'the general appearance of things'. It is a science which, although

> it much excels both in universality and exactness, the loose judgements of the senses and the imagination; yet never attains a perfect precision and exactness. Its first principles are still drawn from the general appearance of objects; and that appearance can never afford us any security, when we examine the prodigious minuteness of which nature is susceptible. Our ideas seem to give a perfect assurance, that no two right lines can have a common segment; but if we consider

these ideas, we shall find, that they always suppose a sensible inclination of the two lines, and that where the angle they form is extremely small, we have no standard of a right line so precise as to assure us of the truth of this proposition.

(T 1.3.1.4)

We cannot know that our ideas are exact, and so we cannot attain full certainty about what the fundamentals of geometry are.

THE ORIGIN OF THE IDEAS OF SPACE AND TIME

Hume considers a whole host of objections to his views on space and whether it is infinitely divisible or not, but we shall not discuss these. Instead, let us consider his account of the origin of our ideas of space and time. This is offered in T 1.2.3, 'Of the other qualities of our ideas of space and time'. We have impressions of extended items and by 'considering the distance betwixt these bodies, [we] acquire the idea of extension' (T 1.2.3.2). How so? The idea of space is an abstract one, acquired in the manner we discussed in the previous chapter. We experience different extended items, and then differences—such as their colour—are omitted in order to isolate what is common, namely 'that disposition of points, or manner of appearance, in which they agree' (T 1.2.3.5). Resemblances in this respect, and also between dispositions of tangible points and coloured points, help to form the abstract idea of space.

What of the idea of time? The origin of this idea lies in the succession of perceptions, and not merely the extended ideas and impressions. Impressions 'of reflections as well as sensation, will afford us an instance of an abstract idea, which comprehends a still greater variety than that of space' (T 1.2.3.6). This means that we do not have an idea of time distinct from objects. It is their ordering which gives us the idea of time. This has a significant consequence. Since time is the manner of succession, it seems that we cannot conceive of an unchangeable or 'stedfast' object enduring through time (T 1.2.3.11). This seems counterintuitive. We seem to be able to imagine an object continuing to exist in time even though it does not change, but for Hume '[w]herever we have no successive perceptions, we have no notion of time' (T 1.2.3.7). This is because the idea of time derives from succession. Nevertheless, we imagine we have an idea of certain objects enduring through time: "tho it be impossible to show the impression, from which the idea of time without a changeable existence is deriv'd; yet we can easily point out those appearances, which make us fancy we have that idea' (T 1.2.5.29). This is because unchanged objects can coexist embedded in change. So, for example, I can watch my cat running around in a box. The box itself remains unchanged, whilst the cat (or the collection of perceptions I identify as the cat) constantly changes, so I come to think that both the box and the cat continue through time.

Similar considerations apply to the supposed idea of a vacuum. Since the 'idea of space and extension is nothing but the idea of visible or tangible points distributed in a certain order', then 'we can form no idea of a vacuum, or space, where there is nothing visible or tangible' (T 1.2.5.1), even though, like that of unchanging duration, we 'falsely imagine we can form such an idea' (T 1.2.5.14). To explain how we do so, Hume distinguishes between what he calls 'two kinds of distance' (T 1.2.5.19). Imagine two visible objects separated from each other 'in the midst of utter darkness' (T 1.2.5.15). The 'utter darkness' is not itself an impression but rather the absence of any impression, and so itself cannot give rise to an idea of space. Nevertheless, the two objects occupy different parts of the visual field, and we conceive this separation to be 'an invisible and intangible distance' (T 1.2.5.16). This contrasts with when there is a visible or tangible distance between two objects, i.e. when we have experience of an extended thing between the two. Hume then argues that we come to think that there is an idea of unoccupied space—an idea of a vacuum—because we are apt to mistake distinct but resembling things.

Now, we shall not follow Hume in the details of his explanation here, but it is worth pausing to record something he says at this point. Recall that resemblance is one of the 'natural relations' or the principles of association. Resemblance, says Hume, is 'the most fertile source of error; and indeed there are few mistakes in reasoning, which do not borrow largely from that origin...Of this we shall see many instances in the progress of this treatise'

(T 1.2.5.21). Such mistakes will be particularly important in Hume's account of our belief in the external world and in the idea of an enduring self, and we shall discuss these in Chapter Four. What is significant here, though, is that Hume feels the need to engage in some physiological speculation in order to explain how resemblance has its effects. He writes that it would

> have been easy to have made an imaginary dissection of the brain, and have shown, why upon our conception of any idea, the animal spirits run into all the contiguous traces, and rouze up the other ideas, that are related to it. But tho' I have neglected any advantage, which I might have drawn from this topic in explaining the relation of ideas, I am afraid I must here have recourse to it, in order to account for the mistakes that arise from these relations.
>
> (T 1.2.5.20)

This I mentioned in the previous chapter. Hume's *Treatise* is written against a background where the phenomenon of the association of ideas is thought to have a physiological basis. Association lies in the brain having its physical nature configured by repeat experience, which leaves traces in the brain's physical structure, and in turn affects the passage of thought. Resemblance is conducive to error because resembling, but distinct, stimuli leave contiguous brain traces, through which run 'animal spirits'. A stimulus can lead to a thought-flow which is not direct but 'falling into the contiguous traces, present other related ideas in lieu of that, which the mind desir'd at first to survey' (T 1.2.5.2). Whatever we might think of the details of this explanation, it is a useful reminder of the naturalistic assumptions that run throughout the *Treatise*.

OF THE IDEA OF EXISTENCE, AND EXTERNAL EXISTENCE

Hume closes Part Two by addressing two related issues. The first concerns the notion of existence. What do we mean by existence? For Hume, of course, this issue turns on what our idea of existence might be. To illuminate an idea, Hume generally seeks an appropriate impression, but he finds no impression distinct from particular perceptions. That is to say, when he conceives of any object (that is, of any perception), there is no separate idea of existence which is added to that perception. Instead, everything that is conceived is also conceived as existing:

> The idea of existence, then, is the very same with the idea of what we conceive to be existent. To reflect on any thing simply, and to reflect on it as existent, are nothing different from each other...Whatever we conceive, we conceive to be existent. Any idea we please to form is the idea of a being; and the idea of a being is any idea we please to form.
> (T 1.2.6.4)

So, there is no separate idea of existence. That is not to say that anything we *conceive* to exist we also *believe* to exist. As we shall see in the next chapter, Hume has an account of what it is to believe rather than to conceive something. The claim here is that to think of a thing is to think of the thing existing. What is unclear, however, is whether Hume thinks there is an idea of existence, but one that is not separable from particular ideas, or that the event of conceiving something—the having of an idea—is the same with conceiving that thing as it existing. Even if we were to decide that issue, there is a further one. In the first *Enquiry*, Hume writes that 'the non-existence of any being, without exception, is as clear and distinct an idea as its existence' (EHU 12.28). So, he holds, as he should, that we can conceive of any being as *not* existing. The problem is to see how this is possible, given that he has told us that to form an idea of something is the same as forming the idea of its existing. I can clearly form an idea of Spider-Man and conceive that he does not exist. However, the idea of existence is not separable from any idea, so it cannot be that my thought that Spider-Man does not exist is a matter of my separating existence from that idea. Nor will the absence of the idea function as a way of conceiving the non-existence of Spider-Man. An idea is required to provide the content for the thought of whatever is conceived to be non-existent.

As well as the idea of existence, Hume considers the topic of 'external existence'. All that we are immediately aware of is perceptions. How is it possible to conceive of any existence external to perceptions? At first sight, it seems straightforwardly that we cannot conceive of anything beyond perceptions.

> Let us fix our attention out of ourselves as much as possible: Let us chace our imagination to the heavens, or to the utmost limits of the universe; we never really advance a step beyond ourselves, nor can we conceive any kind of existence, but those perceptions, which have appear'd in that narrow compass. This is the universe of the imagination, nor have we any idea but what is there produc'd.
>
> (T 1.2.6.8)

To think of something requires having ideas, but the only things of which we have ideas are our impressions. We have no idea of anything beyond impressions and so we cannot conceive of any external existence.

However, Hume seems to be a little more liberal than this statement suggests. We can form what he calls a 'relative idea' of an object. If we think of any objects, we must think of them to be like perceptions, since perceptions are the only things of which we have any positive conception. However, we can suppose them to be 'specifically different from perceptions...without pretending to comprehend' such external objects (T 1.2.6.9). So, we can think that there is some object other than a perception, one which is different in some specific way from any perception, even though we cannot form any idea of what that difference might be. We saw an instance of this earlier in this chapter, when Hume writes that:

> any conclusion we form concerning the connexion and repugnance of impressions, will not be known certainly to be applicable to objects... As an object is suppos'd to be different from an impression...
>
> (T 1.4.5.20)

So, we do suppose that external objects are different from perceptions but in some unspecified way. Hence our idea of them is a 'relative idea', one where we do not 'comprehend the related object'. This allows of some conception of a world beyond experience, albeit a very thin one. We can suppose that the world is somehow different from our perceptions, but we can have no positive conception of the way(s) in which it differs.

Hume makes one more point in this connection. He writes that we do not generally suppose objects to be 'specifically different' from perceptions. Instead, we think of external objects to be *like* perceptions but to have 'different relations, connexions and durations' (T 1.2.6.9). We suppose, that is, that objects that are not perceptions (but which resemble perceptions) continue to exist when we do not perceive them, and are distinct from our experience of them. How we come to believe that this is so, is the topic of T 1.4.2, 'Of scepticism with regard to the senses', which we shall discuss in Chapter Four of this book.

NOTES

1 HL, II, p.253.
2 See Slavov (2016) for discussion.
3 An anonymous reader for this book suggested that Hume means something different by 'adequate' here and so there isn't the tension I identify but I see no reason to think that Hume is departing from the standard usage of 'adequate' by Locke, Spinoza, Arnauld and others.
4 For discussion of this, see Kail (2003).

FURTHER READING

Book-length studies of Part Two include Frasca-Spada (1998), Jacquette (2001), and Baxter (2008). See also Flew (1986), Chapter Three, Fogelin (1985), Chapter Three, Garrett (1997), Chapter Two, Falkenstein (1997) and (2009), and Baxter (2016).

3

OF KNOWLEDGE AND PROBABILITY

INTRODUCTION

Part Three of Book One of the *Treatise* contains Hume's discussion of reason. It also contains his discussion of the relation of causation and his account of belief, and all three of these topics are intertwined. The views expounded in this part of the *Treatise* are among the most profound and original aspects of Hume's philosophy and, as we shall see, constitute an integrated expression of Hume's brand of naturalism.

As I mentioned in the introduction, Hume's account of human cognition undermines the view that there is a difference in kind between human beings and the rest of animal creation, and it is in this part of the *Treatise* where a supposed difference in terms of reason comes into focus. Recall this passage from Leibniz:

> Beasts pass from one imagining to another by means of a link between them which they have previously experienced. For instance, when his master picks up a stick the dog anticipates being beaten... This could be called 'inference' or 'reasoning' in a very broad sense.

But I prefer to keep to accepted usage, reserving these words for men and restricting them to the knowledge of some *reason* for perceptions' being linked together. Mere sensations cannot provide this: all they do is to cause one naturally to expect once more the same linking that has been observed previously.[1] Hume will argue that what Leibniz thinks is reason in only a broad sense is actually what constitutes the bulk of what human reason is.

Within this chapter we shall also explore whether Hume was a sceptic about probable inference, his account of belief, and his views on the relation of causation.

T 1.3.1 OF KNOWLEDGE

Hume opens this part of the *Treatise* by introducing seven 'philosophical relation[s]'. Some of these are the objects of knowledge, whereas one, cause and effect, is the object of probability, which we shall discuss in the next section. In Chapter One we discussed the natural or associative relations. Philosophical relations comprise those ways in which objects can be compared, regardless of any associative effect they may have on the mind. In comparing ideas, we can discover that they stand in one or more of the following relations, namely *resemblance*, *identity*, *relations of time and place*, *proportion in quantity or number*, *degrees in any quality*, *contrariety*, and *causation*.

Such relations can be divided into two different classes, 'constant' and 'inconstant'. The latter relations can change without the objects themselves changing in their intrinsic character, whereas the former relations depend essentially on the intrinsic character of the ideas compared. This requires some explanation. Relations in place are inconstant because that type of relation can change without the objects being compared changing in their character. A square on the left-hand side of a triangle might swap position and then be on the right-hand side of the triangle. The relation has now changed, even though the triangle and the square have not changed in themselves. Consider now the relation of degree in quality. Suppose we think that one shade of blue B is n-degree deeper than a different shade of blue B*. If we change B so as to make it lighter, then its relation to B* changes because we have changed the intrinsic character of B. The class of relations of the former, inconstant type, comprises identity, situations in time and place, and cause and effect. The class of constant relations comprise the remaining four, namely resemblance, degree in quality, proportion in quantity of number, and contrariety.

What, though, does this have to do with knowledge? These relations are the *objects* of knowledge, or rather, the four constant relations are the objects of knowledge (causation is the object of probability, as we shall see). In three cases—resemblance, degree in quality, and contrariety—we come to know that objects exhibit these relations through 'intuition', a kind of immediate cognition or mental 'seeing'. Once we 'see' that ideas resemble, are related by degree in quality, or are contrary, the mind 'assents' to the fact intuited and is 'necessarily determin'd to conceive the ideas according to the proposition' (T. 1.3.7.3). Intuition of these relations compels us to knowledge of their truth. We simply 'see' that two shades of red resemble each other, or that one shade is deeper than the other. Contrariety is more difficult. Hume gives us only one example, that the idea of existence and the idea of non-existence 'destroy each other, and are perfectly incompatible and contrary' (T 1.3.1.2). It seems that we can have intuitive knowledge that two things can exclude each other, though Hume also claims that no two ideas are contrary, except those of existence and non-existence.[2] Perhaps what we cognize when we discover contrariety is that the existence of one thing excludes the existence of another.

Hume thinks that mental intuition yields certainty, and hence it is why it yields knowledge. Knowledge affords no room for doubt. As well as the three relations which we have just discussed which 'can be the objects of knowledge and certainty' (T 1.3.1.2), there is a fourth, namely proportion of quantity of number, or, in other words, mathematical relations. Some simple mathematical relations we are capable of grasping by intuition. We simply 'see' that 2+2=4. However, the number of intuitively knowable mathematical relations is vanishingly small in comparison to the extent of all mathematical relations. 5491÷19=289 is a relation between numbers that is not known intuitively. These relations are discoverable by *reason* or, more precisely, *demonstrative* reason. Such knowledge involves starting from intuitively grasped relations and 'seeing' further relations between these and other truths. We follow each link in the chain in order to discover some conclusion that is not intuitively certain but, via this sequence of intuitively certain steps, we come to see as *demonstratively* certain.

One important sense in which demonstration is *reason* is that it involves inference, namely arriving at a new judgment on the basis of previous judgments. It is a psychological process. This will be very important when we come to discuss *probable* reason. We need to note three further important things about demonstration. First, that it should not be confused with a different notion, namely *deduction*. Second, and relatedly, an otherwise puzzling feature of the status of conclusions drawn from demonstration. The conclusions are those of which it is impossible to conceive the contrary. Third, Hume offers an important qualification regarding geometry.

It is sometimes said that demonstration for Hume is simply what is now known as deduction. Deductive arguments are arguments that have a particular *form*, and are valid in virtue of this, where 'validity' means that it is impossible for the premises of such an argument to be true and its conclusion to be false. We could then say that deductive reasoning is simply drawing conclusions in line with the rules that govern deductive validity. Consider this very basic deductive form (which is known as *modus ponens*):

$$p$$
$$p \supset q$$
$$\therefore q$$

Here 'p' and 'q' refer to propositions (roughly the meanings of sentences). 'p $\supset$ q' is a complex proposition, complex because it is made up of two propositions p and q, related by a *connective*, in this case '$\supset$', which means, roughly, 'if p then q is'. 'p' and 'p $\supset$ q' are the two *premises* of this argument, and 'q' is the *conclusion* (the '$\therefore$' symbol stands for 'therefore'). What is important for our concerns is that the validity argument does not depend on what the sentences involved *mean* but only on the *form* of the argument.

To make this more concrete, consider the following two arguments, both of which are valid.

(1) Snow is white
    If snow is white, eagles have wings
    Therefore, eagles have wings.
(2) Cats purr
    If cats purr, guitars are expensive
    Therefore, guitars are expensive

Both of these arguments are valid because of their *form*, and not their *content*—the meaning of—the premises.

Demonstration is *not* like this: instead, one infers by becoming aware of what the meaning of a concept or idea implies. Thus, Hume tells us "'tis from the idea of a triangle, that we discover the relation of equality, which its three angles bear to two right ones' (T 1.3.1.1). We are, that is, unpacking what is implied by the concept or idea of a triangle. I can intuitively know that a triangle implies its three-sidedness and by further mental reflection or the application of demonstrative reason, I can come to see that the idea of a triangle implies that its angles all sum to 180 degrees. What is important to demonstration then is not the form of arguments but what the concept or idea implies.

This brings us to a second feature of demonstration, one which also distinguishes it from deduction. When we demonstrate some proposition we come to an awareness that it is *impossible* for what we have demonstrated to be false, something that Hume expresses by saying that we cannot *conceive* of its falsity. By contrast, I can have a perfectly valid argument for a conclusion, but nevertheless be able to conceive of the falsity of its conclusion. I can argue that all men are mortal, that Socrates is a man, conclude validly that Socrates is mortal, and yet still be able to conceive that Socrates is immortal. Hume, however, often argues that a proposition cannot be the object of demonstrative reason because we find it possible for that proposition to be false. For example, he tells us that there can be no demonstrative proof for the proposition that nature will remain constant because we can conceive of a change in the course of nature:

> We can at least conceive a change in the course of nature; which sufficiently proves, that such a change is not absolutely impossible. To form a clear idea of any thing, is an undeniable argument for its possibility, and is alone a refutation of any pretended demonstration against it.
>
> (T 1.3.6.5)

What underlies this feature of demonstration? It seems to rest on the idea again that certain concepts imply consequences. When, for example, I come to see that the concept 'bachelor' implies that of 'unmarried man' it becomes impossible to conceive of a bachelor who is *not* an unmarried man. Properly grasping the implications of concepts reveals some things to be impossible relative to what the concept implies. But we should note further that ideas or concepts are exact copies of their objects, namely impressions, and so fundamentally the ideas or concepts and the relations among them reflect relations among those objects.

There is a good question to be asked about how we determine what things are implied by concepts. One popular answer is that such truths are simply determined by what the concept means. Thus, it is true that a triangle has three sides because that is part of what the concept 'triangle' means. 'Some triangles are yellow' is certainly true as well, but we can certainly conceive as possible that there are no yellow triangles, and this is so because it is not part of the meaning of 'triangle' that some are yellow. It just happens to be true that some triangles are that colour.

For Hume, the notion of a concept's implications, and what it does not imply, is bound up with what is known as the 'separability principle', which is stated early in the *Treatise*:

> ...whatever objects are different are distinguishable, and...whatever objects are distinguishable are separable by the thought and imagination. And...whatever objects are separable are also distinguishable, and...whatever objects are distinguishable are also different.
>
> (T 1.1.7.3)

This principle is fundamental to a good deal of what Hume discusses, but he does not offer too much in the way of explanation of it. What we can say is that we know that, for Hume, ideas are centrally images, and so 'separation' could be understood in terms of the possibility of imagining one thing without the other. My idea of a triangle is distinct from my idea of a square because I am able to think of the one without the other by forming an image of the one without the other. When it comes to a triangle, and its three-sidedness, I am *not* able to imagine a triangle without its three sides. I am able to make what Hume calls a 'distinction of reason' (T 1.1.7.18), that is to consider the triangle at one time, and one of its sides at another, but the two things are not distinct and so not separable in the sense that I cannot imagine the existence of the one without the other.

There is a final thing to note about demonstration before we turn to probability. Mathematics is an area where it is plausible to think we have *a priori* knowledge. For a truth to be knowable *a priori* means, roughly, that we can know that truth independently of what we can learn from experience. Thus, I know that 2+2=4 no matter what else I might discover about the world through my senses. I will not, for example, travel to Australia, and learn, to my surprise, that 2+2=5. *A priori* contrasts with *a posteriori* since our knowledge of *a posteriori* propositions is dependent on experience. So, one might come to the belief that all swans are white, but, when arriving in Australia, come across some black ones.

There might seem to be something mysterious about *a priori* knowledge. How can we know something in a way that does not depend on our experience of the world? One way to dispel this mystery would be to say that what we gain knowledge of is simply more knowledge of what our concepts imply. Thus, we can know *a priori* that 'all bachelors are unmarried men' because we come to know what the relevant concepts mean. Similarly, we know that 2+2=4 because we know what '2', '+', '=' and '4' mean. So, knowledge of mathematics is *a priori*, and its objects are relations among ideas or meanings.

So far so good, but there is a little wrinkle to note about Hume's treatment of geometry. It is not a subject matter where we can attain 'a perfect precision and exactness' (T 1.3.1.4). As we noted briefly in the previous chapter, our ideas of triangles or squares, or anything geometrical, are ultimately dependent on experience, and are 'drawn from the general appearance of the objects'. Furthermore, 'appearance can never afford us any security, when we examine the prodigious minuteness of which nature is capable' (T 1.3.1.4). We saw something of this in the previous chapter, but its relevance here is that the ideas with which we are employed are taken to represent the world, but those representations may fall short of the world. In this respect, geometry is not *a priori*, even though it concerns constant relations of ideas which are capable of demonstration.

T 1.3.2 OF PROBABILITY; AND OF THE IDEA OF CAUSE AND EFFECT

At the heart of Book One, Part Three, is Hume's account of causal reason. This is the account he offers of how we infer effects from causes and causes from effects. He is often taken to be a sceptic about such inferences, holding that such inferences have no epistemic value. We shall be discussing this reading later, but it is important to go through matters slowly since the issues surrounding causal or probable reason are complicated and delicate. In this section, we look at Hume's initial discussion of the causal relation, and its connection to inference and reasons for belief. We then discuss the causal maxim, before turning to Hume's treatment of causal inference.

Two of the three remaining philosophical relations, identity and situations in time and place, are known by perception. This leaves us with the relation of cause and effect, and this relation is the object of *probable* reason. We noted above that reason is tied to the notion of *inference*, understood as the psychological transition from what is believed to a new belief. The inferences distinctive of probable reason are the inferences related to the philosophical relation of cause and effect, and so the question concerns the transition of the idea of one to the other.

Why is cause and effect the important relation here? Fundamental to our existence is our capacity to form beliefs about what we do not presently observe. Every action I take requires the capacity to predict what is going to happen, either in the immediate or remote future, and so that requires me to be able to form beliefs about the future. Now, if I know that some object is the cause of another, then I can predict that its effect will follow. If I know that steam causes scalding, then when I see the steam, I will be able to predict that I will be scalded were I to get too close to it. Hence, Hume is interested in causation because it is the only relation 'that can be trac'd beyond our senses, and informs us of existences and objects, which we do not see or feel' (T 1.3.2.3).

This brings us to a different sense of 'reason'. I mentioned 'reasoning' as the movement from one thought or belief to another, but one might counter that this is not a particularly precise way of putting matters. Reasoning is not simply one thought being followed by another, but instead forming a new thought by coming to appreciate that there is some support or *reason in favour* for that thought. Consider what we would think of someone who saw a duck and, on the basis of this observation, arrived at the thought that it will rain bananas. Our reaction to such a thought would be that it is unjustified, unreasonable, or, perhaps, just plain crazy. We would have this reaction because we think that there is no connection whatsoever between the presence of a duck and its raining bananas. In the case of the steam and scalding, however, there *is* some connection, namely that steam *causes* scalding. My inference is a form of reasoning not merely because it is a movement from one thought to another, but one that is made in the light of my knowledge that there is a causal connection between the two. Such knowledge is my *reason* or support for the inference. Hence, Hume says the relation of cause and effect alone gives 'us an assurance from the existence or action of one object' (T 1.3.2.2) to that of another.

Let us put this together with Hume's claim that all 'kinds of reasoning consist in nothing but a *comparison*, and a discovery of those relations...which two or more objects bear to each other' (T 1.3.2.1). Probable reason is the faculty that compares objects and discovers whether they stand in the causal relation. In other words, probable reason, in discovering causal relations, discovers *reasons* for beliefs. So, quite naturally, Hume turns to consider our idea of the relation of cause and effect, since it is 'impossible to reason justly, without understanding perfectly the idea concerning which we reason' (T 1.3.2.4).

What we might expect then is to be offered a definition of 'causation' before going on to discuss probable or causal inference. But this is not what Hume does. Hume only offers definitions of 'cause and effect' *after* he has examined causal inference. This is puzzling. Probable reason is reason based on the causal relation, so it would seem we would need to know what that relation is before we can explain causal reasoning. Hume shows that he is aware of how puzzling this is when he writes of his 'seemingly preposterous' method of 'examining our inference from the relation before we had explain'd the relation itself' (T 1.3.14.30). Hume's 'seemingly preposterous' method is of first importance to understanding his originality on the topic of causation, and we will discuss it fully when we come to discuss that topic. Nevertheless, Hume does make a number of claims about the causal relation when discussing causal inference which we shall note here.

In T 1.3.2 Hume makes three observations about the causal relation. First, he notes that any relation which we deem causal involves *contiguity*. When we think of something as the cause of something else, Hume claims, we do not think that there is action at a distance, either in a spatial or temporal sense. Nothing 'can operate in a time or place, which is ever so little remov'd of each other' (T 1.3.2.6). Second, he notes that we think in terms of a temporal *priority* of cause over effect—we hold that causes are always prior to effects, never after, or simultaneous with, effects (T 1.3.2.7).

Hume is extremely swift in his treatment of both claims. First, in claiming that cause and effect must be contiguous, he breezily passes over the problem generated by Newton's physics, namely that it seems precisely to require action at a distance. Hume simply claims that in such cases we generally *presume* that there is some yet to be discovered contiguity. We can, he says, 'suppose' that contiguity is 'essential' to causation 'according to the general opinion' (T 1.3.2.6) that it is so. With respect to temporal priority, Hume does not stop to consider cases where cause and effect might plausibly be thought to be simultaneous. My cat sitting on a pillow is the cause of the depression in the pillow, and it seems here that cause and effect are simultaneous. Hume offers an argument in favour of temporal priority, but is remarkably insouciant about it, writing that 'if the argument appear satisfactory, 'tis well. If not, I beg the reader to allow me the...liberty...of supposing' that causes are prior to effects. We 'shall find, that the affair is of no great importance' (T 1.3.2.8).

The third thing Hume notes about the idea of causation is something he deems to be 'of much greater importance' (T 1.3.2.11) than contiguity or priority. We think that causes have powers in virtue of which they bring about their effects. Hume calls this 'power or necessary connection'. Hume notes that no such powers are observable and postpones his discussion of the idea of power until later in the *Treatise*, and we shall do the same as well.

So far, Hume treats the causal relation as a relation between objects, where the cause is prior to, and contiguous with, an effect. But later (T 1.3.6.3) Hume adds another component to our idea of cause and effect, that of *constant conjunction*. Why he includes this in the idea of cause and effect is itself a fascinating matter, but we shall talk about it when we discuss Hume's view on the causal relation towards the end of this chapter. But what is 'constant conjunction'? We don't think that a is the cause of b if a is only followed by b occasionally. Instead to think of a as the cause of b we must take it that *every* instance of a is followed by an instance of b. To put it slightly differently, a is the cause of b when they instantiate a universal regularity holding between type A and type B, of which a and b are tokens.

In summary, probable reason concerns the relation of cause and effect, the relation which gives 'us an assurance from the existence or action of one object' to that of another (T 1.3.2.2). Knowing that a and b are causally related therefore provides a reason for drawing an inference from what we have observed to what we have yet to observe. Our *idea* of that relation is a matter of any cause being prior to, contiguous with, and constantly conjoined with another object which is its effect. This leaves a question outstanding. How do we draw such inferences from cause and effect? This question will take us to the heart of Hume's discussion, and we shall turn to it in the section after next. First, however, we need to discuss what is known as the 'causal maxim'.

T 1.3.3 WHY A CAUSE IS ALWAYS NECESSARY

Before discussing the inferences that we draw from cause and effect, Hume considers the assumption that, necessarily, everything that exists has a cause. This, Hume phrases as the question of why 'we pronounce it *necessary*, that everything whose existence has a beginning, shou'd also have a cause' (T 1.3.2.14). This thesis has become known as the 'causal maxim'. Hume's positive explanation of why we *think* that every event necessarily has a cause is rolled into his discussion of why we think that causes necessitate effects: he 'will find it more convenient to sink [the] question in the following, *Why we conclude, that such particular causes must necessarily have such particular effects, and why we form an inference from one to another?*' (T 1.3.3.9). What concerns him, and us, at this stage, is showing that we cannot have knowledge of the causal maxim by intuition or demonstration.

If it is not something we can know through intuition, the question is whether we can have any demonstrative proof of this 'causal maxim'. Hume argues that any such demonstrative proof is impossible, writing that:

> as all distinct ideas are separable from each other, and as the ideas of cause and effect are evidently, 'twill be easy for us to conceive any object to be non-existent this moment, and existent the next, without conjoining to it the distinct idea of a cause or productive principle. The separation, therefore, of the idea of a cause from that of a beginning of existence, is plainly possible for the imagination; and consequently the actual separation of these objects is so far possible, that it implies no contradiction nor absurdity; and is therefore incapable of being refuted by any reasoning from mere ideas; without which 'tis impossible to demonstrate the necessity of a cause.
>
> (T 1.3.3.3)

The thought here is as follows. Demonstration is a matter of awareness of relations, and here we are looking for a relation of necessity between some object O and its having a cause or 'productive principle' C. That is, what we would have to be aware of is the *impossibility* of O without there being a C. Such awareness would be constituted by finding it impossible to *conceive* O without some cause C. But the ideas of effect and of cause are distinct, so we can always conceive one without the other. Hence, we cannot by reason show that any event must have a cause, because that would require seeing that the event is inconceivable without a cause.

The thesis that the ideas of cause and effect are distinct, and hence that we can never perceive a necessary connection between the two, is a constant refrain in Hume's discussion, and I shall reserve discussion of it until later. Here we should note that he briefly considers, and rejects, three further arguments for the causal maxim. One, which he attributes to Samuel Clarke, argues that if an event does not have a cause, it must therefore be self-caused. But this simply begs the question, since it assumes that everything must have a cause. The second, which he attributes to John Locke, is the claim that an event without a cause would have nothing as a cause, but nothingness cannot be a cause. This yet again begs the question.

The third argument, which is first in Hume's order of presentation, he attributes to Hobbes, and it runs as follows:

> All points of time and place...in which we can suppose any object to begin to exist, are in themselves equal; and unless there be some cause, which is peculiar to one time and to one place, and by which that means determines and fixes the existence, it must remain in eternal suspense; and the object can never begin to be, for want of something to fix its beginning.
>
> (T 1.3.3.4)

The thought here is that there must be something which explains why A occurs just in that place and just at the time, since there is nothing in the particular times and places which explains why just there and just then. But again, although this sounds plausible, there is no evident reason why things might not just pop into existence. We might search for an answer but there is no logical impossibility to things just popping into existence.

T 1.3.6 OF THE INFERENCE FROM THE IMPRESSION TO THE IDEA: SCEPTICISM, NATURALISM, AND THE PROBLEM OF INDUCTION

We shall skip a couple of sections and discuss what is the heart of Hume's discussion of probable reason, T 1.3.6, 'Of the inference from the impression to the idea'. The focus of this section is on how the mind moves from an impression of a cause to the idea of its effect. That is, the nature of the inference from one to the other.

There are two broad interpretations of what Hume is trying to say in this section, a *sceptical* interpretation and a *naturalistic* one. The sceptical interpretation holds that Hume is offering a negative epistemic evaluation of those inferences. Recall the example offered above of someone who sees a duck and comes to the belief that it will rain bananas. We hold that this is a *bad inference*, an *unreasonable* one, or an *unjustified* inference, whereas the inference I make from seeing steam to the belief that I would be scalded were I to put my hand in it is a good, reasonable, or justified inference. At the first approximation, we think that the latter kind of inference is a good one because our experience of what has happened in the past provides a reason for beliefs about what we have not observed. My belief that I would be scalded is based on the fact that in the past people who have got too close to steam have been scalded. On the sceptical reading, Hume holds that causal inferences provide *no* justification or epistemic warrant for such beliefs, and all such inferences are epistemically on a par with the inference about banana rain from the observation of ducks.

The naturalistic reading does not see Hume as passing negative judgment on the epistemic standing of causal inferences. His concern instead is to tell us something about *how* such inferences are drawn, and relatedly, something about our nature and the nature of our reason. Hume holds that causal inferences are epistemically good ones, and his concern is simply with how causal inference operates. And, following one of the themes of this book, his concern is to show us that our reason is no different in kind from the mechanism operative in animal inference.

Before we turn to look more closely at Hume's texts, let us first consider the argument supposed to support scepticism about such inferences. This scepticism is known as the 'problem of induction', and though it was inspired by readings of Hume, it is worth getting to grips with it independently of the question of how to interpret his texts since it is a problem that stands independently of Hume's own views. Suppose I warn my son not to put his hand in the steam, and he asks me why. I reply by saying that every time anyone has put their hand in steam in the past they have been scalded. Here, it seems, I am offering my son a *reason* for my claim, something that purports to *justify* it. My claim also expresses an underlying assumption, namely that the future will resemble the past. When my son asks me why the fact that people have been scalded in the past is a reason to think that he will be scalded this time, I will say that what has happened in the past is a guide to what will happen in the future because the future resembles the past. Call this assumption the 'Uniformity Principle' (UP). But now my argumentative son might say this: if I don't have a reason to think that the future will resemble the past, then I don't have any good reason to think that I will get scalded when I get too close to the steam. My claim is a good reason only on the condition that I have a good reason to believe the UP, or, in other words, on the assumption that the future will resemble the past. But we cannot justify any belief in the UP. We cannot know *a priori* that the future will resemble the past. Nor can we argue that we have observed that the future has previously resembled the past, and so will continue to do so. Such an argument would be circular or begging the question, in the sense that the conclusion is assumed in the premises of the argument, and therefore the conclusion has no support. Hence, we have no reason to believe the UP and so we have no reason for any of the beliefs that rest on that assumption.

Before we turn to the details of Hume's argument, let us consider some textual evidence which suggest that Hume holds that all causal inferences are unjustified.[3] First, he says that it is 'impossible for us to satisfy our reason' (T 1.3.6.11) as to why we should infer effect from cause, and that there is 'no reason to determine us' to infer effect from cause (T 1.3.6.12). Elsewhere in the *Treatise*, he writes that there is 'nothing in any object, consider'd in itself, which can afford us a reason for drawing a conclusion beyond it' and that we have 'no reason to draw any inference concerning any object beyond those of which we have had experience' (T 1.3.12.20). Indeed, in the *Enquiry Concerning Human Understanding*, Hume calls one section 'sceptical doubts concerning the operations of the understanding', and the discussion in 'Of the inference from the impression to the idea' resembles the logic of the argument for the problem of induction sketched above. So, it can sound as if Hume thinks that no probable inference is justified.

There are, however, also strong reasons to think that the sceptical conclusion is not Hume's. First, recall that the subtitle of the *Treatise* describes the work as 'an attempt to introduce the experimental method of reasoning into moral subjects'. It is precisely an attempt to draw conclusions on the basis of observation, which is the 'only solid foundation' (T Intro. 7) for the science of human nature. If Hume thinks that past experience does not support any probable inferences, then he must think that there is no reason to believe the conclusions about human nature which he offers in the *Treatise*. Second, he often describes the conclusions of probable inference in terms redolent of success. Thus, causal inference allows us to 'discover the real existence or the relations of objects' (T 1.3.2.2), 'informs of existences and objects, which we do not feel or see' (T 1.3.2.3), and 'brings us acquainted' (T 1.3.9.4) with such existences. Third, he refers to causal inferences as 'just'. Thus, 'cause and effect is the only [relation] of objects on which we can found a just inference from one object to another' (T 1.3.6.7). Fourth, he draws a contrast between such inferences and others that bestows a positive evaluation on the former and a negative evaluation on the latter. Thus, he contrasts beliefs that arise from 'the relation of cause and effect' and those that are 'merely the offspring of the imagination' (T 1.3.9.4). Fifth, Hume makes distinctions in degrees of evidence that causal inference affords, discussing 'the kinds of probability…receiv'd by philosophers, and allow'd to be reasonable foundations of belief and opinion' (T 1.3.13.1). Sixth, and relatedly, Hume offers eight 'Rules by which to judge of causes and effects' in T. 1.3.15. Seventh, and finally, in his discussion of the belief that there are external objects that cause perceptions in us, he writes that reason cannot 'afford us any just conclusion from the existence or qualities of our perceptions to the existence of external continu'd objects' (T 1.4.2.54). The reason why we can form no just conclusion is that we can never observe an external object causing a perception, but what is relevant here is the implied contrast. In cases where we can observe both cause and effect, a just inference is possible, and no just inference is possible when we cannot.

Let us now turn to 'Of the inference from the impression to the idea' to see how we should understand Hume's conclusion. Hume opens this section by rejecting the idea that we can infer effect from cause by grasping the essences of objects, and later he discusses the idea that reason determines inferences by supposing that objects have 'secret powers' (T 1.3.6.8). I am going to postpone discussion of these matters until we come to examine the notion of necessary connection since the two topics are intimately connected. The key point for the present discussion is that in order to tell what effects a given cause has, we have to have observed both. We cannot simply peer at some object and predict what effect it will have, "Tis therefore by EXPERIENCE only, that we can infer the existence of one object from that of another' (T 1.3.6.2). That is, we observe one thing following another, where one is contiguous with another. But that is not sufficient to make us infer effect from cause. Hume further adds that our experience of causation involves another component: constant conjunction. So, steam causes scalding because, all things being equal, every time one puts one's hands into the steam, scalding follows. Hence the 'transition from an impression present to the memory or the senses to the idea of an object, which we call cause or effect, is founded on past *experience*, and on our remembrance of their *constant conjunction*' (T 1.3.6.4).[4] Hume then asks:

> [w]hether experience produces the idea by means of the understanding or the imagination; whether we are determin'd by reason to make the transition, or by a certain association and relation of perceptions.
> (T 1.3.6.4)

Now, it is vitally important to note that this is a *causal* question. What *causes* us to move from the impression of some cause (or effect) to the idea of its effect (or cause). It is either caused by reason or caused by the association of ideas. Reason consists in 'nothing but a *comparison*, and a discovery of those relations...which two or more objects bear to each other' (T 1.3.2.2). On this model, when we infer by reason we simply compare objects, discover that they stand in the causal relation, and this discovery causes as to draw the inference. But Hume rejects that claim. How?

He begins by stating that:

> If reason determin'd us, it wou'd proceed upon that principle, *that instances, of which we have had no experience, must resemble those, of which we have had experience and that the course of nature continues always uniformly the same.*

(T 1.3.6.4)

This is the Uniformity Principle that we introduced when we discussed the classical problem of induction. There, its role centred on the justification of such inferences. Inductive inferences are only justified if we have a justification for the UP, but since we cannot justify the UP, none of the inferences based upon it are justified. Hume's own discussion of the role of the UP is, however, crucially different.

The causal relation involves constant conjunction, and this notion is intimately related to the UP. For A to be the cause of B, every instance of A has to be followed by B, which expresses the assumption that the course of nature remains the same. Reason's 'discovery' that A and B stand in the philosophical relation of cause and effect is equivalent to its discovery of the UP. Reason would then be the *cause* of the inference only if it 'discovers' the UP. There are two forms of reasoning, demonstrative and probable. Can demonstrative reason 'discover' the UP? It cannot. That is because the idea or concept of nature does not imply unchangeability. Were it to do so, we would find it impossible to conceive of a change in the course of nature, just as it is impossible to conceive of a triangle without three sides. Thus:

> We can at least conceive a change in the course of nature; which sufficiently proves, that such a change is not absolutely impossible.

To form a clear idea of any thing, is an undeniable argument for its possibility, and is alone a refutation of any pretended demonstration against it.

(T 1.3.6.5)

What then of probable reason? Could that discover the UP? Hume writes that probable reason is

founded on the presumption of a resemblance betwixt those objects which we have had experience, and those, of which we have had none; and therefore 'tis impossible this presumption can arise from probability. The same principle cannot both be the cause and the effect of another.

(T 1.3.6.7)

There are two key features to this passage. The first is the notion of 'founded'. That sounds like what we were talking about in connection with the problem of induction. My claim that my son would scald himself were he to put his hand in the steam rests on the assumption that the future resembles the past, and, according to the inductive sceptic, since we have no reason to believe that assumption, then I have no reason to believe that my son would be scalded were he to put his hand in the steam. And it is quite true that Hume thinks that probable reason cannot itself provide a reason to believe the UP, since it presupposes it. Thus, a little later, Hume writes that

even after experience has inform'd us of...*constant conjunction*, 'tis impossible for us to satisfy ourselves by our reason, why we shou'd extend that experience beyond those particular instances, which have fallen under our observation. We suppose, but are never able to prove, that there must be a resemblance betwixt those objects, of which we have had experience, and those which lie beyond the reach of our discovery.

(T 1.3.6.11)

But remember also that Hume is concerned about the *causation* of the inference. Probable reasoning is not *caused* by a grasp of the UP, since to reason probabilistically just is to *assume* the UP. But were such inferences determined by reason, then we would have to know the UP *prior* to making such inferences for that principle to cause or 'determine' those inferences. Thus, as Hume says, 'the same principle cannot be both the cause and effect of another' (T 1.3.6.5). Hume, therefore, thinks that the causal inferences we make are not caused by a grasp of the UP, which is a principle that would justify those inferences.

What this shows so far is that a particular model, whereby inferences owe themselves to reason, cannot be right. This is the model I said that Leibniz best expresses. Thus:

> Beasts pass from one imagining to another by means of a link between them which they have previously experienced. For instance, when his master picks up a stick the dog anticipates being beaten.... This could be called 'inference' or 'reasoning' in a very broad sense. But I prefer to keep to accepted usage, reserving these words for men and restricting them to the knowledge of some *reason* for perceptions' being linked together. Mere sensations cannot provide this: all they do is to cause one naturally to expect once more the same linking that has been observed previously.[5]

Genuine reason is a matter of drawing inferences in light of an awareness of some connection between A and B as opposed to the associative inferences of beasts. Elsewhere, Leibniz calls such associative inferences the 'shadow of reason' or 'pseudo-reason'. Thus:

> The thought sequences of beasts are only a shadow of reasoning, that is, they are nothing but a connection in the imagination—a passage from one image to another; for when a new situation appears similar to its predecessor, it is expected to have the same concomitant features as before, as though things were linked in reality just because their images are linked in the memory.[6]

Furthermore, Leibniz reserves the term 'reason' for the faculty that is aware of such connections:

> A *cause* in the realm of things corresponds to a *reason* in the realm of truths, which is why causes themselves...are often called 'reasons'...

> [T]he faculty which is aware of this connection among truths i.e. the faculty for reasoning, is also called 'reason'... [T]his faculty is exclusive to man alone and does not appear in any other animals on earth.[7]

Hume, however, argues that this model is impossible. Reason would have to discover the UP in order for it to cause our inferences but, Hume argues, it cannot. What *does* cause us to infer is the association of ideas, which is what Leibniz and others think is responsible for animal inference. What Hume is then doing here is trying to show that a certain form of naturalism is true. Our reason—our inferential faculty—is no different in kind from that operative in other animals. Thus, in the first *Enquiry* he writes:

> the experimental reasoning itself, which we possess in common with the beasts, and on which the whole conduct of life depends, is nothing but a species of instinct, or mechanical power, that acts in us unknown to ourselves; and in its chief operations, is not directed by any such relations or comparison of ideas, as are the proper objects of our intellectual faculties.
>
> (EHU 9.6)

So, the inferences we draw cannot be a matter of grasping some relation that constitutes a reason in favour of the inference. The fact that our inferences cannot be so caused does not yet mean that we must evaluate such inferences as epistemically unjustified or unwarranted, which would be the sceptical conclusion. It is quite true that Hume says that 'we have no reason to draw the inference', but scepticism would follow only if he held that inferences can only be justified if they are made in the light of reasons. Nowhere, however, does Hume make such a claim. But why might we think that such inferences are epistemically good ones?

Hume's stress is on the mechanical, associative nature of such inferences, writing further that our 'reason shou'd be consider'd a kind of cause, of which truth is the natural effect' (T 1.4.1.1). What this suggests is what is known in contemporary epistemology as *reliabilism*. What makes a belief an epistemically good one is that it is a product of a mechanism or process that tends to produce true beliefs. This idea is reflected in ordinary practice.

We tend to rely on answers to questions that stem from sources that are generally reliable in that sense. We look for good books, trustworthy news sources, or reliable friends. The fact that such beliefs come from reliable sources make them epistemically good ones.

Do we not need to *know* that such sources are reliable? Philosophers are divided on this general issue, but a little reflection makes it far from obvious. When I put cat food in the bowl, my cat, Tails, goes to the bowl (with a happy meow) and eats. Intuitively, many of us seem prepared to say that Tails *knows* there is food in his bowl. His belief (which is revealed in his behaviour) is true, and what is more, his belief is no accident. His sensory capacities are naturally geared towards sensing what is edible, and so his belief is true and the product of a reliable source. But it would of course be absurd to think that Tails knows, or even thinks, that his sensory mechanisms *are* reliable. He simply lacks the cognitive wherewithal to form such beliefs. To change the example, a five-year old child, it seems, will know that her father is home because she can see him, and her reliable seeing produces true belief. It would again be absurd to say that she knows or even believes that her eyesight is reliable. Nevertheless, she has a true belief, and, again, this is no lucky belief but the product of a reliable mechanism.

Examples like these are sometimes used to illustrate another, related, notion in contemporary epistemology known as 'externalism'. Let me introduce the doctrine in the following way. It seems evident that knowledge is different from mere true belief. One can acquire a true belief by luck or accident, and we think that this is not knowledge. Knowledge seems to require not mere true belief but also something that eliminates the luck. There are many such candidates in philosophy for what turns true belief into knowledge, but for our purposes, let us consider it to be the product of a reliable mechanism. Knowledge amounts to true belief that is the product of a reliable mechanism, i.e. one that typically produces true belief. But crucially, a creature who has such knowledge does not need to *know* that his belief is the product of a reliable mechanism in order so to know. Tails the cat and the five-year old above *know* what they know *without* knowing what it is that turned their respective true beliefs into knowledge. In this sense, what turns true belief into knowledge is 'external' to the knowers, in that they have no knowledge of it. Indeed, we can be even more radical here. In the case of the cat, turning true belief into knowledge is 'external' to the cat in the sense that the cat has no chance of even forming a concept of a reliable mechanism, let alone knowing that his sensory mechanisms are reliable. So, to put matters slightly more precisely, an externalism in epistemology holds that what turns true belief into knowledge is something to which the knower need not have any 'cognitive access'.

As one might imagine, the opposite position to 'externalism' is 'internalism'. This holds that in order for some feature to turn true belief into knowledge, the knower must have some kind of cognitive access to whatever turns true belief into knowledge. One must, in other words, be in a position to identity what it is that turns one's true belief into knowledge in order to be in a position to answer the question, 'how do you know?', when it is posed to them. What's more, one cannot just guess but one should have good reason for one's claim.

Externalism and internalism, at least in the most basic forms, part company quite dramatically on this issue. The relevance of all this to Hume, though, concerns how we understand what Hume says about reason as a kind of cause of which truth is its natural effect as well as the issue of scepticism. The internalist view would lead to scepticism quite straightforwardly. In order for reason to be a source of knowledge it is not enough for it to be a reliable cause of true belief. We must both *think* that it is reliable and have good reasons for thinking it to be so. But notice that if we demand to have a reason to think that it is reliable, we are in effect asking for a reason to think that the UP is true, and we know already that neither demonstrative nor probable reason can provide such a reason. Hence an internalist would claim even if the UP were true, and probable reason were reliable, we could not have knowledge or justified belief.

We, however, noted above that the way Hume talks about reason suggests that he is no such sceptic. He thinks causal inferences are 'just' and that they allow us to 'discover the real existence of objects', and, of course, his entire philosophy is 'experimental', resting on arguments based on experience. Furthermore, he is prepared to credit animals and children with knowledge. Hume then seems much more in line with the externalist and takes reason to be a mechanism productive of true belief and hence a just source of belief in virtue of it. That is not to say that he has a full-blown epistemological theory based around an explicit commitment to an externalist view. It is rather that he refigures reason away from one view of it, exemplified in Leibniz, as a faculty distinct from the natural world, and toward a natural, mechanical view. Of course, we can ask whether the UP is true and that might bring disquiet, but that is far from thinking that reason is not an epistemically good source of belief. Hume and everyone else assume that the UP is true and that probable reason thus produces true belief. We cannot prove that it is, but that is an impossible aspiration that encourages the mistaken view of reason exhibited by Leibniz. As Hume puts it in the first *Enquiry*, he shows

> the whimsical condition of mankind, who must act and reason and believe; though they are not able, by their most diligent enquiry, to satisfy themselves concerning the foundations of those operations.
> (EHU 12.23)

Nevertheless, Hume's central claim is about the *nature* of our reason, and not a negative evaluation of its epistemic standing.

> Here, then, is a kind of pre-established harmony between the course of nature and the succession of our ideas; and though the powers and forces, by which the former is governed, be wholly unknown to us; yet our thoughts and conceptions have still, we find, gone on in the same train with the other works of nature. Custom is that principle, by which this correspondence has been effected; so necessary to the subsistence of our species, and the regulation of our conduct, in every circumstance and occurrence of human life. Had not the presence of an object instantly excited the idea of those objects commonly conjoined with it, all our knowledge must have been limited to the narrow sphere of our memory and senses.
> (EHU 5.21)

T 1.3.7 OF THE NATURE OF THE IDEA OR BELIEF

In the *Abstract*, Hume claims that the *Treatise* asks a 'new question unthought of philosophers' (*Abstract* 17). The question posed is what the difference is between merely *conceiving* of such and such and *believing* that such and such is the case. I can, for example, easily imagine that when I touch the keyboard on my computer, flowers will grow from my fingers—it is something of which I can conceive—but I clearly do not believe that it will happen. What then is the difference? Hume has an answer, but it has not been well received. It is one of the topics he reviews in the *Appendix*, and about which he inserts a new passage into the main text, writing that belief consists in the 'manner of conception' of ideas and their 'feeling to the mind', but that 'I confess, that 'tis impossible to explain perfectly this feeling or manner of conception' (T 1.3.7.7). Clearly, he was not particularly happy with his account. Nevertheless, as we shall see, he is moving in the right direction even if he does not arrive at the right place.

A first thing to note is that his discussion of belief is mainly focused on beliefs about what we presently do not observe. Probable reason, which we have just discussed, involves bringing ideas to mind via the associative relation of cause and effect, but the associative relations of contiguity and resemblance can also bring to mind ideas of the unobserved. What Hume wants to know is how the ideas produced by such associative transitions become beliefs and what it is that makes them beliefs. But note that I said, 'mainly focused'. Before Hume makes belief the forefront of his discussion in the *Treatise*, he writes in T 1.3.5, 'Of the impressions of the sense and memory', that the '*belief* or *assent*, which always attends the memory and the sense, is nothing but the vivacity of those perceptions they present' (T 1.3.5.7). We can believe what we see, and we can believe what we remember, and this consists in those perceptions having a 'superior force and vivacity' (T 1.3.5.3) to mere ideas. This brings up all the issues we noted about the 'difference betwixt feeling and thinking' in Chapter One, and, as we shall see, some further ones. But the basic idea is that believing is a matter of some perception having a certain degree of force and vivacity.

Hume's discussion in T 1.3.7, 'Of the nature of the idea or belief', begins immediately after his discussion of causal inference. We have an impression of a cause and infer its effect. In other words, we come to have an idea of what we presently do not observe. The impression can either be an impression of the sense or an impression of memory. When we make such inferences, not only do we have an idea of the unobserved object, but we also *believe* that it will occur. In what does this consist? Hume discusses, and rejects, some alternatives and we shall come to these presently, but he quickly arrives at his first statement of his account of belief. A belief is, 'A LIVELY IDEA RELATED TO OR ASSOCIATED WITH A PRESENT IMPRESSION' (T 1.3.7.5). The relevant idea is an idea of what is unobserved, and the impression (of the senses or memory) is of what is seen or remembered and which, via association, produces the idea. So, my seeing the steam produces the idea of scalding. I *believe* that I will get scalded because the idea of scalding becomes more lively or forceful by 'borrowing' some of the force and vivacity from the present impression. The impression 'communicates to...[the idea] a share of its force and vivacity' (T 1.3.8.2, italics removed).

How are we to understand this view of belief? The first thing to note is that, like Hume's account of probable reason, this view of belief is modelled on views of animal cognition. The vivacity of ideas is borrowed from the vivacity of impressions (or the repetition of less vivacious impressions). Thus Leibniz writes of the 'potent imagination' of beasts which 'strikes and moves them',[8] and that the potency of the ideas in the imagination comes either from a 'forceful impression' (*une impression forte*) or from repeated impressions. Repeated experience can produce as 'deep and vivid [an] image' (*profounde et...vive*)[9] as one that is brought about by a single, more forceful, impression. Now, the key point here is that such ideas strike and move the animal. That is, the borrowed force of the idea from the impression affects the *behaviour* of the animal. When Hume reviews his account of belief, he notes that the ideas that figure in beliefs 'have more force and influence; makes them appear of greater importance; infixes them in the mind; and renders them the governing principles of all our actions' (T 1.3.7.7).

The second thing to note is that this emphasis on influence and behaviour is where Hume heads in the right direction. One plausible account of belief is based on what is known in contemporary philosophy of mind as 'functionalism'. This, in the sketchiest of sketches, holds that what makes a mental state the kind of mental state it is, should be understood in terms of the causal role it plays in the mental economy of the mind. It is a state that, given certain kinds of inputs, typically causes certain kinds of outputs. For example, my imagining that flowers will grow out of my fingers when I touch the keyboard differs from my belief partly in terms of what each mental event causes. My imagination might cause some things (a little wry amusement on my part), but my *belief* that the flowers would actually grow would have very different effects. First, it would cause all sorts of different mental states, depending on my disposition, like panic or bewilderment. Second, it would, in turn, affect my behaviour. For one thing, I would certainly avoid touching my keyboard. I would no doubt inform my family straight away and try to seek appropriate help, and so on. Furthermore, the inputs into forming that state are different. In the case of my imagining, the cause was imaginative effort to find an example for this book. In the case of the belief, the cause is likely something different, such as, for example, witnessing the event happening to all those sat around me in the library, or hearing a warning from someone whom I trust. These inputs are typically concerned with how the world is, either by direct sensory engagement or indirect engagement via sources of information such as the testimony of others. So, putting these two together, we might view Hume's account of belief in the following light. First, the impression (of the senses or memory) that is the input into belief formation expresses, albeit inchoately, a view that belief requires inputs that connect the mind to the world. Second, his appeal to the vivacity of the connected idea expresses the thesis that belief impacts behaviour in a way that mere imagination does not.

As I mentioned, Hume's account begins with a somewhat more successful criticism of other possible views of belief. First, believing is not simply a matter of adding the idea of existence to some other idea. There is no separate idea of existence to add to another idea, and, in any case, simply conceiving of the existence of something is far from *believing* that that thing exists. Second, believing cannot be the addition of any other idea. The reason for this is that thinkers can take very different attitudes to the very same content or proposition. Philosophers commonly employ the notion of 'propositional attitudes', of which belief is one such attitude. Such attitudes are the ones picked out by expressions such as 'hopes that', 'fears that', 'worries that' and 'believes that'. The 'that' picks out something that is the object of the attitude, which is referred to as a proposition, which is, very roughly, a way of expressing a way the world is or might be. So 'Fred is late' is a way of expressing the way the world is, or might be, and one can take different attitudes to that proposition. One can hope that Fred is late, fear that Fred is late, worry that Fred is late, or believe that Fred is late. With this in place, we are now able to understand why Hume holds that believing is not a matter of some additional idea. A change in idea would not be a change in the attitude but in the proposition towards which believing is the attitude. You may believe that Fred is late, but I may not believe that Fred is late. We are taking different attitudes to the very same proposition, namely, that Fred is late, so believing cannot be a difference in the ideas that compose it. Finally, if belief *were* a matter of the addition of some idea, then it would have the consequence that we could simply decide to believe at will. 'The mind', he writes, 'has the command over all its ideas, and can separate, unite, mix, and vary them as it pleases; so that if belief consisted merely in a new idea, it wou'd be in a man's power to believe what he pleas'd' (T App. 2). But it seems impossible simply to believe as a direct result of a decision. Certainly, one can decide to imagine that there is an elephant sat beside them, but one cannot simply decide to *believe* that there is an elephant beside them.

All of these observations seem good ones, but there are problems with Hume's positive account. As it stands, the account implies that a belief is a conscious mental occurrence. Conscious since it is a lively idea, and an occurrence in the sense that the belief lasts as long as that lively idea lasts. But most beliefs are neither conscious nor short-lived occurrences. I am very confident that the present reader of this book believes that they are located more than two miles away from the sun, and I am equally confident that that belief has never entered their consciousness. No doubt, it is in your consciousness right now, but, equally, you believed that proposition yesterday and will continue to believe it when you forget what is being discussed on these pages. Most beliefs, then, are not conscious, though they can become so. This also helps to show why it is wrong to think that beliefs are occurrences. Your (presumed) conscious agreement with the statement about your location expresses a dispositional fact about you, a tendency to act and think in accordance with your attitude to your location with respect to the sun. To possess a belief involves being disposed to act and think in certain ways, and these are typically not short-term occurrences. Such a view fits well with the functionalist account briefly mentioned above, but it is not something that Hume himself neither explicitly recognises nor considers.[10]

As mentioned, Hume was also unhappy with his initial account, spending a good part of the *Appendix* reviewing it. A different view emerges here, which carried into the *Abstract* and, later, the first *Enquiry*, where the difference is a matter of some peculiar feeling or sentiment. Thus, 'belief is nothing but a peculiar feeling, different from the simple conception', a 'feeling or sentiment' (T App. 3). On the face of it, that sounds like a change from the particular idea being more vivid to a separate feeling that attaches itself to the relevant idea. Even here, however, Hume is not consistent because he also writes in such a way that suggests he is simply thinking in terms of the idea itself having more 'force and influence' (T App. 9). Now, the discussion in the *Appendix* is guided by a contrast between belief and fiction, and part of what might be worrying Hume here, though he is not explicit about it, is a distinction between the force and vivacity he associates with belief and the force and vivacity that can attend good and engaging fiction. Thus, Hume writes in a section that he asks to be inserted into the main text that

> how great soever the pitch maybe, to which this vivacity [of the ideas involved in poetry and madness] rises, 'tis evident, that in poetry it never has the same *feeling* with that which arises in the mind, when we reason....The mind can easily distinguish betwixt the one and the

> other; and whatever emotion the poetical enthusiasm may give to the spirits, 'tis still the mere phantom of belief or perswasion.
>
> (T 1.3.10.10, emphasis original)

We can reinforce this with a different example. When one is watching an engaging film, one's responses to it can be quite potent. One might cry, gasp, or even move in response to what one is viewing, and, at the same time, one does not believe what one is seeing. Mere vivacity and liveliness are not going to distinguish fiction from belief, nor is the appeal to belief having greater force and vivacity. So, Hume has to resort to appealing to some 'peculiar feeling or sentiment', a 'certain *je-ne-scai-quoi*, of which 'tis impossible to give any definition or description' (T 1.3.8.16). It seems he is looking for some introspectable feature to distinguish belief from other mental phenomena, but that is not the place to look for the kind of emphasis on belief's causal nature, a nature which Hume dimly recognises.[11]

THE CAUSAL RELATION: T 1.3.14 OF THE IDEA OF NECESSARY CONNEXION

We have examined what causal inference is, but we have yet to focus on just what Hume might think the causal relation to be. After discussing further aspects of belief and some varieties of probability, Hume offers in T 1.3.14, 'Of the idea of necessary connexion', two definitions of 'cause'. Let us begin with these two definitions.

First, he says that we may define a cause as an 'object precedent and contiguous to another, and where all the objects resembling the former are plac'd in like relations of precedency and contiguity to those objects, that resemble the latter' (T 1.3.14.31). This defines 'cause' as a philosophical relation. This definition is often understood as a statement of what is known as the 'regularity theory of causation', a theory with which Hume's name is closely associated. Indeed, it is often called the 'Humean theory of causation'. Very roughly, the claim here is that for one thing to cause another is for every object of type A (the cause) to be followed by an object of type B (the effect), together with the conditions that A occurs before B, and that A and B are contiguous. The fact that things of type A are always followed by things of type B constitutes a regularity, and so a particular instance of causation is a matter of some token *a* of type A being followed by a token *b* of type B (and where the contiguity and priority conditions are met).

This is far from an intuitive account of what we ordinarily think causation to be. We tend to think in terms of one thing *bringing about* another, or *making it* happen, whereas on this view, there is no such relation between a cause and its effect. It is simply a matter of one thing following another. And, relatedly, we also find it intuitive that there could be such regularities and yet we do not think of them as exhibiting a causal relation. Thomas Reid, an early critic of Hume, pointed out that night follows day regularly, but we do not think that day *causes* night. Furthermore, we also think that there can be cause and effect when there is no regularity. The assassination of Franz Ferdinand arguably caused the First World War, but this was a one-off event.

Now, the point here is not that these objections cannot be met. It is rather that the regularity view is not an obvious or straightforward conclusion from our ordinary causal beliefs. But there is also a second sense in which viewing Hume's account of causation as a simple statement of the regularity theory is radical. It is difficult to overstate just how subtle, sophisticated, and varied discussions of the nature of causation were during the period before Hume. The theories included, but are not exhausted by, emanation, occasionalism, *influxus*, forms, plastic natures, modal transfer, a distinction between primary and secondary causes, final causation, and agency models. The subtly of the discussions of these different notions is often complicated enough to make one's head spin. What is remarkable about Hume in this second sense is that a definition of cause as regularity seems simply to bypass all of this subtly in one fell swoop.

We shall return to the radical nature of the account presently, but as we noted, Hume offers not one but two definitions of 'cause'. The second definition runs as follows. A 'CAUSE is an object precedent and contiguous to another, and so united with it, that the idea of the one determines the one to form the idea of the other, and the impression of one, to form a more lively idea of the other (T 1.3.14.31). This definition, at first glance, is very puzzling. On the assumption that a definition is an attempt to capture what we mean by the term 'cause', this looks flatly wrong. When we say that smoking causes cancer, we are not referring to the effect that some observation has on our minds. We are simply referring to the relationship between smoking and cancer. Be that as it may, the fact that Hume offers a second definition raises further problems in itself. If both definitions are definitions of the same thing, namely 'cause', then at least one of them must be incorrect. A definition is supposed to state the meaning of a term, but the definitions are different in meaning from each other. To put the point slightly more technically, the definitions are not *intensionally* equivalent. The terms 'bachelor' and 'unmarried man' are intensionally equivalent since the two terms are synonymous. Hume's definitions are not synonymous. Nor are Hume's definitions even *extensionally* equivalent. That is to say, they do not pick out the same set of items. 'Bachelor' and 'unmarried man' are both intensionally and extensionally equivalent since the terms mean the same thing and are true of exactly the same set of objects. Nevertheless, it is possible for two terms to differ in intension—mean something different—and yet have the same extension. Thus, to borrow an example from the American philosopher, W. V. O. Quine, the term 'cordate' means 'animal with a heart', and the term 'renate' means 'animal with kidneys', and clearly these two terms differ in meaning. Nevertheless, they are extensionally equivalent, since every animal with a heart has a kidney and *vice versa*. But, as mentioned, Hume's definitions are not extensionally equivalent: there can be pairs of objects which satisfy the first definition, but are not observed by anyone, and so fail to meet the second. The definitions do not mean the same thing and nor do they pick out the same set of things.

In sum, Hume offers very radical accounts of causation, and two definitions that are not equivalent. So, we should look very carefully at how he arrives at this remarkable view. The reader will recall a further peculiarity which I mentioned when we began our discussion of causal inference. Hume does not start with a definition of 'cause' when he begins to explain causal inference, but instead arrives at the definitions from the account of the inference. He pursues the 'seemingly preposterous' method of 'examining our inference from the relation before we had explain'd the relation itself' (T 1.3.14.30). How are we to understand this? Hume's approach is an instance—the first to my knowledge—of what Australian philosopher Huw Price calls 'subject naturalism'.[12] I have said quite a lot about naturalism thus far, but this is a further, and important, notion. So far, we have considered Hume's naturalism in terms of any attempt to model human nature in a way that makes human beings continuous with other animals, and a key element to this is an attempt to explain human cognition by appeal to materials used to explain animal cognition. But to arrive at the notion of 'subject naturalism', we need to approach things from a somewhat different angle. The natural sciences study nature, and we might therefore hold that to count as a natural thing or object, it must be something that features in those sciences. By itself, that leaves open the existence of non-natural things. It leaves open the possibility of a transcendent God and, furthermore, the existence of things which cannot be understood in terms of the natural sciences. Thus, one might hold that moral facts or facts about minds are 'non-natural' in the sense that they cannot be understood in terms of the natural sciences.

The issue of natural and non-natural (though not put in quite those terms) emerged in the early modern period because of a new conception of the natural world as extended matter in motion. Descartes, for example, takes minds to be fundamentally different from what is described by the natural sciences and so in that sense Cartesian minds are 'non-natural'. This conception of the natural world also generated puzzles about causation. If matter is just pure extension, then there seems no place for active power, the power to initiate change. For some this required a solution that went beyond the material world. So, for example, occasionalist philosophers like Nicolas Malebranche placed active power in the omnipotent will of God, whose activity kept the world in motion, and hence his position in the end is non-naturalist. Others, such as Ralph Cudworth, decided that the conception of the natural world as pure extension must be wrong, and he rejected it in order to allow for active power. Indeed, the new conception of the natural world led to the very sophisticated and intricate discussions of causation and power mentioned previously, which constitute attempts to reconcile material substance and causal power.

All of these attempts focused on the metaphysical: that is, they sought something 'in the world' or 'in the objects' to play the role of causal power, or, failing that, something non-natural, such as the will of God. Furthermore we can see from what I have briefly said that philosophers of the period are willing to allow something that is non-natural in the sense given above, something which philosophers nowadays are far more reluctant to do. Many philosophers are 'naturalists' in an ontological sense, holding that all that exists is natural, and that what constitutes the 'natural' is what is recognised by the sciences. For the sake of exposition, let us say that the relevant science is physics. Such naturalism throws up what are known as 'placement problems'. If the world is just physical, how can there be moral facts? How do we place morality in a world that is just physical? How are we to understand consciousness in a world where only the physical exists. What are we to make of causation, aesthetic phenomena, or the taste of apple when all that exists is physical?

The fact that such a naturalism seeks to solve placement problems by seeking something 'in the objects' is why, unsurprisingly, it is called 'object naturalism'. *Subject* naturalism, by contrast, approaches placement problems by looking not at the world but by looking at us, the *subjects*. Instead of asking *what* causation or morality is, the relevant issue is that of explaining how we come to *think* and *talk* in terms of, say, morality or causation. If we come to explain why we think and talk in the way we do, we may no longer think that the ontological issue is a pressing one. What Hume is doing is precisely what a subject naturalist does. He does not begin with asking what the metaphysics of causation might be but instead with explaining how we come to think in causal terms.

Let us look at this in action. How does Hume arrive at the first definition? Causation, considered a philosophical relation, comprises three components, contiguity, temporal priority, and succession or constant conjunction. His grounds for positing the first two of these components in our concept of causation are broadly observational or empirical, based on examining with 'the utmost accuracy those objects, which are commonly denominated causes and effects' (T 1.3.14.31). So, although he says contiguity is 'essential' to causation, he nevertheless treats it as contingent and provisional, writing, 'at least [we] may suppose it such, according to the general opinion, till we can find a more proper occasion to clear up this matter' (T 1.3.2.6). Later, he drops it in connection with causal relations among certain perceptions (T 1.4.5). It is included because we *typically* include it in our idea of causation. For temporal priority, Hume again offers empirical support, but also adds an *a priori* argument, though, significantly, he does not attach much weight to it, writing that if 'this argument appear satisfactory, 'tis well. If not, I beg the reader to allow me the same liberty, which I have us'd in the preceding case [i.e. contiguity], of supposing as such. For he shall find, that the affair is of no great importance' (T 1.3.2.8), as 'experience in most instances seems to contradict' the non-priority of causes.

This leaves us with constant conjunction. Hume adds this component in the context of his discussion of what determines us, causally speaking, to draw causal inferences, stating that '[c]ontiguity and succession are not sufficient *to make us pronounce* any two objects to be cause and effect, unless we perceive, that these two relations are preserv'd in several instances' (T 1.3.6.3, my emphasis). It is because constant conjunction enters into the *causation* of the inference that it is included in the definition of 'cause'. It is what makes us judge causally. Hence, we have 'insensibly discover'd' the relation of constant conjunction while discussing 'another subject' (T 1.3.6.3).

Notice then that the philosophical relation, and especially the key component of constant conjunction, emerges because these elements are those which *make* us infer. It constitutes the *input* into causal thinking. The second definition we can think of as the mental *output* of this input. Thus, Hume writes, 'tho' causation be a *philosophical* relation, as implying contiguity, succession and constant conjunction, yet 'tis only so far as it is a *natural* relation, and produces an union among our ideas, that we are able to reason upon it, or draw any inference from it' (T 1.3.6.16). Hence, the second definition of 'cause' which makes reference to the mind's inference is the mind's reaction to the input of the philosophical relation.

The second definition might seem simply a restatement of Hume's account of belief. After all, it refers the impression of one thing forming the lively idea of another. But there is something more to it than that. Recall that near the beginning of his discussion of causal inference, Hume mentions necessary connection, deeming it to be 'of much greater importance' than the other components of the causal relation (T 1.3.2.11). Hume is quite clear that we can have no impression of necessary connection and so no idea of it, or at least no idea of it that reflects a genuine experience of power. Instead, he famously claims that the impression of necessity we have is merely the 'determination' (T 1.3.14.1) of the mind to pass from one object to another, or the 'propensity, which custom produces, to pass from an object to the idea of its usual attendant' (T 1.3.14.20). It is nothing but a feeling of a particular kind, which is then projected onto objects. This projection fools us into thinking that we perceive causal power in the world.

In what sense is this determination of the mind the impression of necessary connection? 'Necessary connection' is a synonym for 'causal power' and, as noted above, we ordinarily think that causation involves power. For *a* to cause *b* it is not enough for all *a*s to be followed by *b*s but *a* must bring about *b*. So whence that thought? Here again Hume's subject naturalism comes to the fore. Noting that power or necessary connection is not immediately observable, he declares he will 'beat about the neighbouring fields' rather than directly examine the 'nature of that necessary connexion' (T 1.3.2.13). He consciously approaches things by quitting 'the direct examination' of necessary connection and asks instead 'why we conclude that 'such particular causes must *necessarily* have such particular effects' (T 1.3.2.15). That is, he bypasses *what* necessity or power *is* and examines why we *think in terms of necessity*.

What, then, is the explanation of the thought? Hume hints at his answer to this at T 1.3.6 where he writes that perhaps ''twill appear in the end, that the necessary connexion will depend on the inference, instead of the inference's depending on the necessary connexion' (T 1.3.6.3). To understand this, we first need to know how the inference *would* depend on the necessary connection. If we were able to grasp the power or necessary connection that relates cause and effect, we would be able (a) to infer *a priori* what effect the cause must have and (b) to find it inconceivable that any other effect could happen. Thus, Hume writes that the 'true manner' of perceiving the 'real force or energy, by which such a particular effect necessarily results' involves being 'able to pronounce from a simple view of the one, that it must be follow'd or preceded by the other' (T 1.3.14.13). This is put in the first *Enquiry* in this way:

> were the power or energy of any cause discoverable by the mind, we could foresee the effect, even without experience; and might, at first, pronounce with certainty concerning it, by the mere dint of thought and reasoning.
>
> (EHU 7.7)

Thus, we would simply read off effect from cause were we to have a grasp of necessary connection. Why? To cut a long and complicated story short,[13] powers are essences and it is the nature of an object to have the effects that it has, and if we were to know that nature, we could read off what effect the object must have.

We have, however, no such experience and hence no impression of power. This is because the ideas of cause and effect are distinct, and hence separable, and so there is no possibility of drawing such inferences, which would be equivalent to the demonstrative inferences we discussed near the beginning of this chapter. Furthermore, we cannot read off what effect some cause would have but we can also conceive of any cause having a different effect from its usual. Thus, to quote at length:

> the inference we draw from cause to effect, is not deriv'd merely from a survey of these particular objects, and from such a penetration into their essences as may discover the dependence of the one upon the other. There is no object, which implies the existence of any other if we consider these objects in themselves, and never look beyond the ideas which we form of them. Such an inference would amount to knowledge, and wou'd imply the absolute contradiction and impossibility of conceiving anything different. But as all distinct ideas are separable, 'tis evident there can be no impossibility of that kind. When we pass from a present impression to the idea of any object, we might possibly have separated the idea from the impression, and have substituted any other idea in its room.
>
> (T 1.3.6.1)

We now have a sense of what would be involved if the inference depended on the necessary connection. We also now know why Hume thinks we have no impression of genuine necessary connection. Let us now turn to the view that the necessary connection depends on the inference. We noted above that Hume argues that our impression of necessary connection is a feeling of determination. But saying that the impression is some feeling of determination does not really help to explain why we come to have thoughts about power or necessity. The key point is that the effect of the repeated experience of constant conjunction mimics what a genuine experience of necessary connection *would* be like. It resembles the experience of simply reading off an effect from a cause and it makes it seem as if one cannot conceive of the cause without the effect. Thus we gain 'long habit, such a turn of mind, that, upon the appearance of the cause, [we] *immediately* expect with assurance its usual attendant, and *hardly conceive it possible that any other event could result from it*' (EHU 7.21, my emphasis), and because 'custom has render'd it difficult to separate the ideas, [people are commonly] apt to fancy such a separation to be in itself impossible and absurd' (T 1.4.3.9). This determination of the mind is then projected onto regularities so that the 'generality of mankind...suppose that...they perceive the very force of energy of the cause, by which it is connected to its effect' (EHU 7.21). It is in this sense that the necessary connection depends on the inference. We come to think in terms of necessary connection not because we perceive necessary connection but because of the effect that causal inference has on our minds.

Having seen how Hume arrives at his two definitions in terms of the input to our causal inferences and its output, we should consider this question: does Hume think that all there *is* to the causal relation is what is stated in these two definitions or is he trying to say that all we can *understand* by the causal relation is what is stated in the two definitions? The former seems eminently plausible and is the view of the majority of Hume commentators. After all, he offers us definitions of the term 'cause', and we have no idea of any power other than the determination of the mind. Crucially, Hume also thinks that we lack an idea of real necessary connection and so we cannot *mean* anything by the expression 'necessary connection in the objects'. Thus:

> We wou'd not willingly stop before we are acquainted with that energy in the cause, by which it operates on its effect....And how must we be disappointed, when we learn, that this connection, tie, or energy lies merely in ourselves....Such a discovery not only cuts off all hopes of ever attaining satisfaction, but even prevents our very wishes; since it appears, that when we say we desire to know the ultimate and operating principle, as something, which resides in the external object, we either contradict ourselves, or talk without a meaning.
>
> (T 1.4.7.5)

It is this consideration which persuades most commentators that Hume thinks that the two definitions exhaust what there is to causation. However, a number of things should give us pause for thought.

First in a number of places in the *Treatise*, and more extensively in the *Enquiry*, Hume refers to unknowable powers. Thus:

> It has been observ'd already, that in no single instance the ultimate connexion of any objects is discoverable, either by our senses or reason, and that we can never penetrate so far into the essence and construction of bodies, as to perceive the principle, on which their mutual influence depends.
>
> (T 2.3.1.4)

In the *Enquiry* he writes that we 'are ignorant, it is true, of the manner in which bodies operate on each other. Their force or energy is entirely incomprehensible' (EHU 7.25), and:

> These ultimate springs and principles are totally shut up from human curiosity and enquiry...The most perfect philosophy of the natural kind only starves off our ignorance a little longer.
>
> (EHU 4.12)

There are plenty of other such avowals. There are many attempts to offer what we can call 'deflationary readings' of such passages, i.e. readings that try to show that we cannot take such passages at face value. It is arguable whether such attempts are successful, but we do not have the space to pursue this issue here.[14] Second, quite generally, Hume refrains from making claims about the world beyond experience. We should content ourselves with:

> knowing perfectly the manner in which objects affect [the] senses, and their connexions with each other, as far as experience informs [us] of them. This suffices for the conduct of life; and this also suffices for my philosophy, which pretends only to explain the nature and causes of our perceptions, or impressions and ideas.
>
> (T 1.2.5.26).

His intention, he says, 'never was to penetrate into the nature of bodies', since that is an 'enterprize [that] is beyond the reach of human understanding' (T 1.2.5.26). We should 'confine our speculations to the *appearances* of objects to our senses, without entering into disquisitions concerning their real nature and operations' (T 1.2.5.26n12). This general feature is relevant inasmuch as it shows that Hume does not wish to draw conclusions about the nature of the world independently of experience, and the conclusion that there *is* nothing to causation except regularity seems an unwarranted or cognitively immodest conclusion. We may have no understanding of what power might be, and so it is unintelligible to us, but that does not imply there is no such thing. 'I am', he writes,

> ready to allow, that there may be several qualities, both in material and immaterial objects, with which we are utterly unacquainted; and if we please to call these *power* or *efficacy*, 'twill be little consequence to the world. But then instead of meaning those unknown qualities, we make the terms of power and efficacy signify something, of which we have a clear idea, and which is incompatible with those objects, to which we apply it, obscurity and error begin then to take place, and we are led astray by a false philosophy.
>
> (T 1.3.14.27)

Now to be clear, the claim is not that Hume definitely thinks that there *is* or must be something more to causation. The point is rather that Hume's interest in naturalising human beings is consistent with a studied agnosticism about the nature of causation in the world. What is intelligible *to us* about causation is what is given in the two definitions.

But if Hume is *defining* 'cause', is he not telling us what causation is? What he tells us in the *Enquiry*, however, seems to suggest something weaker. He writes that 'so imperfect are the ideas which we form of [cause and effect], that it is impossible to give any just definition of cause, except what is drawn from something extraneous and foreign to it' (EHU 7.29). What we should be aware of, as Galen Strawson points out,[15] is that the eighteenth-century sense of 'definition' is rather different from that of giving an exhaustive account of the thing defined. Edmund Burke, writing a few years after Hume, tells us that

> when we define, we seem in danger of circumscribing nature within the bounds of our own notions, which we often...form out of a limited and partial consideration of the object before us, instead of extending our ideas to take in all that nature comprehends....A definition may be very exact, and yet go but a very little way towards informing us of the nature of the thing defined.[16]

A final point. We noted above that Hume explicitly refrains from making claims about the nature of the world beyond our experience, and this should not be a surprise given how we have understood the project of the *Treatise* which is the naturalisation of the human being. As such, this project can be carried out without making any claims about the nature of reality beyond our cognition. It is important to emphasise, as I mentioned above, that the claim that Hume is really only interested in circumscribing what we can understand by causation rather than making a positive claim about the metaphysics of causation should not be taken to be stronger than it is. Hume is not interested in arguing that there are such powers, or that the supposition that there might be any should play any serious role in our thought. It is simply that we, like the rest of animal creation, can only have access to regularities. Hence, to repeat a passage quoted earlier:

> Here, then, is a kind of pre-established harmony between the course of nature and the succession of our ideas; and though the powers and

forces, by which the former is governed, be wholly unknown to us; yet our thoughts and conceptions have still, we find, gone on in the same train with the other works of nature. Custom is that principle, by which this correspondence has been effected; so necessary to the subsistence of our species, and the regulation of our conduct, in every circumstance and occurrence of human life. Had not the presence of an object instantly excited the idea of those objects commonly conjoined with it, all our knowledge must have been limited to the narrow sphere of our memory and senses.

(EHU 5.2.21)

OF THE REASON OF ANIMALS

After offering his two definitions of 'cause', Hume then offers eight rules by which to judge cause and effect. These, he thinks, are easy to comprehend, but difficult to apply. The first three of these comprise a recapitulation of the definition of 'cause' as a philosophical relation. The fourth involves the assumption that like effects have like causes and vice versa, and so when we discover the one 'we immediately extend our observation to every phenomenon of the same kind' (T 1.3.15.6). Where different objects produce like effects, they must have some common quality (rule five), and where two similar objects produce different effects then we must suppose some difference in the object (rule six). Rule seven discusses how different causes can interact to produce compound effects, and rule eight tells us that if an object exists without bringing about its effect, it must be an incomplete cause, requiring some other principle.

Let us now turn to the final section of Part Three of Book One of the *Treatise*, 'Of the reason of animals'. Here Hume offers an argument to show that 'beasts are endow'd with thought and reason as well as men' (T 1.3.16.1). Before we come to discuss Hume's argument, it is worth noting that this claim embodies what I like to call a serious joke. Why I like to call it a joke is the fact that Hume has given us an account of human reason which, as we have seen, is modelled on animal accounts of inference. The serious aspect is of course that this claim is part and parcel of Hume's substantive naturalism, which aims to show that human beings are no different in kind from other animals.

The argument he offers is based on the idea that like effects have like causes. The external behaviour of animals, Hume claims, generally resembles that of human beings, and so we should assume that the inner causes are generally the same. It is

> from the resemblance of the external actions of animals to those we ourselves perform, that we judge their internal likewise to resemble ours; and the same principle of reasoning, carry'd one step farther, will make us conclude that since our internal actions resemble each other, the causes, from which they are deriv'd, must also be resembling.
>
> (T 1.3.16.3)

For Hume, the fact that his account applies to non-human animals is a signal advantage over other philosophies which, he says, 'suppose such a subtility and refinement of thought, as not only exceeds the capacity of mere animals but even children and the common people of our own species' (T 1.3.16.3).

Hume acknowledges that some animal behaviour expresses instincts that cannot be seen as operative of probable reason, which he calls the 'more extraordinary instances of sagacity' (T 1.3.16.5). Probable reasoning is a matter of learned inference, and when Hume discusses this in animals it is, in effect, simply a recapitulation of the main discussion of Part Three of Book One. Impressions of the sense or memory, together with experience of past conjunctions of objects, yield inference to the unobserved. The beliefs of animals are given the same account as human belief. Beasts do not draw inferences either because they perceive necessary connection, or in the light of argument that the future resembles the past. It is 'by means of custom alone, that experience operates on them' (T 1.3.16.8). In conclusion, then, to 'consider the matter aright, reason is nothing but a wonderful and unintelligible instinct in our souls, which carries us along a certain train of ideas' (T 1.3.16.9).

NOTES

1 Leibniz, *New Essays on Human Understanding*, p.143. Hereafter NE.
2 For a good discussion see Kemp (2007).

3 Here I am following Loeb (2002), who lays out these points in a very clear manner.
4 We can infer cause from effects as well as effects from causes. In the former case, I can observe footprints in the snow and infer that there was a fox in the garden.
5 NE p.143.
6 NE p.51.
7 NE p.457.
8 Leibniz, *Monadology*, Section 27.
9 NE p.271.
10 Loeb (2002) tries to read Hume as implicitly exploiting a dispositional account of belief. For criticism of Loeb, see Marušić (2010).
11 An old, but still very useful, discussion of Hume on belief is Gorman (1993).
12 See e.g. Price (2011).
13 For the longer story, see Kail (2007a), Chapter Four.
14 I remain unconvinced that such strategies work—see Kail (2007a) and (2015). For a trenchant defence of the traditional view, see Millican (2009).
15 Strawson (2011), p.24.
16 Burke, *A Philosophical Enquiry into the Origin of our Ideas of the Sublime and Beautiful*, pp.4–5.

FURTHER READING

Part Three of Book One is among the most discussed parts of Hume's philosophical writings. Below are some relatively recent classics. On knowledge and demonstration, Owen (2000), Chapter Five, and Schmitt (2014), Chapter Two are highly recommended. The literature on Hume's account of probable inference is vast. For views that are similar to the one sketched here see Owen (2000), Chapters Six to Nine, Garrett (1997), Chapter Four, and Schmitt (2014), *passim*. For more traditional sceptical readings, see Millican (2002b) and Winkler (2016). On belief, see Gorman (1993), Bell (2002), Loeb (2002), Chapter Three, and Marušić (2010). Like the literature on probable reason, the literature on Hume's account of causation is vast. For discussions of the two definitions, see, for example, Garrett (1997), Chapter Five, Beebee (2011), and Boehm (2014). On the question of Hume's attitude to whether his two definitions exhaust all there is to the causal relation, see the papers in Richman and Read (eds.) (2007), Millican (2009), Strawson (2011), Chapter One, and Kail (2007), Chapter Four. On Hume's subject naturalism, see Kail (2014b), and on the relation between reason and Hume's naturalism, see Kail (2007b) and Kail (2019).

4
OF THE SCEPTICAL AND OTHER SYSTEMS OF PHILOSOPHY

INTRODUCTION

There are two aspects to Part Four of Book One of the *Treatise*. The first is relatively obvious. It comprises sections that discuss particular philosophical topics, such as the self and the external world. The second aspect is more subtle. As the discussion of different topics progresses, Hume becomes more reflective about philosophy and the sceptical problems it generates which leads him to evince less and less psychological confidence as Part Four progresses. Near the beginning of Part Four Hume discusses scepticism about reason itself but seems quite sanguine about the worries that such reflection generates. He tells us that 'nature breaks the force of all sceptical arguments in time, and keeps them from having any considerable influence on the understanding' (T 1.4.1.12). In discussing scepticism about the external world, he tells us that 'sceptical doubt arises naturally from a profound and intense reflection' (T 1.4.2.57) but we nevertheless continue to believe that there is one when we cease profound and intense reflection. Generally speaking, reflection does not undermine belief and confidence. However, in the conclusion to Part Four he writes:

> But what have I here said, that reflections very refin'd and metaphysical have little or no influence upon us? This opinion I can scarce forbear retracting, and condemning from my present feeling and experience. The *intense* view of these manifold contradictions and imperfections of human reason has so wrought upon me, and heated my brain, that I am ready to reject all belief and reasoning, and can look upon no opinion even as more probable or likely than another.
>
> (T 1.4.7.8)

Gradually Hume comes to realise that reflection does indeed affect confidence. This second aspect of Part Four is something we shall consider alongside the particular topics that Hume considers in each section. What we see enacted is not merely a discussion of topics but an attitude to philosophy and its goals.

T 1.4.1 OF SCEPTICISM WITH REGARD TO REASON

T 1.4.1 presents an argument purporting to show that 'all the rules of logic', when correctly applied, demand 'a total extinction of belief and evidence' (T. 1.4.1.6). This dramatic conclusion has two aspects. First, it suggests that if we reason according to all the rules of logic, we arrive at the conclusion that we have no evidence for any belief. This is an (extreme) *epistemological* conclusion. Second, talk of the 'total extinction of belief' suggests that the application of all the 'rules of logic' produces a *psychological* effect, namely the destruction of the psychological state of belief. At first blush these two aspects are connected in the following manner. The 'rules of logic' somehow imply that there is no evidence for any belief whatsoever (the epistemic aspect). The extinction of belief is not then so much a psychological claim but instead a normative demand based on the idea that one should not believe without evidence. Belief *should* be abandoned when there is no evidence. This leaves us with the question of the relationship between the normative and its actual psychological consequences, but let us first discuss the sceptical argument.

Hume begins by distinguishing the rules and norms that govern reasoning and our application of them:

> The rules are certain and infallible; but when we apply them, our fallible and uncertain faculties are very apt to depart from them, and fall into error...Our reason must be consider'd as a kind of cause, of which truth is the natural effect; but such-a-one as by the irruption of other causes, and by the inconstancy of our mental powers, may frequently be prevented.
>
> (T 1.4.1.1)

Our reason is a cause of true belief, but a fallible one, and its fallibility is something we learn from experience. Our awareness of its past fallibility provides us with a reason to check any judgment we make with a further judgment that factors in our past mistakes and the likelihood of our being mistaken in this instance. Call the demand to make such judgments the 'Assurance Norm'.

The Assurance Norm is what leads to Hume's conclusion that 'all knowledge degenerates into probability' (T 1.4.1.1). The new judgment reduces first judgment's certainty by introducing the memory of our fallibility, and so removes the absolute certainty that demonstration appeared to promise. We should factor in the possibility of having gone wrong which then makes the conclusion of the first judgment less than certain. Hence, knowledge degenerates into probability in that its conclusions are no longer 100% certain. But things do not stop here. The Assurance Norm applies to the inferences of probable reason as well. When we make an inference, we are obliged to consider that in light of our memory of past mistakes. This higher-order judgment dictates that we should reduce our confidence in the first judgment. But this higher-order judgment—the judgment about the original judgment—is itself an instance of probable reasoning and is itself subject to the Assurance Norm. So, this now third-order judgment adds a further source of doubt, which is transferred down to the first-order judgment and further decreases one's confidence in that judgment. Since this itself is a judgment of probable reason, it is itself subject to the Assurance Norm and we continue on a regress of higher-order judgments, each of which decreases one's confidence in the first-order judgment until it reaches zero.

I noted above that when talking about the extinction of belief and evidence, we can see this from either a psychological or epistemic perspective, and that these two might be connected by seeing the epistemic as guiding the thought that one ought not believe because there is no evidence. However, matters are rather more complicated than represented here. The key thing to note is that, epistemically, the argument just presented is not a good one. It is not inevitable that obeying the Assurance Norm lowers the probability of the first judgment. We might double-check a judgment without that itself reducing the epistemic stand of that judgment. It could actually reinforce or confirm rather than diminish the first judgment by showing that the evidence is good. This is one reason why some commentators think that we should not read what Hume says here epistemically. Instead, Hume is merely talking about our psychology. The scepticism should be thought of as a matter of the destruction of belief by reflection, independently of whether it is epistemically correct to conclude that no belief has any evidence. The scepticism is that if we followed the Assurance Norm remorselessly, our beliefs, *qua* psychological states, would be destroyed. The judgment that emerges by combining the first judgment and the second-order judgment will be one with slightly less force and vivacity than the first judgment. Further iterations gradually produce further combined judgments with ever decreasing force and vivacity. On this view, when Hume is talking about 'all the rules of logic' he is referring to remorseless use of the Assurance Norm, the outcome is the extinction of belief. 'Evidence', on this view, is not taken to be an epistemic term but rather the degree of force and vivacity.

This latter view has its attractions and seems to fit well with Hume's response to the argument. He writes:

> My intention [in offering this argument] is only to make the reader sensible of the truth of my hypothesis, *that all our reasonings concerning causes and effects are deriv'd from nothing but custom; and that belief is more properly an act of the sensitive, than the cogitative part of our natures.*

(T 1.4.1.8)

The key point, as Hume observes, is that we are psychologically incapable of following the argument to its end point, namely the destruction of belief. 'Nature, by an absolute and uncontroulable necessity has determin'd us to judge as well as to breath' (T 1.4.1.7). Were belief free of the natural mechanisms Hume describes in Part Three, then such extinction would be possible. Instead those mechanisms, when operating at an artificial and abstract level—such as when higher-order judgments are far removed from the first judgement—thankfully fail to have a causal effect of destroying belief:

> Where the mind reaches not to objects with easiness and facility, the same principles have not the same effect as in a more natural conception of the ideas; nor does the imagination feel a sensation, which holds any proportion with that which arises from its common judgments and opinions.
>
> (T 1.4.1.10)

So, Hume is trying to show that, fortunately, belief is not psychologically responsive to the iterative version of the Assurance Norm, and he treats this fact as confirmation of his account of the nature of the mechanism which he identifies as reason. The sceptical argument is not intended to be an *epistemic* conclusion.

Other commentators are nevertheless unsatisfied with this response and see the scepticism as offering an epistemic conclusion. Some point out that Hume's use of the term 'evidence' elsewhere in the *Treatise* seems epistemic rather than psychological.[1] Others hold that although the epistemic conclusion is literally unbelievable, it is nevertheless the case that Hume is theoretically committed to the sceptical conclusion that all beliefs lack any epistemic warrant, and, as he puts it, 'our judgment is not in *any* thing possest of *any* measures of truth and falsehood' (T 1.4.1.7). Hume does not believe that conclusion because it is psychologically impossible to do so, but nevertheless that is merely a psychological fact. The argument is sound (or at least Hume thinks it is), but because we cannot, psychologically speaking, follow reason as the Assurance Norm demands, we cannot 'sincerely assent' to its destructive conclusion. So, we are left with the view that, although we continue to believe, we recognise that reason would yield the *evaluative* conclusion that all beliefs lack justification or evidence.

I agree with those commentators that take Hume's argument to be epistemic in character. However, Hume's considered response is reserved for the conclusion to Part Four and so we shall turn to his answer when we discuss that conclusion.

T 1.4.2 OF SCEPTICISM WITH REGARD TO THE SENSES

The next section of Part Four considers the external world. It is a long, complicated, and much discussed part of the *Treatise*. Among the remarkable things about it is that Hume appears to change his attitude to the subject matter through the course of his discussion.

In the opening section he says that the subject of this section concerns 'the *causes* which induce us to believe in the existence of body' (T 1.4.2.2) and that it is 'in vain to ask' whether body exists (T 1.4.2.1). We cannot but help believe in the existence of body. However, towards the end of his discussion he acknowledges that he said that 'we ought to have an implicit faith in our senses, and that this wou'd be the conclusion, [he] shou'd draw from the whole of my reasoning', and then voices 'a quite contrary sentiment', that he is 'inclin'd to repose no faith at all in [his] senses, or rather imagination, than place in it such an implicit confidence' (T 1.4.2.56). Somehow, then, Hume's examination of the causes of the belief in body undermines his initial confidence.

We shall return to this at the end of this section. At the beginning Hume tells us that he is trying to explain the belief in body. What is that belief? At a first approximation, which we shall qualify later, Hume is considering the objects which we immediately perceive by our senses which we hold to be external objects. These are objects which have two features. Such objects *continue* to exist when we are not perceiving them, and such objects are *distinct* from our experience of them. Continuity is straightforward. We assume that the things we perceive continue to exist when we do not perceive them. The notion of distinctness is a little more complicated, where Hume says this includes the 'external' position as well as the 'independence of their existence and operation'

(T 1.4.2.2). There are two different thoughts here. The latter is that things do not depend on us for their existence: that is, they do not come into existence in virtue of our perception of them. The former is that the things we perceive are spatially distinct from our person.

Let us say that these two features constitute the core content of our belief about bodies or material things. We believe that continuous and independent things exist, and we perceive things of that kind. But, to add further complexity, there are two versions of this belief, the vulgar and the philosophical. The 'vulgar view' is the view of people who are not troubled by philosophy, and its important feature is as follows. We *immediately* perceive continuous and distinct objects. When I open my eyes, my mind is simply aware directly or immediately of the objects and their qualities. I am not aware of anything else but those objects. When we come to discuss the philosophical view, we shall see how the vulgar view differs from it, but Hume's explanation of the belief in body begins with the vulgar view.

So how do we get the belief in continuous and independent existence? Hume turns to three possible sources, the senses, reason, and the imagination, arguing that the first two cannot be what produces the belief, so it must be down to the imagination. The senses cannot inform us that objects continue to exist unperceived: it is 'a contradiction in terms, and supposes that the senses continue to operate, ever after they have ceas'd all manner of operation' (T 1.4.2.3). As for independence, it is important to bring out some key assumptions with which Hume is working. At this stage, Hume is thinking of perceiving as a matter of an object, or thing perceived, being immediately present to the perceiver. When we perceive an object, it is simply 'there' before the mind of the observer. This is what Hume primarily means by 'the senses', and so when we believe in body, we hold that some of the things immediately present to the mind have a continued and distinct existence. Pains do not have a continuous and distinct existence, but chairs do. However, Hume also thinks that all that is really immediately present to the mind are *perceptions*, and that these are 'internal and perishing existences' (T 1.4.2.15). These are neither independent of us nor spatially distinct. Since what is immediately present to the senses is not distinct, the senses cannot be the source of the belief that there are distinct objects.

We shall leave reason as a possible source of this belief for the time being and turn to Hume's appeal to the imagination as an explanation of the belief. Hume holds that the belief emerges because of our psychological reaction to two features of impressions which he calls 'coherence' and 'constancy'. These are relational features of impressions. Hume begins with coherence, and this involves connecting different sets of impressions together at different times. So, for example, I might at one time have impressions of a fire burning brightly and emitting intense heat but I later have impressions of ash and faint heat. I suppose that there is a certain relation between the two sets of impressions since there is a regularity between them, a supposition bolstered by the belief in bodies. However, this conclusion should not be thought of as an instance of probable or causal reasoning, as Hume is at pains to emphasise (T 1.4.2.21). When we reason upon cause and effect, we do so on the basis of observing both cause and effect. However, when we suppose a continued object to make sense of two different sets of perceptions, we do not observe it: we simply suppose its continued existence. Instead, we come to think in terms of coherence simply because of the associative principles of the imagination. Even then, Hume thinks coherence alone is insufficient to explain the belief in continuous and distinct objects. What is required is constancy.

What is 'constancy'? Let us begin with an illustration. Focus on what is before your eyes right now. Now very briefly close your eyes and open them again. Your experience—the impression—on either side of the interruption is most likely to be the same. But the 'same' is ambiguous between two senses of the term, *numerical* and *qualitative* sameness or identity. Very roughly, qualitative identity is a relation between two or more things, all of which share the same properties. Imagine I have two teacups, both of which are the same size, colour, weight etc., and, indeed, it is difficult to tell one from the other. We can say they are qualitatively identical or the same. The teacups are not, however, numerically identical. Numerical identity is a relation that concerns one, and only, one object, and is often discussed in connection with change.

If, for example, I replace the engine, lights and upholstery in my car, and spray it a new colour, one might ask whether, given all the changes, the car is the same car as the one before the changes or not. We touched upon Hume's complicated views on the idea of numerical identity earlier in this book and he mentions them again in this part, but what is important for our concerns here is that constancy relates to numerically different, but qualitatively the same, items. When one shuts one's eyes in the situation described above, there are two sets of perceptions, numerically distinct, but qualitatively the same. This relation between these perceptions is constancy. And constancy gives rise to a certain temptation. Because the two different sets of perceptions are so similar, the mind is tempted to think of them as numerically identical. And yet their interruption tells against their numerical identity. This has an uncomfortable effect upon the mind. Hume writes that we 'find ourselves somewhat at a loss, and are involv'd in a kind of contradiction'. Hence:

> [i]n order to free ourselves from this difficulty, we disguise, as much as possible, the interruption, or rather remove it entirely, by supposing that these interrupted perceptions are connected by a real existence, of which we are insensible.
>
> (T 1.4.2.24)

Hume then examines the details of this account, but we shall only note one. He tells us that the 'kind of contradiction' felt by the mind—the conflict between the pull to see both sets of perceptions as identical, and yet recognising that they are not—produces a 'sensible uneasiness', and the mind 'will naturally seek relief from the uneasiness' (T 1.4.2.37). This 'uneasiness' is relieved by simply yielding to the tendency to think of the two different sets of perceptions as identical. We simply yield because it removes the psychological discomfort by the supposition of 'continu'd existence'.

Notice, that on the face of it, Hume seems to be describing quite an elaborate mental process. Prior to the belief, it looks as if we have various beliefs about the non-identity of resembling perceptions, of the relations of coherence, and a belief in the existence of perceptions. All that seems rather sophisticated, and what is more, given that children come to think of a continuous world fairly early in life, it seems that we have to credit infants with such beliefs, which seems quite absurd. But we can alleviate some of this absurdity by drawing upon a contemporary distinction between personal and sub-personal levels in psychology. *Very* roughly, the personal level is the level of common-sense psychology, where we talk of persons, beliefs, hopes, thoughts etc., which involve conscious goals and conscious control. At the sub-personal level, we are picking out mechanisms that operate without the person's knowledge or awareness of their operation, and which are not in the person's control, nor consciously attached to goals. They are processes that, nevertheless, contribute to psychology at the personal level. So, for example, when you understand a sentence, you do so at personal level, but how information such as the sounds or shapes that enter your senses is then processed to yield that understanding occurs at the sub-personal level. Such mechanisms do not involve beliefs, let alone sophisticated ones, though they may yield them. So, we can think that Hume's explanation is couched at something akin to a sub-personal level, even if, of course, he does not describe it as such.

At the end of this process, the belief in body which emerges can be described as follows. Some of the things with which we are immediately acquainted are deemed to be bodies, that is, are thought to continue to exist when unperceived and are independent of our experience of them. Once we acquire the belief in constancy, the coherence of experience suggests a world of continuous and distinct objects. Importantly, those objects are conceived to be things of which we have immediate awareness. This is the vulgar view. But, Hume thinks, the vulgar view is false, and 'contrary to the plainest experience' (T 1.4.2.44). What is immediately perceived is dependent on fleeting perceptions and not continuous and distinct objects.

One might think that this is the end of the matter. However, Hume notes, philosophers do not rest content which acknowledging the falsity of this view. Instead, they formulate a different, philosophical version, of the ordinary or 'vulgar' belief in body. Another term for the philosophical view is 'the doctrine of double existence', a term which gives a clue to its distinctive content. The philosophical system acknowledges that those things which are immediately perceived are perceptions, and that these are neither continuous nor independent. What the view supposes is that there are continuous and independent objects (physical objects), that our perceptions are *caused by* those objects, and that our perceptions *represent* those objects. Instead of the perceptual relationship being one of our direct immediate awareness, we are directly aware of perceptions, but *indirectly* aware of bodies or continuous objects. Perceptions manage to represent objects, on this system, in virtue of resembling the objects that cause those perceptions. This view is sometimes also known as 'indirect realism'. 'Indirect' because our perceptual relation to bodies is mediated by perceptions, 'realism' because there are physical objects, i.e. continuous and distinct objects. Such a view is most associated with John Locke and was the subject of severe criticism by George Berkeley. What does Hume have to say about the philosophical system?

For him it is only a 'palliative remedy, and…contains all the difficulties of the vulgar system, with some others, that are peculiar to itself' (T 1.4.2.46). The philosophical system 'has no primary recommendation either to reason or the imagination, but acquires all its influence on the imagination' (T 1.4.2.46) from the vulgar view. Let us unpack this claim. When it comes to reason, the key point is that the belief can neither be caused nor justified by reason. What is supposed is that there is a causal relation between a physical object and our perceptions. However, we cannot directly experience such a relation since our experience is limited to our own perceptions: we cannot 'climb out of minds', as it were, to experience a physical object causing a perception since all of our experience involves perceptions. We 'may observe a conjunction or a relation of cause and effect betwixt different perceptions, but can never observe it betwixt perceptions and objects' (T 1.4.2.47).

What of the system having no primary recommendation to the imagination and gaining all its influence from the vulgar system? Hume thinks that, since the system cannot be caused or justified by reason, what most motivates the philosophical system is the grip that the vulgar system has on the imagination. Despite recognising that the vulgar system is false, philosophers still *want* to believe in the continuous and distinct existence of physical objects, and this pull of the imagination leads them to invent a new set of objects that are continuous and distinct. As Hume puts it:

> Nature is obstinate, and will not quit the field, however strongly attack'd by reason; and at the same time reason is so clear in the point, that there is no possibility of disguising her. Not being able to reconcile these two enemies, we endeavour to set ourselves at ease as much as possible, and successively granting to each whatever it demands, and by feigning a double existence, where each may find something, that has all the conditions it desires. (T 1.4.2.52)

So, the philosophical view is invented simply because philosophers cannot escape the pull of the vulgar view. Not only this, but it is a system also 'over-loaded' with an additional 'absurdity'. Recall that, according to the philosophical system, physical objects differ from perceptions in being continuous and distinct but nevertheless they are supposed to resemble perceptions. But what we can conceive is only perceptions and so what the philosophers conceive when supposedly conceiving physical objects is really 'a new set of perceptions'. We may, Hume writes, 'suppose in general, but 'tis impossible for us distinctly to conceive objects in their nature any thing but exactly the same with perceptions' (T.1.4.2.56). This is something to which Hume alluded much earlier in the *Treatise*, in T 1.2.6. Here Hume tells us that 'external objects become known only by those perceptions they occasion' (T 1.2.6.7), but it is 'impossible for us to conceive any specific difference between perceptions and objects' (T 1.2.6.8). Instead, we generally do not 'suppose them specifically different; but only attribute to them different relations, connexions and durations' (T 1.2.6.8).

Does this mean that an external world of continuous and distinct objects is not only not caused by reason but, worse still, is literally unthinkable since any attempt to think of external objects really only results in thoughts about perceptions? Some commentators think so, but we shall postpone discussion of this topic until we get to the section called 'Of the modern philosophy'. Now though, we are in a position to see why Hume's tone shifts from confidence at the beginning of 'Of scepticism with regard to the senses' to his 'quite contrary sentiment' of being 'inclin'd to repose no faith at all in [his] senses, or rather imagination, than place in it such an implicit confidence' (T 1.4.2.56).

What is key here is the kind of causes Hume identifies as central to the emergence of the belief. First, and quite obviously, neither version of the belief is caused by reason, that is a kind of cause that has truth as its natural effect. Second, and more importantly, the kind of cause that Hume identifies is a kind that normally casts suspicion on beliefs. Suppose you ask Fred where the train station is located. Consider now three different situations under which Fred answers. First, you know Fred, and you know he is a very trustworthy person. When you receive the answer, you feel justified in believing it because you know he is quite generally a reliable source of information. Second, Fred is someone whom you do not know, but you ask on the street as you are unsure of the location of the train station. In this case, although you do not know Fred, you have no particular reason to mistrust him and so you take his word on the matter. Third, Fred gives you an answer, but you subsequently learn that Fred is, generally speaking, a deceiver. The fact that you learn that he is generally a deceiver provides a reason to be suspicious of the answer he gave you. The causes of the belief in body resemble the third case. As Hume writes in an unpublished essay entitled 'Of the immortality of the soul', 'all doctrines are to be suspected which are favoured by our passions',[2] and the reason for this, very roughly, is that here beliefs are settled upon and sustained not because they are likely to be true but because we *want* the belief to be true because we find it comforting. The 'simple supposition of continued existence' emerges, not because the mind takes the evidence to suggest it, but because that supposition removes the irksome 'uneasiness' the mind feels when confronted with two contrary inclinations. It is the relief from this uneasiness that motivates the belief. With respect to the philosophical system, what sustains the 'arbitrary' invention of a new set of objects, is that philosophers are loathe to give up the false system of the vulgar and so 'seek some pretext to justify' the opinion (T 1.4.2.52).

We can then think of Hume's shift in the text from trust to a 'quite contrary sentiment' as a dramatic presentation of our coming to be aware that the causes of a belief, which we previously had implicit faith in, are such that they cast suspicion on that belief. It is like trusting Fred initially and then learning that Fred is the kind of person who habitually deceives. We cannot have 'implicit faith' in a belief sourced in the kind of cause which we have reason to think has suspect results. Hence, Hume asks:

> What can we look for from this confusion of groundless and extraordinary opinions but error and falshood? And how can we justify to ourselves any belief we repose in them?
>
> (T 1.4.2.57)

Notice that Hume does not answer these questions at this stage. He does not, that is, say that the philosophical belief *is* false and that it *cannot* be justified. Indeed, he notes a little earlier that the denial of any continuous and distinct existence is 'peculiar to a few extravagant sceptics; who after all maintain'd that opinion in words only, and were never able to bring themselves sincerely to believe it' (T 1.4.2.50). During 'profound and intense reflection', the 'contrary sentiment' has its grip, only to disappear when leaving the study. Nevertheless, 'sceptical doubt, both with respect to reason and the senses, is a malady which can never be radically cur'd', and 'carelessness and inattention alone afford any remedy' (T 1.4.2.57). This, however, is not Hume's final word on the matter as we shall see.

ANCIENT AND MODERN PHILOSOPHIES

In two successive sections Hume discusses two philosophical views. The first, under the title 'Of the antient philosophy', discusses variations on the notion of substance. The second, under the title 'Of the modern philosophy', discusses the distinction between primary and secondary qualities, something central to early modern philosophy.

In 'Of the antient philosophy', Hume offers a psychological explanation of the invention of the concept of substance. As is now familiar, Hume holds that what is immediately presented to the mind are impressions and we have seen that their constancy and coherence lead us to ascribe to some of them a continued and distinct existence. A further issue arises when we consider whether one thing can continue to exist even though all its qualities change. It is here that one key role for the notion of substance is secure identity through change. The substance is conceived to be the thing that possesses qualities, and it remains constant even though those qualities change. The 'imagination', Hume says, 'is apt to feign something unknown and invisible, which it supposes to continue the same under all these variations; and this unintelligible something it calls a *substance*' (T 1.4.3.4).

Another role for substance in versions of ancient philosophy—and their scholastic variants—is to be the bearer of powers in the explanation of change. We have already seen that Hume thinks that we cannot perceive or grasp any such powers. Here Hume notes that philosophers correct the vulgar error of thinking that powers are perceivable, but instead of resting content with that observation, their imagination again produces a different idea of that which they fail to discover by observation. This 'consolation principally consists in their invention of the words *faculty* and *occult quality*' (T.1.4.3.10). Sometimes what is invented is merely the word, and sometimes something more than words, Hume suggests, when some start talking in terms of the sympathies, antipathies, and horrors of a vacuum. He sees such talk as reflecting a general disposition to personify nature, an inclination found in poets 'by their readiness to personify every thing' and in children 'by their desire of beating the stones, which hurt them':

> And in the antient philosophers, by these fictions of sympathy and antipathy. We must pardon children because of their age; poets, because they profess to follow implicitly the suggestions of their fancy: But what excuse shall we find to justify our philosophers of so signal a weakness?
>
> (T 1.4.3.11)

The cumulative effect of Hume's discussion is an attitude of suspicion. The philosophical views they espouse are fictions of the imagination. But this raises a question which Hume confronts in the next section, 'Of the modern philosophy'. It may be objected, Hume says:

> that the imagination, according to my own confession, being the ultimate judge of all systems of philosophy, I am unjust in blaming the antient philosophers for making use of that faculty, and allowing themselves to be entirely guided by it in their reasonings.
>
> (T 1.4.4.1)

Since everything in the mind is governed by the imagination via the principles of association, what is wrong with the views of ancient philosophers since they are products of the imagination? In answer, Hume distinguishes between principles of the imagination which are 'permanent, irresistible, and universal', and those which are 'changeable, weak, and irregular' (T 1.4.4.1). He gives the example of our causal inferences to illustrate the former kind of principles, and the views of ancient philosophers as an example of the latter. The former are 'the foundation of all our thoughts and actions, so that upon their removal human nature must immediately perish and go to ruin', whereas the latter are 'neither unavoidable to mankind, nor necessary, nor so much as useful in the conduct of life' (T 1.4.4.1). This distinction, at first blush, seems to afford a pragmatic justification of the belief in the continued and distinct existence of physical objects. We know that the vulgar view is false, and that the philosophical view is not justified by reason, but the supposition of continued and distinct objects might be thought of as one of those principles which are necessary to human nature, and Hume tells us that it is. The propensity to believe in external objects is 'equally natural and necessary in the human mind' as our probabilistic inferences (T 1.4.7.4). This then provides an answer to the question Hume posed at the end of 'Of scepticism with regard to the senses', namely 'how can we justify to ourselves any belief we repose' in our senses. Although we cannot give an epistemic reason for the belief, we can give a practical reason: we should retain the belief because without it all action would cease, and we would go 'to perish and ruin'.

It is worth pausing to develop this thought a little and beyond anything to which Hume explicitly commits himself. Our belief in a stable world is necessary for action. It is this supposition which makes the coherence of experience 'much greater and more uniform, [and]... gives us a notion of a much greater regularity among objects' (T 1.4.2.22). Without it we would not be able to act successfully. Yet we cannot give any epistemic reason for the belief. To offer some pragmatic justification for the belief we need to say why it is better to have the belief than not to have the belief. There are two possibilities in play here: either there are continued and distinct existences or there are not. If there are such things, and one acts in accordance with that belief, one's actions will lead to success, all other things being equal. If there are no such objects, then one's actions will not be successful. However, whether or not there are external objects, actions will never be successful if you lack the belief, partly because you will not form beliefs about the future because those rest on a supposition about regularities among objects. So, it is better to have the belief than not.

This seems promising. However, 'Of the modern philosophy' brings out a conflict between two 'equally natural and necessary' principles. In brief, causal reasoning suggests a conclusion that deprives us of any notion of continued and distinct existence. As Hume puts it in the conclusion of this section, there is

> a direction and total opposition betwixt our reason and our senses, or more properly speaking, betwixt those conclusions we form from cause and effect, and those that perswade us of the continu'd and independent existence of body.
>
> (T 1.4.4.15)

Notice that nothing Hume says at this stage decides between the 'opposition' here. That is to say, he does not decide that we should reject belief in the external world because reason appears to dictate that we should. Instead, he notes that there is a severe 'opposition' between these two 'equally natural and necessary' principles. How Hume navigates this 'total opposition' will be discussed when we come to Hume's own conclusion to Book One. But first we should understand how it is generated.

The refence to the 'modern philosophy' in this section is to a distinction between the primary and secondary qualities of physical objects, which is intimately related to the philosophical view of perception and the external world. Physical objects are presented as having a range of different qualities including smell, tastes, colour, extension, and solidity. Our impressions represent those properties in virtue of them *resembling* those physical objects in those respects. So, our extended impression represents the extension of a physical object in virtue of the impression resembling the object in that respect. However, not all of the qualities that we assume to be qualities of physical objects are actually so. Consider the distinctive smell of a rose. We think it to be an indefinable sensuous quality that is a quality of that flower. According to modern philosophy, the rose itself possesses nothing like that quality. Instead, in virtue of its primary qualities, the object causes in us a sensation that yields the distinctive rose smell, but there is nothing like that quality in the rose. What lies behind this line of thought is a view that science only needs a limited range of qualities for physical objects in order to explain their behaviour. Roughly, everything physical is extended stuff in motion or at rest, and so the only qualities required are extension, shape (figure), number, and, at least according to some philosophers, solidity. Furthermore, material objects are composed of atoms or corpuscles that are arranged in various patterns. These different arrangements affect other physical objects, and also affect our impressions or sensations. One arrangement causes in us one kind of sensation, a different arrangement a different one.

Hume claims that this philosophy has the implication that the secondary qualities—colour, smell, taste, and others—are 'nothing but impressions in the mind' (T 1.4.4.3). Physical objects are not coloured. Instead, colours are the effects on the mind of the interaction of colourless objects, and we mistakenly attribute colours to those physical objects. Commentators routinely criticise Hume here, claiming that he misunderstands the distinction. Philosophers like Locke and Descartes understand secondary qualities like colour not as perceptions of the mind but work instead with a distinction between colours as we experience them and colours in the objects. Objects do have colours, and those are the arrangements of corpuscles which constitute the power of the object to produce a distinctive kind of experience or sensation which we associate with red. Redness is the power of an object to produce those particular sensations in us, and so redness is not a mere perception in the mind. Hume therefore misunderstands, or at least misrepresents, the primary and secondary distinction.

Hume, however, is not making any mistake. Instead, his view reflects a criticism of the view of Locke and Descartes by philosophers like Pierre Bayle and Nicolas Malebranche, who, very roughly, hold that what we understand by properties like colour is the distinctive qualitative character and so it is wrong to identify colours with such powers.[3] And, like his French influences, Hume also focuses on a particular argument in favour of the distinction. The taste, colours, and other perceivable qualities vary according to both the circumstances of the observer and the particular observer. Given that the object itself does not change, we have to admit that, in at least some cases, the particular colour impression does not resemble the object that causes that impression in that respect. That is, as Hume puts it, 'many of our impressions have no external model or archetype' (T.1.4.4.4). To derive the conclusion that such qualities are impressions in the mind, Hume reminds of one of the rules by which to judge cause and effect, namely that like causes have like effects, and *vice versa*. Since, in some cases, we must admit that the cause of our impression does not resemble the colour of the object, we have to admit, by this rule, that none does. Hence there is nothing resembling colour in objects.

That which remains of physical objects then is their primary qualities. But Hume thinks that this position is unstable. If we deprive physical objects of the secondary qualities, then 'nothing we can conceive of is possest of a real, continu'd, and independent existence; not even motion, extension, and solidity, which are the primary qualities chiefly insisted on' (T 1.4.4.6). Very briefly, the argument goes as follows. Bare motion does not exist on its own: it is a matter of *something's* being in motion or rest. So, we need a conception of a body, and, on this view of matter, a conception of an extended and solid thing that is devoid of other qualities such as colour. When it comes to forming an idea of extension, our primary idea is visual in character. But how, if we deprive ourselves of all colours (including black and white) can we conceive of something that is extended and yet has no colour? The only other option seems to be to appeal to solidity, which Hume glosses as the idea of two bodies 'which being impelled by the utmost force, cannot penetrate each other' (T 1.4.4.9). But that notion presupposes that we have a prior conception of two bodies, which is the point in question. Hume considers and rejects the sense of touch as a source of the idea of solidity and concludes that we cannot form any idea of any body that supposedly consists in solely primary qualities.

It is possible to question every step of this argument, but for our purposes the key point is this: Hume thinks that the causal reasoning that supports the drawing of the primary and secondary quality distinction and its conclusion is 'as satisfactory as can possibly be imagined' (T.1.4.4.4). Hence it is one of those 'conclusions we form from cause and effect' (T.1.4.4.15). But from it we 'utterly annihilate all those [external] objects and reduce ourselves to the opinions of the most extravagant scepticism concerning them' (T 1.4.4.6).

T 1.4.5 OF THE IMMATERIALITY OF THE SOUL

T 1.4.6, 'Of personal identity', is one of the most famous and influential parts of Hume's *Treatise* and proposes a view of the human mind as nothing but a collection of experiences or perceptions bundled together. Often this topic is discussed separately from the section that precedes it, T 1.4.5, 'Of the immateriality of the soul', but what Hume says in T 1.4.5 bears crucially on his view of the mind as a bundle of perceptions. So, we shall start there.

'Of the immateriality of the soul' is a long and complicated section. A number of different issues lurk in the background which Hume does not explicitly raise but which are important to note. The self or soul is supposed to be an immaterial substance that is responsible for thought and experience, a notion that had both philosophical and religious ramifications during the period. Descartes had argued that the mind was an immaterial substance distinct from the material world, a thesis which provoked some profound philosophical responses. Some argued that two different kinds of substance could not possibly interact with each other. Spinoza argued that the correct response to Descartes' reflections on substance was that there is only one true substance, God or nature. According to Nicolas Malebranche, there are two kinds of substance but any apparent interaction between the two depends on the will of God. Leibniz and Berkeley, by contrast, decided (for very different reasons) that there is no material substance. The doctrine of the immateriality of the soul is also linked to the idea of its being naturally immortal. Berkeley and many others saw a threat in materialism to this idea, one which stemmed from John Locke's speculation that matter might itself think, leading to the worry that the soul would cease to exist when the body does.[4]

'These philosophers' Hume says 'are the curious reasoners concerning the material or immaterial substances' upon which our perceptions are supposed to depend (T 1.4.5.2). His approach is to argue that we cannot have any idea of what substances are supposed to be, and so the whole debate is fundamentally misconceived. We have mentioned the notion of substance a number of times in this book already. There are some key aspects to the ontology of substances. First, they are the 'owner' of properties. We distinguish between a thinker and her thoughts, and a substance view holds that the thinker is the substances upon which thoughts depend. This brings us to a second and related point. Substances are independent entities, upon which other entities, variously called 'modes' or 'accidents', depend. I can exist without thinking about my cat, but the thought of my cat cannot exist without me. I am a thinking thing, and all my thoughts depend on me. Third, substances help to individuate things into *kinds*. This is particularly relevant to the issue of the immateriality of the self. What makes one substance of one kind as opposed to another depends on its *essence*, the property which a thing cannot lose and yet still exist. I am a thinking substance, and whilst it is possible for me to exist without this or that particular thought, I cannot exist without thinking. What it is to be a soul or self is to be an essentially thinking thing. Material substance by contrast is a different kind and so has a different essence: to be a material object is to be extended in space. For Descartes and others, there are two fundamentally different kinds, minds and material substance, each of which supports their own modes. Fourth, as briefly mentioned previously, substances sometimes serve to underwrite the identity of individuals. I mentioned the idea that a substance is the 'owner' of different properties or modes and so it provides a sense in which there is a 'something' that is the possessor of properties and that there is therefore a single unitary thing. Furthermore, we tend to hold that the same thing can continue to exist even though its properties change over time. That is, an individual can remain *numerically identical* even though lots of things about that individual change over time. So, although my thoughts and experiences constantly change, I still believe I persist through these changes, and the sameness of substance ensures that I remain the same person through change.

Hume's response to the issue of the immateriality, or otherwise, of the soul is to attack the very notion of substance. A substance is supposed to be the unchanging owner of modes, but we have no impression of such a thing and hence no idea. This attack we have seen before in the *Treatise*, but Hume adds a further argument here which is going to be relevant to 'Of personal identity'. Substances are independent entities, whereas modes are dependent entities. The immaterial substance that is me is an independent entity and my particular thoughts and perceptions are all dependent modes. But how do we determine what is a substance and what is a mode? Here an appeal is made to conceivability. Very roughly, if we can conceive of x existing independently of anything else, then it meets the condition of substancehood, but if we cannot conceive of x without y, then x is a mode of y. So, since I can conceive of my mind existing independently of anything else, it is a substance, but since I cannot conceive of a thought of a cat without a thinker, thoughts are modes. Hume then considers a definition of substance as 'something which may exist by itself' (T 1.4.5.5), and attempts to show, by using conceivability, that this definition yields an absurd conclusion. Since our perceptions are distinct and separable, we can clearly conceive of these existing independently of anything else, and so perceptions would count as substances on this definition. But perceptions were supposed to depend on a substance that is a self. The definition of substance fails and, further, since we have no idea of substance, 'what possibility then of answering the question, *Whether perceptions inhere in a material or immaterial substance,* when we do not so much as understand the meaning of the question?' (T 1.4.5.6).

Besides this, Hume also considers a different argument that supposedly supports the immateriality of the soul. Hume's discussion here is long and complex, but very briefly we can sum it up as follows. Matter is extended and so capable of dividing into parts. But thoughts are not so capable of division, and so thought and matter are incompatible. Further, Hume argues, the mind contains both extended and non-extended perceptions. The question is how can something that is not extended, such as a desire, be placed in an extended thing, a notion which Hume agrees is absurd, and so identifying perceptions with material things is absurd. Furthermore, since some perceptions are themselves extended, there is a further absurdity in the 'local conjunction' of a non-extended perception with an extended perception. But this is not the same as adopting the view that there is an immaterial substance. Instead, Hume thinks that we should really 'separate the question concerning the substance of the mind from that concerning the cause of its thought' (T 1.4.5.30). Here enters Hume's account of causation. There is no *a priori* reason why matter cannot cause thought or *vice versa*, since our idea of causation simply requires that the relata meet constant conjunction. Thus:

> To pronounce, then, the final decision upon the whole; the question concerning the substance of the soul is absolutely unintelligible: All our perceptions are not susceptible of a local union either with what is extended or unextended; there being some of them of the one kind, and some of the other: And as constant conjunction of objects constitutes the very essence of cause and effect, matter and motion may often be regarded as the causes of thought, insofar as we have any notion of that relation (T 1.4.5.33).

T 1.4.6 OF PERSONAL IDENTITY

As I mentioned at the beginning of the previous section, 'Of personal identity' is sometimes treated as a self-standing section but we should read it in conjunction with 'Of the immateriality of the soul', and this is what we shall now do. Here Hume is concerned with our idea of self and what is implicit in the opening stretch of 'Of personal identity' is a conception of the self as a substance that is the owner of different thoughts and feelings. What *I* am is a substance and I continue to exist through the various changes of thought and feeling because the substance that I am continues to exist, something that exists 'invariably the same, thro' the whole course of our lives', and to which our 'impressions and ideas are suppos'd to have a reference' (T 1.4.6.2).

Hume's first objection to this position turns on the Copy Principle. We have no idea of a self, so construed, since we have no appropriate impression. There is 'no impression constant and invariable' (T 1.4.6.2). The second objection turns on considerations drawn from 'Of the immateriality of the soul'. Hume writes:

> what must become of all our particular perceptions upon this hypothesis? All these are different, and distinguishable, and separable from each other, and may be separately conceiv'd, and may exist separately, and have no need for any thing to support their existence. After what manner, therefore, do they belong to self; and how are they connected with it?
>
> (T 1.4.6.3)

This is a variant on the argument present at T 1.4.5. A standard way of distinguishing substances from modes, when applied to perceptions, delivers the wrong answer.

Instead, Hume holds that the self is nothing but a collection of perceptions. We are 'nothing but a bundle or collection of different perceptions, which succeed each other with an inconceivable rapidity, and are in a perpetual flux and movement' (T 1.4.6.4). Hume then turns to consider why we ascribe identity to this bundle. Hume's primary sense of 'identity' in this context is diachronic identity, or identity through time. You are very different now, and in many respects, from how you were when you were five years old, and yet we do not think that you are not *numerically* the same person as the five-year old you. There are not two things—you and a five-year old you—but a single thing that continues to exist through change. If I were a substance, then my diachronic identity would be accounted for by the fact that that substance continues to exist through time even though my thoughts and feelings constantly change. Many philosophers these days agree with Hume that the self is not a substance, holding that it is something like a collection of thoughts and experiences, and ask what makes it true that I remain numerically the same person today as I was when I was five years old. What makes it true that I am numerically identical to the five-year-old is that there is a causal chain linking his thoughts and experiences to those I have right now. In such cases when philosophers talk of 'personal identity' they have in mind specifying the necessary and sufficient conditions for identity through time.

Hume's topic is somewhat different. He thinks that there is no identity through change. He is what is known as a 'strict identity' theorist and so he thinks that it is false that I am numerically identical to the five-year-old. Instead, he wants to explain what he takes to be an *illusion*, namely the belief that we have that we persist through change. To that end, Hume's account resembles his account of our belief in the continued existence of physical objects. When we 'contemplate' an unchanging object and a succession of different, but closely related, objects, we tend to confound the two since the 'feeling to the mind' is very similar, and we tend to acquiesce to this confusion. We nevertheless are aware of the change in perceptions, and, in order to sustain the illusion, we feign something else, namely the 'notion of a *soul*, and *self*, and *substance*' or something 'unknown and mysterious connecting these parts' (T 1.4.6.6).

After a discussion of what relations generally lead to the ascription of identity to successive objects, Hume discusses the principles of association in connection to the generation of the belief in personal identity. Hume sees no role for contiguity, and so the weight of the explanation rests on causation and resemblance. With respect to causation, Hume writes:

> that the true idea of the human mind, is to consider it as a system of different perceptions or different existences, which are link'd together by the relation of cause and effect, and mutually produce, destroy, influence, and modify each other.
>
> (T 1.4.6.19)

Causation is central to Hume's account of self since it is causation that binds perceptions into bundles.

Resemblance contributes to the belief in the following way. Part of our sense of an enduring self obviously involves our memory which provides a sense of having a past. To remember, for Hume, is to have a perception that resembles, and is caused by, a past perception. So, the resemblance between the two perceptions itself contributes to the bundling. Causation also relates to memory, but in a different sense. We remember because of causal relations between past and present perceptions, but once we have the idea of causation in general, we are able to extend our sense of self beyond what we can remember and fill in the gaps. Thus, I might remember what I did last Thursday and last Tuesday, but Wednesday is a blank. Nevertheless, we can suppose causal relations among perceptions in the gap and connect one bundle with another. Thus, Hume says 'memory does not so much *produce* as *discover* personal identity, by shewing us the relation of cause and effect among our different perceptions' (T 1.4.6.20). This last remark is very probably aimed at Locke, who was commonly held to propose that personal identity is determined by how far back one's memory extends. "Twil be incumbent', writes Hume, 'on those, who affirm that memory produces entirely our personal identity, to give a reason why we can thus extend our identity beyond our memory' (T 1.4.6.20).

In the *Appendix*, Hume expressed profound dissatisfaction with his account of personal identity, and the topic was not revisited in *An Enquiry Concerning Human Understanding*. This is not to say that Hume abandoned the bundle account of the mind or self: in his *Dialogues Concerning Natural Religion*, published posthumously, we are told that the 'soul' is a 'composition of various faculties, passions, sentiments, ideas; united, indeed, into one self or person but still distinct from each other' (DNR 4.2). Nevertheless, Hume felt that there was something wrong with his account. Before we come to what that might be, we should note a qualification Hume makes in 'Of personal identity' that will be important when we discuss the self in his account of the passions. He writes that we 'must distinguish between personal identity, as it regards our thought or imagination, and as it regards our passions or the concern we take in ourselves' (T 1.4.6.5). Hume does not elaborate on this distinction at this stage but we will see in Chapter Five that the sense of personal identity in Book Two is rather different from the one offered in Book One.

What does Hume think is deficient in his account? Certainly, one can think of objections to Hume's account. One standard worry is as follows. Does the account not presuppose a self? That is, we are told that there is a confusion between viewing a steady, unchanging object and a series of distinct, but related, objects, but surely there must be someone prior to all of this that is thus confused? This is not a particularly compelling objection, however. There is no reason to think that we cannot understand 'mistake' in terms of a mechanism composed of perceptions, just as a clock telling the time is simply a matter of the joint co-operation of its parts. A deeper worry concerns the 'ownership' of thoughts and experiences. On Hume' view, for an experience to be mine is for it to be the member of a bundle of experiences or perceptions. Your perception is yours because it is a member of the bundle that constitutes you. But why could a single perception not be both causally related to my bundle and your bundle? Would that mean that there is actually one, larger bundle, and so one person? Furthermore, the nature of the ownership of experience seems wrong. It is not that it is mine simply because it is part of my bundle as, say, a pen happens to be a member of the collection that constitutes a set of pens. Instead, the particular experiences I am having is *necessarily* mine. They could not belong to someone else. Sure, somebody could have qualitatively similar ones, but they would be numerically different ones. Treating experiences as if they were independent objects that happen to be bundled together cannot account for the fact that someone's experience is necessarily his or hers.

Such problems could be multiplied, but they do not seem to be the problem that Hume has in mind. So, what is *his* particular problem? The frank answer to this question is no one knows. There are over twenty different versions in the literature, and no consensus at all over what Hume's problem is.[5] In the *Appendix* he retraces the arguments that induced him to 'deny the strict and proper identity and simplicity of a self or thinking being' (T App. 10), and he seems to find them satisfactory. But 'when [he] proceed[s] to explain the principle of connexion, which binds them together, and makes us attribute to them a real simplicity and identity; [he is] sensible, that [his] account is very defective' (T App. 20). His hopes vanish 'when [he] come[s] to explain the principles, that unite our successive perceptions in our thought and consciousness' (T App. 20). So far so good, but it is what Hume says next that creates a real puzzle. He says that there are two principles which he can neither renounce nor render consistent. These are:

(1) All our distinct perceptions are distinct existences, and
(2) The mind never perceives any real connexion among distinct existences.

What is puzzling is that these two principles *are* consistent. Both can be true together. The first principle explains why we perceive no real connection. The perceptions are distinct existences. The second we saw when discussing necessary connection. To perceive a necessary connection, one would be able to infer *a priori* what effect some object must have and, further, find it inconceivable that it be followed by anything other than its effect. But since perceptions are distinct, we cannot make such *a priori* inferences and we can always conceive of some object being followed by something other than its customary effect. So, if these principles are inconsistent, they are inconsistent not with each other but with some other principle or principles that Hume does not explicitly mention here.

Even then, it is still obscure what Hume thinks the problem might be. To see if we can get any further, let us distinguish between two broad locations in which Hume's problem might lie. First, he might think that the problem lies in how we move from minds being bundled to the false belief in the self's identity and simplicity. There is no problem with minds being bundled, but instead one lies in how we come to believe in a substantial self. Alternatively, we might instead hold that his puzzlement lies in how perceptions become bundles in the first place. The problem lies not in the explanation of the belief in substance but in securing the input into the belief-forming mechanism. The large majority of commentators think Hume's problem is of the first kind, and a small minority hold that it is a problem of the second kind. In support of the first, commentators point to the fact that Hume says that 'thought alone finds personal identity, when reflecting on the train of past perceptions, that compose a mind, the ideas of them are felt to be connected together', and that his hopes vanish when he tries to 'explain the principles, that unite our successive perceptions in our thought or consciousness' (T App. 20). That sounds very strongly like his failure, whatever it might be, lies in the account of the belief in the unity of the mind.

However, it seems to me that this is not where his problem lies. For Hume himself tells us that there 'wou'd be no difficulty in the case' if 'our perceptions inhere in something simple and individual, or did the mind perceive some real connexion among them' (T App. 21). If the solution to Hume's problem lies in a stronger principle of connection among perceptions, either by a substance or necessary connection, then the problem lies with what bundles perceptions together. Somehow, something stronger is required. But although this allows us to identify Hume's problem as with the bundling of perceptions, it is difficult to go further than this, since it is unclear why Hume thinks his account requires stronger connections than he allows for in the rest of the *Treatise*.

T 1.4.7 CONCLUSION OF THIS BOOK

We now turn to T 1.4.7, Hume's dramatic conclusion to Book One. The tone at the beginning is despondent and melancholic:

> I am first affrighted and confounded with that forlorn solitude, in which I am plac'd in my philosophy, and fancy myself some strange uncouth monster, who...has been expell'd all human commerce, and left utterly abandon' and disconsolate....When I turn my eye inwards, I find nothing but doubt and ignorance. All the world conspires to oppose and contradict me, thou' such is my weakness, that I feel all my opinions loosen and fall of themselves, when unsupported by the approbation of others.
> (T 1.4.7.2)

One aspect to Hume's melancholy here is the solitude in which his 'profound' philosophy has placed him. His present opinions seem to conflict with general opinions of humanity and this itself has a psychological effect. But it is not just that that is the source of his melancholy. For he reviews some of his reflections, and one yields a 'manifest contradiction', the other a 'dangerous dilemma'.

The 'manifest contradiction' is the problem identified in 'Of the modern philosophy'. There are two 'equally natural and necessary' operations in the human mind that are, in certain contexts, 'directly contrary'. It is not 'possible for us to reason justly and regularly from causes and effects, and at the same time believe the continu'd existence of matter' (T 1.4.7.4). How can we reconcile these two, and so not 'embrace a manifest contradiction'? The 'dangerous dilemma' recalls 'Of scepticism with regard to reason'. Awareness of our fallibility encourages the Assurance Norm of checking a first-order judgment with a second-order judgment, the joint verdict of which decreases the probability of the original judgment being correct. The norm requires that this process is iterated, leading eventually to 'a total extinction of belief and evidence' (T. 1.4.1.6). When Hume first discussed this argument, he met it with insouciance. Our psychology does not respond to the norm and we keep on believing. Here, however, matters are different. He considers whether we should simply abandon such refined reasoning, and then notes that to do so would 'cut off entirely all science and philosophy' (T 1.4.7.7). But if we do continue with refined reason, it is only by means of a 'singular and seemingly trivial property of the fancy', namely our incapacity for our belief to follow the Assurance Norm. Yet 'we do not, and cannot establish it for a rule, that [refined reasoning] ought not to have any influence'. We have, Hume says, another 'manifest contradiction' (T 1.4.7.7).

He continues:

> But what have I here said, that reflections very refin'd and metaphysical have little or no influence upon us? This opinion I can scarce forbear retracting, and condemning from my present feeling and experience. The *intense* view of these manifold contradictions and imperfections in human reason has so wrought upon me and heated my brain, that I am ready to reject all belief and reasoning, and can look upon no opinion even as more probable or likely than another.
>
> (T 1.4.7.8)

Hume notes that this 'philosophical melancholy and delirium' can be met by leaving this 'bent of mind' behind, and entering life outside the study, something he noted in reaction to the sceptical anxiety recorded in 'Of scepticism with regard to the senses'. He finds himself 'absolutely and necessarily determin'd to live, and talk, and act like other people in the common affairs of life' (T 1.4.7.10). So, it might seem that we should simply turn our back on philosophical reflection and live according to common life. This would be in line with a rather broad understanding of Pyrrhonian scepticism as an ancient philosophy that held that knowledge is impossible, and so, it seemed to them, one ought to live merely by appearance. But this is not what Hume is recommending. He certainly wants to continue with science and philosophy, but now considers just why he should. When he strives against the natural current of ordinary life in pursuit he will have 'good reason for [his] resistance' and will be 'led a wandering into such dreary solitudes, and rough passages, [he has] hitherto met.' If he is to be a fool, 'as all those who reason and believe any thing certainly are, [his] follies shall at least be natural and agreeable' (T 1.4.7.10).

Hume doesn't abandon reflective enterprises and will pursue them to the extent to which he finds them natural and agreeable, and no further. Notice that this implies that Hume had not previously considered his motivations for rational reflection: he simply followed reflection to its (bitter) end.[6] He thinks that there is no reason to push reason beyond the extent to which he finds it natural and agreeable. But that does not quite deal with the epistemic issue, and the related normative one. Reflection destroys all 'belief and evidence', and Hume has simply stated that he will not pursue reflection where it is unnatural and disagreeable. Yet, the Assurance Norm suggests we should, and what is more, doing so has its profound sceptical conclusion. So, Hume might hold that he only has a reason to reflect when he finds reflection natural and agreeable, but we might think that, from a purely epistemic perspective, we have no evidence for any belief. If we are interested solely in following reason, regardless of our own inclination, scepticism is the result.

However, this is not the end of his response. He states that these are 'sentiments' of 'his spleen and indolence', and that it is a result of his returning to 'a serious good-humor'd disposition, [rather] than from the force of reason and conviction' (T 1.4.7.11). We can continue with philosophy, but 'upon sceptical principles, and from an inclination which we feel to employing ourselves in this manner'. Again, this sounds perfectly consistent with thinking that, epistemically, beliefs are unjustified. However, the paragraph concludes with the following principle, which has become known as the 'Title Principle':[7]

> When reason is lively, and mixes with some propensity, it ought to be assented to. When it does not, it can never have any title to operate upon us.
>
> (T 1.4.7.11)

Quite how to interpret this Title Principle is a delicate matter, but a number of things can be said here. First, the notion of 'mixes with some propensity' should be understood as the natural and agreeable inclinations Hume alluded to earlier. In the paragraph after the statement of the Title Principle, he elaborates a little by mentioning that he has a natural curiosity about the subject matter that will go on to comprise the subsequent books of the *Treatise*, as well as an ambition of 'contributing to the instruction of mankind'. Hence his motivation for reflection. Second, we know what is meant by 'lively reason', namely where force and vivacity attach to the ideas produced by reason. Third, the principle is evidently *normative*. It tells us when we *should* assent to reason, and when it makes no such demand.

We will come to what the grounds for the Title Principle might be. But its immediate significance lies in its helping us to resolve Hume's two 'manifest contradictions'. In 'Of scepticism with regard to reason', we know that liveliness of belief does not follow the iteration suggested by the Assurance Norm. But Hume noted that we 'do not, and cannot establish it for a rule, that [refined reasoning] ought not to have any influence'. However, the Title Principle establishes such a rule. Not only does refined influence have no influence on belief, it also *ought* not to. The conclusion that all beliefs have no evidence is something not only that we cannot believe but that we *should* not. So, we should not believe the sceptical conclusion of 'Of scepticism with regard to reason'.

How does the Title Principle resolve the manifest contradiction between causal reasoning and the supposition of continued and distinct objects? Hume is not explicit in the *Treatise*. Presumably if it is to be resolved by appeal to the Title Principle then the causal reasoning that evacuates the content of our idea and so leaving nothing with a continued and distinct existence must violate it. It must be reason that is not lively and so we ought not believe the conclusion. Significantly, in the *Enquiry Concerning Human Understanding*, Hume attributes the sceptical argument that results in our having no conception of continued and distinct arguments to Berkeley, and says such arguments 'admit of no answer, and produce no conviction. Their only effect is to cause that momentary amazement and irresolution and confusion, which is the result of scepticism' (EHU 12.15n32). This might simply seem to record our psychological inability to believe the conclusion, but in light of the Title Principle, it is more than that. The lack of conviction for Hume is the lack of vivacity and so the arguments do not produce vivacity.

What, however, grounds the Title Principle? It is hardly clear from the text, and those commentators who do think the Title Principle brings a resolution to Hume's sceptical worries differ on how to understand it and its grounds. Here is one suggestion. We think of reason as a causal mechanism that produces true belief, and our interest in its products is a matter of our wanting true belief. Our reason, that is, for reasoning and the Assurance Norm, is that we seek true and/or probable belief. Awareness of our fallibility and our desire for true belief warrant the Assurance Norm, but this norm and its iteration imply the conclusion that no degree of probability attaches to any belief. If we come to think that extreme iteration destroys all probability, and we started the process of reflection in the first place *because* we wanted probable belief, then we no longer have any reason to engage in iterative reflection, since the argument suggests that it does not lead to what we wanted in the first place. Some degree of evidence still attaches when reason is lively, but none does when it is not. Hence, we have no reason to follow iteration to its end point and it has no 'title to operate' upon us. Hume, of course, does not say that this is what lies behind the Title Principle. Indeed, he says nothing that explains it. Nevertheless, read in this way, we can see how it addresses the manifest contradictions.

Hume, in seeking to satisfy his curiosity and desire to contribute a little to the world of learning, decides to continue with philosophy, admitting also that he has a weakness for enquiry in general. Contrasting the activity of philosophy with superstition, he thinks errors in the former are merely ridiculous, whereas in the latter, dangerous. Rather than intense reflections, his subsequent philosophical investigations will be conducted in a 'careless manner' guided by the natural passions of humanity.

NOTES

1 See, for example, Meeker (2013).
2 EMPL, 598.
3 See Kail (2007a), Chapter Seven for a full discussion of this issue. The same accusation is levelled at George Berkeley, and again the accusation is misplaced. See Kail (2014), pp.74–77.
4 Locke's speculation had profound ramifications for philosophical and religious thought. On this, see Yolton (1983).
5 A useful survey remains the relevant chapter in Garrett (1997). See also Garrett (2011).
6 By 'not previously considered' I mean the way in which the narrative in the *Treatise* unfolds. No doubt Hume had considered the motivations for pursuing reflection before putting quill to paper. See the concluding section of Book 2 of the *Treatise*, discussed in Chapter Six.
7 After Garrett (1997).

FURTHER READING

Discussions of Book One, Part Four tend to focus on particular topics within its pages rather than seeing the whole part as a single movement. For an exception, albeit a somewhat idiosyncratic one, see Livingston (1998). See also Garrett (1997), Chapter Ten, who also integrates some of the particular topics discussed in this part of the *Treatise*.

On 'Of scepticism with regard to reason', there are sceptical and non-sceptical readings. For one non-sceptical reading, see Schmitt (2014), Part Four. For sceptical readings, see Fogelin (2009) and Meeker (2013), Chapters One to Three. On the external world, one can begin, yet again, with Stroud (1977), Chapter Five, and then Loeb (2002), Chapters Five and Six, Rocknak (2018), and Kail (2007a), Part One. On personal identity, begin with Stroud (1977), Chapter Six, Garrett (1997), Chapter Eight, McIntyre (2009), Butler (2015), and Strawson (2011).

On Hume's conclusion to Book One, Baier (1991), Chapter One is stimulating, but idiosyncratic. See further Ridge (2003), Kail (2005), and Garrett (1997), Chapter Ten, where the idea of the 'Title Principle' first came to prominence. There is a sizeable literature on the Title Principle. See e.g. Ainslie (2015), Chapter Seven, Qu (2020), and Kail (2016).

5

OF PRIDE AND HUMILITY, LOVE AND HATRED

INTRODUCTION

Book Two of the *Treatise*, 'Of the passions', was until recently, a rather neglected part of the *Treatise*, with only the section, 'Of the influencing motives of the will' gaining much by way of attention. Hume himself, however, says his 'opinions' in this book are 'new and extraordinary' (*Abstract* 30). Whilst it true that one can trace many influences on Book Two, such as Francis Hutcheson, Bernard Mandeville, Nicolas Malebranche, and others, Hume transforms these thoughts into something radically new. Perhaps the most extraordinary aspect of Book Two is the account of the self in a social world, a richer but complementary notion to that offered in Book One.

Book Two is divided into three parts, Part One on pride and humility, Part Two on love and hatred, and Part Three on the will and the 'direct passions'. What 'direct passions' are will be the subject of the next chapter, but for the moment what unites the first two parts is that all four of the passions—pride, humility, love, and hatred—are *indirect* passions. Such passions also have selves

DOI: 10.4324/9781315667874-6

as their object, one's own self in the cases of pride and humility, other selves in the cases of love and hatred. Given their interrelations, we shall treat these indirect passions together in this chapter.

PRIDE, HUMILITY, OBJECTS, SUBJECTS, AND CAUSES

Hume begins Book Two by distinguishing two kinds of impressions and ideas, original and secondary, which he says is the same as the division between impressions of sensation and reflection mentioned right at the beginning of Book One. Original sensations are 'such as without any antecedent perception arise in the soul, from the constitution of the body, from the animal spirits, or from the application of objects to the external organs' (T 2.1.1.1) and include impressions gained by the external senses and bodily pleasures and pains. Passions are secondary or reflective impressions. They are secondary because they arise from original impressions (and our ideas of them). Passions are caused by other impressions and our thoughts of them, whereas original impressions' ultimate causes are not other impressions or ideas. As well as the distinction between original and secondary perceptions, Hume also mentions that passions can be either violent or calm, and distinguishes between direct and indirect passions, but we shall discuss these distinctions later.

With these preliminaries out of the way, Hume turns to pride and humility. The passion of pride plays a central role in Hume's moral psychology. What might not be obvious, however, is that its prominence is no doubt an aspect of Hume's campaign against Christian accounts of human nature. Pride is the deadliest of the seven deadly sins and, as Craig Boyd puts it, pride is viewed 'as a distorted, and thus immoral, evaluation of the self which was seen as a direct threat to moral life'.[1] Augustine saw pride 'as the beginning of all sins' and Aquinas as the 'universal root of all sins', something which makes us blind to our dependence on God. Hume, however, sees things differently. He connects pride with 'greatness of mind' and the virtues, writing that

> many religious declaimers decry those virtues and purely pagan and natural, and represent to us the excellency of the *Christian* religion,

> which places humility in the rank of virtues, and corrects the judgments of the world, and even of philosophers, who so generally admire all the efforts of pride and ambition. Whether the virtue of humility has been rightly understood, I shall not pretend to determine. I am content with the concession that the world naturally esteems a well-regulated pride, which secretly animates our conduct, without breaking out into such indecent expressions of vanity, as may offend the vanity of others.
>
> (T 3.3.2.13)

We shall return to how pride and humility relate to virtue and vice when we turn to Book Three of the *Treatise*, but here we focus on what Hume has to say about the two passions in Book Two.

Hume first, in line with his general view of concepts, identifies the relevant impressions from which the ideas are derived. He declares pride and humility are 'simple and uniform impressions' which cannot be further defined, though it is clear that pride is a distinctive kind of pleasure, humility a distinctive kind of pain (T 2.1.5.4). Nevertheless, he goes on to identify the perceptions that are the causes of those passions and what the object of them is. The *object* of each is the idea of the self 'or that succession of related ideas and impressions, of which we have an intimate memory of consciousness' (T 2.1.2.2).[2] The causes of these passions are various but comprise those which are positively valued and negatively valued. The former cause pride, the latter humility. Some of these include traits of ourselves, both mental and physical. Every 'valuable quality of the mind...[is a] cause[ ] of pride; and their opposites of humility' (T 2.1.2.5), and our physical traits can also be the cause of pride and humility (T 2.1.8.2). Beyond our mental and physical traits, things which are causes of pride and humility include one's country, family, house, or even one's clothes.

Hume then draws a distinction between the *subject* and the *quality* of any given cause, illustrating the distinction with an example of a man proud of his beautiful house:

> The quality is the beauty, and the subject is the house, consider'd as his property....Both of these are essential....Beauty, consider'd merely as such, unless plac'd upon something related to us, never

> produces any pride or vanity; and the strongest relation alone, without beauty, or something else in its place, has as little influence on that passion.
>
> (T 2.1.2.6)

The distinction here is between the object of which one is proud and the aspect or property of the object of which one is proud. Here that is the beauty of the house, and, as mentioned above, this is the positive or negative value which is productive of either pride or humility. It is worth noting that Hume's terminology is a little confusing to a modern reader. When we think of the object and the subject of pride, we think of the object as the thing of which someone is proud and the subject as the person who is proud, whereas Hume uses these terms the other way round, where the subject is the thing of which we are proud and the self is the object of that passion. I will continue by using the term 'object' as the thing of which one is proud.

We are proud of something (the 'subject') which has a quality which is itself valuable: it not just the house but the beauty of the house of which I am proud.

What it is to be a value for Hume is a complicated matter, but at its heart, to be positively valuable is a capacity to produce pleasure, and to be negatively valuable is a capacity to produce pain. It is important to note this now because it is crucial for understanding the associative mechanism that Hume appeals to in the production of the indirect passions and why such passions are 'indirect'. As well as the association of ideas, which underlies the psychology of Book One of the *Treatise*, Hume introduces in his discussion of the indirect passions the association of *impressions*. Here the only relevant relation is that of resemblance (T 2.1.4.4). Both the association of impressions and the more familiar association of ideas are involved in the production of pride and humility, which is why Hume refers to the 'double relation' of perceptions (T 2.1.5.5). The pleasure that is a quality of the object of pride also produces the distinctive pleasure of pride by the association of impressions, and the relation between the subject and the object of pride is secured by the association of ideas. So, the beauty of a house may elicit a pleasure in me, but that is insufficient to produce pride without it being suitably related to me. The association of ideas relates that object to myself.

PRIDE AND HUMILITY: REFINEMENTS AND CATEGORIES OF CAUSE

Hume offers as a 'general system' the claim that 'all agreeable objects, related to ourselves, by an association of ideas and of impressions, produce pride, and disagreeable ones, humility' (T 2.1.6.1). Nevertheless, this claim requires some refinements, and Hume offers five refinements which he lists under the title of 'limitations'.

Hume requires that the cause of pride must be related to the self. But what kind of relation? Here Hume's first refinement or 'limitation' is that the relation should be a close one. Hume offers the example of people at a feast surrounded by many delights. This bounty might produce joy in the attendees, and their attendance constitutes *some* relation between them and the feast, but it is not enough for one to be proud of the feast. Only the host of the feast stands in a sufficiently close relation for him to feel pride. Hume does not tell us just what constitutes a 'close' relation, and so this may seem, as Amelia Rorty puts it, 'stunning for its vagueness'.[3] But, as Rorty herself notes, we can understand Hume as taking the notion of closeness as an *intentional* one: that is to say, one where the subject *takes* the relation to be a close one.

Second, the relation should not merely be close, but also 'peculiar to ourselves, or at least common to us with a few persons' (T 2.1.6.4). If I am a particularly skilled cook in comparison to my friends I will feel pride in my skills, but if I am equally skilled and now in the company of people better than me, then I will not. What is relevant here, Hume observes, is that 'we judge of objects more from comparison than from their real and intrinsic merit' (T 2.1.6.4). When my culinary skills are better than my friends' they are a source of pride, but the very same level of competence when compared to a group of professional chefs might single me out as particularly weak in this regard and hence a source of humility. If I am just average when compared with others, my skill is neither a source of pride or humility.

Hume's third 'limitation' or refinement is that whatever is the cause of pride or humility must be publicly discernible. Our sense of ourselves as proud or humble depends crucially on how others view us, and so the causes must be something others can identify. This idea is intimately related to the important notion of sympathy, so we shall revisit the publicity of the cause of the indirect passions briefly when we discuss that topic.

Fourth, whatever is the cause of the indirect passions, it must be relatively durable in nature. Some of the causes of the indirect passions are durable in a relatively straightforward sense. Thus, virtues and vices are relatively enduring dispositions to act. However, the durability requirement might seem puzzling, since, again following Rorty,[4] some of the things of which we are proud or humble appear rather momentary. So, for example, a cricketer scoring a first century in a Test match celebrates what is in effect a fleeting moment, but he is nevertheless duly proud of that moment. However, it is easy to reconcile this with Hume's durability requirement by considering not the duration of the event but instead its duration in the consciousness and memory of the subject and others. The scoring of his first century is something that is remembered for a long time, both by the players and the spectators.

Fifth, and finally, pride and humility are subject to 'general rules'. The kinds of things which generate pride or humility can vary quite considerably depending on the particular context in which the person is placed, and what would normally generate pleasure and pride might not in fact do so. So, someone might be wealthy and powerful (something that normally generates pride) but nevertheless because of the 'peculiarities of health and temper' they lack any 'enjoyment in their possessions' (T 2.1.6.8).

With these refinements in place, Hume then discusses the general categories of the causes of pride and humility. These include our virtues and vices, physical beauty and deformity, 'external advantages', and property and riches. Aside from these 'original causes', there is a secondary cause which is the opinions of others facilitated by sympathy. We shall now briefly note a few features of these original causes before turning to sympathy and how Hume treats the self in Book Two of the *Treatise*.

Virtues and vices are the causes of pride and humility respectively. We shall discuss what these might be in more detail later in this book, but for present purposes they can be thought of as dispositions to produce certain kinds of action, and, furthermore, to produce moral sentiments in the minds of observers and one's self. These sentiments are peculiar pleasures and pains, pleasure which is the approval of virtue, pain which is the disapproval of vice. It is because our virtues and vices produce pleasure and pain and are parts of ourselves, that they operate via the double relation to produce pride and humility. These character tendencies or dispositions Hume calls 'mental qualities', as opposed to 'bodily qualities', but, nevertheless, bodily qualities can also be the cause of pride and humility. These Hume discusses under the title, 'Of beauty and deformity', and, again, what is beautiful produces a peculiar pleasure, and what is deformed, a pain, which enter into the double relation required to produce the indirect passions. Besides these 'qualities of our mind and body, that is *self*' (T 2.1.9.1), Hume includes other qualities related to ourselves as the causes of direct passions. The relation between the subject and the first two sorts of qualities is relatively straightforward since they are conceived to be part of what constitutes our selves, but, Hume notes that there are other causes which are related in a different manner. These he dubs 'external advantages and disadvantages', and some of the examples he gives include houses, gardens, the particular features of a country such as the fertility of its soil and the quality of its wines, and the antiquity of one's family. Such things are the sources of pride or humility when 'external objects acquire a particular relation to ourselves, and are associated or connected with us' (T 2.1.9.6). Hume takes the relations of contiguity and causation to be the operative relations here. I might take pride in living in a beautiful village because of contiguity but notice that this will be subject to Hume's limitations. It may not produce as much pride if compared to an even more beautiful one, or where everyone lives in a beautiful village. Again, the key feature is that such things produce the pleasure or pain associated with value, and its standing and its being conceived to stand in a close relation to the subject. Finally, Hume adds property and riches as one of the original causes of pride, and, in particular, the sense of power which riches bestow.

SELF AND MIND

Thus far we have primarily focused on describing the structure of Hume's account of pride and humility. Certain inputs, namely valuable qualities of certain things, produce a separate pleasure or pain which, thanks to the double associative relation, produce, as the object of the relevant passion, the idea of the self. In Book One of the *Treatise*, Hume tells us that the 'true idea' of the human mind is 'as a system of different perceptions or different existences, which are link'd together by the relation of cause and effect, and mutually produce, destroy, influence, and modify each other' (T 1.4.6.19). At first blush, things seem a little different in Book Two when Hume says that the object of the indirect passions is 'that succession of related ideas and impressions, of which we have an intimate memory of consciousness' (T 2.1.2.2). However, Hume also told us in Book One that we 'must distinguish between personal identity, as it regards our thought or imagination, and as it regards our passions or the concern we take in ourselves' (T 1.4.6.5). What is this distinction? Hume does not explicitly tell us what it is, but it is possible to discern what the distinction consists in and how it involves a rather different conception of self. The key point, as Donald Ainslie[5] nicely observes, is that Hume gives two different accounts of the self. Ainslie puts it thus

> On the one hand, he investigates (in Book One) the self as the locus of experience—the self as *mind*. On the other hand, (in Book Two) he has a notion of the self as *an embodied person with a distinctive place in the social sphere*.[6]

The following initial considerations support this claim. First, although Hume does offer in Book One what he calls 'the true idea' of the human mind, it is not one with which we ordinarily operate. Instead, in 'common life…the ideas of self and person are never very fix'd nor determinate' (T 1.4.2.6). Secondly, and related to this point, unlike in Book One, Hume is prepared to include the body as part of the idea of self, at least in ordinary life. He notes that this is philosophically controversial but writes '[w]hether we consider the body as part of ourselves, or assent to those philosophers, who regard it as something external' (T 2.1.8.1), its relation to us is so close that it produces the indirect passions, and he contrasts the 'qualities of our mind and body, that is *self*', with 'external advantages' (T 2.1.9.1). Third, whilst Hume uses the 'mind' as a synonym for self or person in Book One, he never does so in Book Two. Fourth, as Ainslie notes, Hume works with a distinction between features of selves that 'define them as who they are' and other features that are accidental.[7] Thus Hume distinguishes between features that are 'connected with our being and existence' and those that are 'accidental' and 'are in a manner separated from us' (T 2.1.8.8). These features are those which characterise a person in such a way that 'we can never think of him without reflecting on…[the] qualities' (T 2.2.3.4), and which are 'infixed' (T 2.3.2.6).

The key feature by which pride and humility facilitate this sense of self, and the distinction between what is part of us rather than merely accidental, lies in the fact that it is only the durable and evaluatively important qualities of the person which are productive of those passions. It is these qualities, rather than mere fleeting experiences, that are the objects of self-consciousness. Durable aspects of one's self produce pleasure or pain, and, thanks to the double relation, those aspects of the self become the object of self-consciousness. We noted above that the durable features include our character dispositions, as well as those moments the significance of which make them live on in memory. Second are those features that are not merely durable but those that are evaluatively important to us, either positively or negatively so. Consider, for example, a feature of my body, namely my height. It is not something I normally think of, nor think of as particularly important to who I am. However, if it becomes evaluatively important in some way, it might become a source of pride or humility and thus enter into my self-consciousness and my sense of who I am. These two features differ from a mere sequence of perceptions—hearing, for example, a sequence of notes—of which I am conscious but which I do not regard as 'connected with [my] being and existence'. As Ainslie says, indirect passions 'pick out from among the many perceptions in our mind some which…play a more significant role than others'.[8]

This yields a sense of self involving a conception of the self 'more or less advantageous' (T2.1.2.3), of its 'qualities and circumstances' (T 2.1.5.6) and as an 'idea of our merit and character' (T 2.1.8.8). This of course is not the same thing as thinking of the self as a substance, but it suggests that our sense of self is that of an embodied person with enduring traits rather than the collection of perceptions that make up a mind. Indeed, something like this is hinted at in Book One when Hume writes that 'the same person may vary his character and disposition, as well as his impressions and ideas, without losing his identity. Whatever changes he endures, his several parts are still connected by the relation of causation' (T 1.4.6.19).

SYMPATHY

We now turn to sympathy and its relation to our sense of self. Thus far we have discussed what Hume calls the 'original' causes of the indirect passions. However, there is a 'secondary' cause which depends on the opinions of others. Thus, he writes that our 'reputation, our character, our name are considerations of vast weight and importance; and even the other causes of pride; virtue, beauty and riches; have little influence, when not seconded by the opinions and sentiments of others' (T 2.1.11.1). Our sense of self depends crucially on the response of others and so our sense of self depends on being related to others. Even our beliefs and opinions depend on how others view us, something Hume had already hinted at in Book One. In the 'forlorn solitude' described in T 1.3.4.7, 'Conclusion of this book', he says that he feels that 'all my opinions loosen and fall of themselves, when unsupported by the approbation of others' (T 1.4.7.2).

Underlying this phenomenon is the mechanism of *sympathy*. In outline, sympathy involves the following. Another person's feeling or opinion is 'first known only by its effects, and by those external signs in the countenance and conversation, which convey an idea of it' (T 2.1.11.3). That is, sentiments or opinions cause observable behaviour, which, in turn causes in us the idea of that feeling. Second, the idea becomes an impression, by acquiring force and vivacity, which is borrowed from the impression of ourselves, an impression which 'is always intimately present with us, and that our consciousness gives us so lively a conception' (T 2.1.11.4). So rather than merely *thinking* that the other person is in distress, the operation of sympathy converts the mere idea into a *feeling* of being distressed, so I too become distraught.

This is facilitated by the associative relations of resemblance, contiguity, and causation. ''Tis obvious', Hume writes, that there is:

> a great resemblance among all human creatures, and that we never remark any passion or principle in others, of which, in some degree of other, we may not find a parallel in ourselves. The case is the same with the fabric of the mind....There is a very remarkable resemblance, which preserves itself admidst all their variety; and this resemblance must very much contribute to make us enter into the sentiments of others, and embrace them....The stronger the relation is betwixt ourselves and any object, the more easily does the imagination make the transition, and convey to the related idea the vivacity of conception, with which we always form the idea of our own person.
>
> (T 2.1.11.5)

But it is not just resemblance that produces this effect. Contiguity has a considerable effect. The 'sentiments of others have little influence, when far remov'd from us, and requires the relation of contiguity, to make them communicate themselves entirely' (T 2.1.11.6). To see this, imagine being sat in the waiting room at an emergency dentist, full of people in pain. One can, of course, imagine what that is like, but were one actually to be sat in the room and near all the patients, our sympathy is such that we would begin to feel their pain and discomfort because of our proximity to it. This is a familiar phenomenon. We tend to wince when we are near someone who, say, drops something heavy onto their toes. But there is a further sense of 'closeness' which differs from mere physical distance, one which is a matter of the particular relationship in which we stand to others. Thus, members of my family, my loved ones, those in my particular circle, engage my sympathy far more than strangers do. This relation Hume subsumes under the relation of cause and effect.

Two things are worth noting before we proceed. First, sympathy is a mechanism and its results are spontaneous and involuntary. We 'catch' the feelings of others, whether we want to or not. Second, what we have described so far are the elements of this particular psychological mechanism, but, as we shall see, its products can be subject to correction and further refinement.

Let us now turn to sympathy's influence on pride and humility. We noted above that one of the 'limitations' to Hume's system was the requirement that whatever causes pride or humility must be publicly discernible. The praise or blame of others that sustains pride or humility requires of course that the sympathizer should be able to *identify* the features that are the original causes of those passions in order to be the recipient of that praise or blame. The observer's recognition of those causes of pride or humility influences our opinions of ourselves which in turn influences our self-conception. As Hume writes:

> nothing is more natural than for us to embrace the opinions of others...both from *sympathy*, which renders all their sentiments intimately present to us; and from *reasoning*, which makes us regard their judgment, as a kind of argument for what they affirm. These two principles of authority and sympathy influence almost all our opinions but must have a peculiar influence, when we judge of our own worth and character.
>
> (T 2.1.11.9)

The approval or disapproval of the observer is felt by sympathy and so converted into our own approval or disapproval of ourselves, thus reinforcing the indirect passion. Given our own partiality, we are 'particularly pleas'd with anything, that confirms the good opinion we have of ourselves, and are easily shock'd with whatever opposes it' (T 2.1.11.9).

The inclusion of the 'authority' of the observer is important here. The observer does not merely approve of me but does so because of her recognition of the causes of pride or humility. As Hume puts it earlier, 'no person is ever prais'd by another for any quality, which wou'd not, if real, produce of itself, a pride in the person possessed of it' (T 2.1.11.9). What is more, the effect of sympathy and its relation to authority is impacted by the extent to which such opinions come from 'whom we ourselves esteem and approve of', and we are 'mortify'd with the contempt of persons, upon whose judgments we set some value' (T 2.1.11.11).

We shall turn to some more complex inflexions of sympathy later in this chapter and its important role in moral judgment later in this book. Hume concludes his discussion of the indirect passions with a discussion of the pride and humility of animals. As we have noted before, a key aspect of Hume's naturalism is his modelling of human nature on principles thought to be operative in non-human animals. He claims that the behaviour of animals, such as the 'gait of a swan, turkey, or peacock' (T 2.1.12.4) expresses pride, though he notes that the causes of animal pride are more limited. They have 'little or no sense of virtue' and cannot possess property (T 2.1.12.5). Two further things about Hume's naturalism in this context are worth noting. First, something very similar to sympathy was deployed by Malebranche, whom we know Hume studied carefully. According to Malebranche 'communication of the passions' owed itself to corporeal and mechanical forces which express our animal embodiment.[9] Second, Hume departs from a moralised view of pride to a purely descriptive approach. Hume's predecessors started examining pride with the assumption that it is morally problematic which is a symptom of the Christian conception of human nature we noted near the beginning of this chapter. So, for example, Bernard Mandeville, again someone who exerted a good deal of influence on Hume's moral psychology, conceived of pride as embodying a key evaluative fault: pride is necessarily an *over*-estimation of our own worth, and is thus of itself dubious.[10] Hume does indeed think that we can sometimes overestimate our own worth, but this is not essential to pride: instead pride and humility are treated as morally neutral, psychological phenomena.

LOVE, HATRED, AND THE COMPOUND PASSIONS

The other pair of indirect passions is love and hatred. As Páll Árdal observed long ago, Hume uses the terms 'love' and 'hatred' in a somewhat technical sense, where 'love' means 'thinking highly of', and 'hatred' its opposite.[11] That is, it is a wider evaluative response to the qualities of others.

As always, Hume begins by noting that each is marked by distinctive hedonic impressions. The causes of these passions are, Hume tells us, 'very much diversify'd, and have not many things in common' (T 2.2.1.4) but include both the mental and physical qualities of the person as well as their external advantages and disadvantages. Again, Hume distinguishes in the causes between the subject and the quality in a manner analogous to that which we noted in the causes of pride and humility (T 2.2.1.5), and again the mechanism involved in producing these passions is the double relation mechanism. As with pride and humility, the cause must bear some close relation to the object of love or hatred, and that it must produce pleasure or pain.

To illustrate this, Hume discusses this mechanism in T 2.2.2, 'Experiments to confirm this system', by varying conditions to determine whether or not we would think that these indirect passions would be produced. We will leave aside some further complications Hume discusses regarding this pair of indirect passions,[12] and turn instead to consider how the indirect passions relate to other passions. This adds some further complexity to his account, with Hume noting that his discussion here 'is no-wise contrary to my system; but only departs a little from that simplicity, which has been hitherto its principle force and beauty' (T 2.2.6.2).

To begin with, Hume notes that there is 'by the original constitution of the mind' (T 2.2.6.6) a connection between love and hatred and benevolence and anger respectively. In this respect they differ from pride and humility, which are 'pure emotions in the soul, unattended with any desire, and not immediately exciting us to action' (T 2.2.6.3). Love and hatred, by contrast:

> are not compleated within themselves, nor rest in that emotion, which they produce, but carry the mind to some thing farther. Love is always follow'd by a desire of the happiness of the person belov'd...[and] hatred produces a desire of the misery and an aversion to the happiness of the person hated.
>
> (T 2.2.6.3)

This relation, in turn, forms the basis of 'compound passions', which proceed from 'a mixture of love and hatred with other affections' (T 2.2.11.1). Compound passions include pity, malice, envy, respect, contempt, and the amorous passion. At the most basic level, as we have noted, benevolence is connected to love, and anger with hatred by 'original constitution', but matters are more complicated in subsequent cases.

First, Hume discusses compassion or pity, and its contrary, malice, which he defines as 'a concern for, and...a joy in the misery of others, without any friendship or enmity to occasion this concern or joy' (T 2.2.7.1). This pair 'arise from secondary principles', arising from benevolence or hatred, but which 'are vary'd by some particular turn of thought and imagination'. Here sympathy re-enters the picture. In the case of pity or compassion, 'their persons...their interests, their passions...must strike upon us in a lively manner, and produce a similar emotion' (T 2.2.7.2). Malice, on the other hand, involves not just sympathy but also comparison. Now, Hume's sense of malice is closer to the German *Schadenfreude* or joy in the suffering of others rather than the modern sense of malice as a desire to cause suffering or injury. It is produced in the following manner. We sympathise with the suffering of others but we are also apt to 'judge more of objects by comparison than from their intrinsic worth or value' (T 2.2.8.2). This Hume takes to be a quite general principle, and it is something we met before when discussing Hume's limitations on his system of pride and humility. I might feel proud of my house when it is better than any other in my village but when compared with the rather grand ones in the next, my pride might dissipate entirely. Our sympathetic reaction varies when we consider our particular situation in comparison with that of the other person. We compare ourselves to the other 'in proportion to the degrees of riches, and power, and merit, and reputation, which we think of ourselves possest of' (T 2.2.8.8). In the case where the other person exceeds us in this respect, we do not feel pity in recognising their suffering but take joy in it. Similarly, envy occurs when the enjoyment of some other person makes us sensitive of our value relative to that person, though this phenomenon is not merely a product of comparison but also of contiguity or 'proximity' (T 2.2.8.13). The soldier does not envy his general, but he can envy his sergeant or corporal.

Hume notes that there is something odd about comparison in these cases, that is, when one receives 'a sensation directly opposite' to that of the other person. Such cases are those where we feel joy in someone else's sorrow, or, in the case of envy, 'grief from their joy' (T 2.2.9.1). Why should a certain kind of sensation yield its contrary, given that Hume has been using resemblance as a key feature of the mechanism productive of the passions? To explain this, Hume appeals to what he calls the 'principle of parallel direction' of passions (T 2.2.9.9). We have noted that impressions are related by resemblance, but they are also related 'when their impulses or directions are similar and correspondent' (T 2.2.9.3). So, for example, benevolence and pity are similar because they both have a tendency towards the happiness of another, and thus travel in a parallel direction, even though benevolence involves pleasure and pity pain. This is key to Hume's explanation of how 'benevolence and anger, and consequently love and hatred, arise when our happiness or misery have any dependence on the happiness or misery' of any person with whom we have no relation (T 2.2.9.5). Hume asks us to consider two persons who are competing in the same trade in the same town where it is not possible for both to be successful, and to compare this case with two merchants cooperating in such a way that the success of one is in the interest of the other. Hatred comes in the first case, because of conflicting interests, and love in the other case because of common interest. The pleasure that the rival takes in his success causes a pain in us, and his pain in his failure a pleasure in us. Since there is no close relation, the passions must arise in virtue of the parallel direction.

This principle of parallel direction is introduced during a discussion of how benevolence and anger are 'mixed' with compassion and malice. The discussion also introduces a complication in the notion of sympathy. So far, we have considered sympathy to be simply the sharing of feelings or passions. However, sympathetic engagement is not 'always limited to the present moment' but can involve 'the pleasures and pains of others, which are not in being, and which we only anticipate by the force of the imagination' (T 2.2.9.13). So, we can sympathise not merely with actual sensations and passions but possible future ones. Hume illustrates this with an example of a person in a field, unaware of the danger of being trampled by horses: we anticipate the pain that person would feel were she to be so trampled. This Hume calls 'extensive' as opposed to 'limited' sympathy. However, our capacity to engage in such extensive sympathy depends on our sense of the present condition of the person with whom we are sympathising, and that depends on the vivacity of that conception. When we have a lively conception of the other person, that is transferred to a lively conception of their likely future pleasures and pains. This 'strong sympathy' is contrasted with 'weak' sympathy, where we sympathise with another person but our conception of their feelings and passions is less vivid, and so does not produce a conception of their future pleasures and pains.

This distinction is used by Hume to explain another complication in his general system, that is when sympathy produces what seems to be contrary responses. The 'same object...causes contrary passions, according to its [i.e. sympathy's] different degrees' (T 2.2.9.16). He illustrates this by considering two different reactions to poverty. Weak sympathy, which involves a painful sensation, may produce contempt because of the painfulness of the sensation, but the strong, extended sympathy, engages pity and compassion. The latter engages the parallel direction of the passions, and so engages love and benevolence rather than the more basic disagreeable sensation alone, giving us a richer view of the person.

Comparison is integral to the production of respect and contempt. When one considers the good qualities of someone without a comparison to oneself, the product is love, but in some instances, when we consider the person superior to us, the product might be humility. However, pride and humility can become mixed when the response to another is that of respect and contempt, produced by a third point of view which is both a grasp of the non-comparative value of the other person *and* a comparison of that person with oneself. It is, as it were, that I am keeping the other and myself in mind in equal measure and so recognising the value of the other and their relative superiority. With Hume's remaining passion, that of amorous love, the principle of parallel direction is again invoked. Here the sense of beauty is connected with bodily appetite, and because of the resemblance of pleasure, there arises 'such a connexion betwixt the sense of beauty, the bodily appetite, and benevolence, that they become in a manner inseparable' (T 2.2.11.4).

The discussion of love and hatred, like that of pride and humility, is capped by a discussion of love and hatred in non-human animals where commonalities and differences are noted, together with a confirmation that everything 'is conducted by springs and principles, which are not peculiar to man, or any one species of animals' (T 2.2.12.1). So, we have a complete system. However, it is not difficult to find merit in James Baillie's suspicion that the complexity in Hume's system of the compound passions involves him in some rather *ad hoc* claims, such as the principle of parallel direction and the two kinds of sympathy.[13] The system of association of ideas and impressions is becoming increasingly complicated in order to deal with various phenomena, such as the fact that we can have different sympathetic reactions to the same objects. Nevertheless, Hume's sensitivity to the complexities is laudable and the distinction between limited and extensive sympathy is a good one, namely one between a mere mechanical response (wincing at someone else's pain), and a more extensive engagement with a person and their situation. This latter conception of sympathy Hume's friend Adam Smith would later greatly develop in *The Theory of Moral Sentiments* (1759).

NOTES

1 Boyd (2014), p.245.
2 I shall note, but not discuss, a potential problem here. When Hume says that the passions have the self as their object, he seems to be saying that the passions are *about* or involve *representing* the self. However, later in Book Two, Hume claims that passions are 'original existences' and contain 'not any representative quality' (T 2.2.3.5), which suggests that passions cannot be about anything else, or, as philosophers say, that are not intentional. We will discuss this in the next chapter.
3 Rorty (1990), p.260.
4 Rorty (1990), p.261,
5 Here I follow Donald Ainslie's excellent discussions in Ainslie (1999) and (2005).

6 Ainslie (2005), p.144. See also Penelhum (2000), p.49 who also makes this distinction.
7 Ainslie (1999), p.478.
8 Ainslie (1999), p.482.
9 On this, and other aspects of the relation between Hume and Malebranche on sympathy, see Wright (1983), p.232, James (2005), and Schmitter (2012).
10 I owe this observation to Gabriel Watts (2019).
11 See Árdal (1989), Chapter Two.
12 See further Árdal (1989), Chapter Two.
13 See Baillie (2000), p.72.

FURTHER READING

The classic study of Book Two is Árdal (1989). A recent and useful introduction is Taylor (2016), and for a full-length study see Taylor (2015). See also Alanen (2006) and Inoue (2003). On the self in Book Two, see McIntyre (1989), Ainslie (1999) and (2005), and Penelhum (2000) and (2015). On sympathy, see Vitz (2016), Mercer (1972), and Waldow (2009).

6

OF THE WILL AND DIRECT PASSIONS

INTRODUCTION

Part Three of Book Two of the *Treatise* discusses a number of topics that fall under the general category of the philosophy of action, including free will, how action is motivated, and the category of 'direct passion'. We also noted at the beginning of the previous chapter a distinction between calm and violent passions, and we shall discuss this distinction in this one. The first two sections discuss free will or 'liberty' and its relation to 'necessity', and Hume claims that his approach to the issue 'puts the whole controversy in a new light' (*Abstract* 34). In section three we discuss 'Of the influencing motives of the will', the part of Book Two that has received the most attention by philosophers. Hume's discussion here appears to embody an account of motivation that remains highly influential in contemporary philosophy, and which is referred to as the 'Humean theory of motivation'. We then follow Hume's turn to the causes of the violent passions and discuss different factors which influence passions. After discussing the direct passions themselves we consider Hume's discussion of curiosity, 'or that love of truth, which was the first source of all our enquiries' (T 2.3.10.1).

T 2.3.1 OF LIBERTY AND NECESSITY

Hume opens Part Three by offering a definition of the 'will', and again he appeals to a distinctive simple impression, holding that the term 'will' is not definable in simpler terms. Nevertheless, he gives us a way of identifying what the will is by saying that it is 'the internal impression we feel and are conscious of, when we knowingly give rise to any new motion of our body, or new perception of the mind' (T 2.3.1.2). 'Knowingly' here picks up on the thought that I am acting on my will when I intentionally or deliberately bring about an action or thought.[1]

Hume does not tell us much more here but instead turns to 'that long disputed question concerning liberty and necessity; which occurs so naturally in treating of the will' (T 2.3.1.2). The dispute concerns free will and it will be useful to lay out the dispute in modern dress before turning to Hume's own position. The issue is whether acting freely is compatible or incompatible with a thesis about causation called 'determinism'. Very roughly, determinism holds that every event is the result of prior events or causes which express laws of nature. Because of this, whatever occurs is 'fixed' by these prior factors. If this thesis holds for everything—that determinism is true universally—then, at first blush, acting freely seems impossible. It seems impossible because of the following. It is highly plausible to think that in order to act freely it must be true that when I act freely it was within my power to have acted otherwise than the way I did. But if determinism is true then what I do is fixed by the past, and so I could *not* have done otherwise. We might therefore conclude that determinism is *incompatible* with freedom.

Notice the issue is whether determinism is compatible with freedom which is independent of the question of whether determinism as a thesis about causation is true. One might think that there are reasons to believe determinism, or reasons to think it is false, but still hold that there is a further question about whether freedom is possible *if* determinism is true. Some philosophers, *compatibilists*, attempt to argue that determinism is not a threat to freedom and so determinism is compatible with freedom. They employ different strategies to support this thesis. First, they might say that to act freely is simply a matter of one's actions being brought about by facts that are, in some relevant sense, 'internal' to you. I desire to have a cup of tea, and that desire, which is mine, causes me to have the tea and so I act freely. However, someone holding a gun to my head and forcing me to have coffee would be me acting without freedom because what causes me to do so is external to me. But what of the intuition that, in order to be free, one should have been able to do otherwise? One response is to say that one still could have done otherwise, in the sense that were one to have had a different desire, one for coffee say, then one would have done otherwise than choose tea. Hence you could have acted otherwise than the way you did. A second response is to argue that it is false that in order to act freely one must have been able to do otherwise. Suppose I am sat in a room the door of which is, unbeknownst to me, locked. So I am unable to leave the room. However, I wanted to stay in the room, anyway. Surely I am acting freely even if I could not have done otherwise?

We will briefly return to these ideas, but Hume's approach to the question is somewhat different to what I just described. He begins by noting that it is 'universally acknowledg'd, that the operations of external bodies are necessary, and that in the communication of their motion...there are not the least traces of indifference of liberty' (T 2.3.1.3). The question arises whether this is also true of 'the actions of the mind', our thoughts and decisions, and with them our intentional actions. Hume then reminds us of some key features of his discussion of necessary connection. When there is a constant conjunction or 'constant union' which also produces in the mind of the observer the impression of necessary connection, then we deem the 'action' necessary. He then goes on to argue that there is such a uniformity in 'the common course of human affairs' (T 2.3.1.5) that we must deem human actions necessary. The actions of the mind are therefore equally necessary as those of matter. He discusses various objections to this claim, such as the fact that human behaviour is sometimes unpredictable, arguing that this indicates only our ignorance of the complex interactions of causes which is equally the case in the natural world.

The key point for our concerns is his claim that there is only one kind of causation operative both in human action and in the rest of the natural world. Much earlier in the *Treatise*—in his discussion of necessary connection—Hume stated that 'the common distinction betwixt moral and physical necessity is without any foundation in nature' (T 1.3.14.33). Why this is important here is as follows.[2] I noted that determinism holds that future events are 'fixed' by past causes, and so if my actions are determined then I cannot act in any other way. An incompatabilist who wants to hold that there is free will would reject the claim that all causation is deterministic. The rest of nature might be related by causes that necessitate their effects but when it comes to the causation of action by rational minds the nature of the causation involved is rather different. Why I act the way that I do is because I come to appreciate that a given course of action is the *right* or *good* thing to do and my decision to act is not brought about by prior events but by my *evaluation* of the action. My agency exercises free choice, and the values involved *incline*, but do not *necessitate*, my will. Here I have what is called 'liberty of indifference', namely that I can always choose other than I do. I choose to drink tea because it is better for me than coffee but it is still within my power to choose the coffee. But what of the 'moral necessity' Hume mentions? Well, some choices are such that, although one could have acted otherwise physically speaking, the evaluative situation is such that there is only genuinely one course of action. Suppose you are told to hand over your car keys, or you will be shot. Physically speaking, it is possible for you to refuse to hand over your keys, but evaluatively speaking the overwhelmingness of being shot means that you can only really do one thing. It is morally necessary to hand over the keys.

This route to avoid the perceived threat of determinism Hume thinks is blocked by his account of causation. There are no grounds for thinking that there is any difference between the causal necessity operative in the physical world and that which is operative between our motives and actions. But notice that the sense of necessity in play here is Hume's newly-minted one. Hume is not saying that there is some metaphysically rich notion of absolute necessity at work in physical objects that is equally operative in our actions. Instead, there is just the conjunction and inference:

> Let no one...put an invidious construction on my words, by simply saying, that I assert the necessity of human actions, and place them on the same footing with the operations of senseless matter. I do not ascribe to the will that unintelligible necessity, which is suppos'd to lie in matter. But I ascribe to matter, that intelligible quality, call it necessity or not, which the most rigorous orthodoxy does or must allow to belong to the will.
>
> (T 2.3.2.4)

Hume concedes that someone might dispute his sense of necessity and refuse to call it necessity or 'maintain there is something else in the operations of matter', but nevertheless, he says, they would have to concede that the regularities and the inferences based on them apply equally to both. Necessity in this sense

> has universally, tho' tacitly, in the schools, in the pulpit, and in common life, been allow'd to belong to the will of man, and no one has ever pretended to deny, that we can draw inferences concerning human actions, and that those inferences are founded on experienc'd union of like actions with like motives and circumstances.
>
> (T 2.3.2.4)

Notice that Hume is reframing the issue away from the metaphysics of causation. The question is not whether there is a different kind of causation operative in action which allows for liberty of indifference, but what experience suggests about actions and the rest of the natural world. The metaphysics of causation is something unfathomable and from the point of view of experience and common life the operations of matter and the relations of motives and actions are on a par. Hume is even more explicit about this in his discussion of the same topic in the first *Enquiry*:

> if men attempt the discussion of questions which lie beyond the bounds of human capacity...they may long beat the air in their fruitless contests, and never arrive at any determinate conclusion. But if the

> question regard any subject of common life and experience, nothing, one would think, could preserve the dispute so long undecided but some ambiguous expression, which keep the antagonists still at a distance, and hinder them from grappling with each other. This has been the case in the long disputed question concerning liberty and necessity.
>
> (EHU 8.1)

There is something right in saying that, nevertheless, Hume presents a compatibilist position in the *Treatise* inasmuch as he allows that there is 'liberty of spontaneity' which he says is 'that which is oppos'd to violence' and is 'the most common sense of the word [free]' (T 2.3.2.1). This idea is the compatibilist one mentioned above, namely that what it is to act freely is simply to act without constraint or external impediment. Nevertheless, we do tend to 'confound' the two senses of liberty (T 2.3.2.1) encouraged by what Hume claims to be 'a false sensation or experience' of indifference (T 2.3.2.2).

What is interesting here is that Hume approaches this matter not from the first-person perspective—the perspective of the agent—but from the third-person perspective, or the perspective of the spectator. We attribute causal necessity when we observe regularities, and it is the spectator of our actions who is often better placed to observe them. We 'may imagine we feel a liberty within ourselves; but a spectator can commonly infer our actions from our motives and character' (T 2.3.2.2). In our own case, we do not feel the determination of the mind that the spectator does. In 'reflecting on human actions we seldom feel...a looseness or indifference, [often] in performing the actions themselves we are sensible of something like it' (T 2.3.2.2). Furthermore:

> we feel our actions are subject to our will on most occasions, and imagine that the will itself is subject to nothing; because when by a denial of it we are provok'd to try, we feel that it moves more easily, and produces an image of itself even on that side, on which it did not settle.
>
> (T 2.3.2.2)

We will something, and we also can imagine willing the opposite, leading us to imagine that we could have chosen and done otherwise. The 'looseness' we feel in our thoughts because of the absence of a feeling of determination together with the imagination producing images of alternative courses of action amounts to the 'false sensation' of liberty of indifference and the thought that we could have done otherwise than we did.

Hume argues further that his claim about the necessity of human action is supported when we consider the relation between action and responsibility. One of the reasons we are interested in distinguishing between free and unfree actions turns on our interest in holding people responsible for actions they did freely and excusing them if they were performed because they were forced or coerced. So, for example, if I take money from the till freely, I am held responsible and consequently blamed for what I do. If, however, I am forced to do so at gunpoint, I am deemed not to be acting freely and hence not held responsible. If one denies that there is necessity, in Hume's sense of the term, in the connection between a person and an action, this would be to deny that there is any causal connection between the person and the action, and so the person could not be held responsible for it. So, a person 'is as pure and untainted, after having committed the most horrid crimes, as at the first moment of his birth, nor is his character any way concern'd in actions' (T.2.3.2.6). Thus:

> [t]he constant and universal object of hatred or anger is a person or creature endow'd with thought and consciousness; and when any criminal or injurious actions excite that passion, 'tis only by their relation to the person or connexion with him. But according to the doctrine of liberty or chance, this connexion is reduced to nothing, nor are men more accountable for those actions, which are design'd and premeditated, than for such as are the most casual and accidental. Actions are by their nature temporary and perishing; and where they proceed not from some cause in the character or disposition of the person who perform'd them, they infix not themselves upon them, and can neither redound to his honour, if good, nor infamy, if evil. The action itself may be blameable....But the person is not responsible for it; and as it proceeded from nothing in him, that is durable or constant, and leaves nothing of that nature behind it, 'tis

> impossible that he can, upon its account, become the object of punishment or vengeance.
>
> (T.2.3.2.6)

I quote at length here because there is something more than a little puzzling in this claim. Hume is telling us that we only hold someone responsible for an action when it is the causal result of something durable in the person. If someone acts 'out of character' then they are not responsible. Here Hume is not saying that actions performed out of character are not causal in nature. He says people are 'less blam'd for such evil actions as they perform ignorantly and causally...Why? Because the causes of these actions are only momentary, and terminate in them alone' (T 2.3.2.7). Again, a 'hasty temper...operates only by intervals and infects not the whole character' (T 2.3.2.7). These actions are caused by something—motives—but are not caused by the durable features of the person. The motive and the durable features are distinct. But this seems rather counterintuitive, as Paul Russell puts it, a 'puzzling and controversial claim'.[3] Surely, we hold people responsible, even if they act out of character? Russell himself has a very useful suggestion about why Hume might think what he does about responsibility. Russell reminds us that moral sentiments, which are themselves particular forms of praise and blame, are intimately related to the indirect passions. We will talk about this further in subsequent chapters, but what is important is that approval or disapproval is connected with the 'durable principles of the mind....Actions themselves, not proceeding from any constant principle, have no influence on love or hatred, pride or humility; and consequently are never consider'd in morality' (T 3.3.1.4). What Hume is saying, says Russell, is made intelligible by the fact that he is trying to describe the mechanisms whereby praise and blame are elicited, and given the connection between the durable aspects of a person, the indirect passions, and praise and blame, the account of responsibility here is a description of the conditions under which a person is *felt* to be responsible—when, that is, the moral sentiments are felt. Whether this is successful is a moot point, but nevertheless it does go some way to explaining what is otherwise an odd view.

T 2.3.3 OF THE INFLUENCING MOTIVES OF THE WILL

T 2.3.3, 'Of the influencing motives of the will' is the most widely read part of Book Two of the *Treatise* outside of Hume scholarship proper. This is because, as I mentioned above, it is supposed to embody a theory now referred to as the 'Humean Theory of Motivation', a theory which is central to discussions in contemporary moral philosophy. Whether this theory is really what Hume is offering in this section is not actually clear. The situation here is somewhat parallel to what we said about induction in Chapter Three. Hume's name is strongly associated with the problem of induction, so much so that it is widely held that he endorses the sceptical conclusion that inferences from past experience have no positive epistemic standing. It is understandable how one might arrive at this conclusion given Hume's texts, but on closer inspection this does not seem to be his view. Nevertheless, this subtle misreading is philosophically interesting and has been highly influential. The same is the case with 'Of the influencing motives of the will'. To see this, we shall begin by sketching the Humean Theory of Motivation and its importance to moral philosophy and then turn to Hume's own text.[4]

We can think of explaining why someone performs some action as giving an account of the agent's motivation. Suppose, for example, one wants to explain why Fred got on some particular train. The first thing one might say is that Fred believes that this train is going to London. We then might ask why he is going to London, and one might reply, because he believes that the cricket is on at the Oval cricket ground and that he believes that the Oval is in London. However, his wife Mabel has just the same beliefs as Fred and yet she has not boarded the train. One way to explain the difference in behaviour is to say that although Fred and Mabel share all the relevant beliefs, they differ in their desires. Fred *wanted* to go to the cricket and Mabel did not. So, in explaining someone's action, we advert to what they believed and what they desired. Implicit in this picture is the idea that one needs to talk about what the agent desires because we can easily conceive of somebody having exactly the same beliefs as someone who acts but who themselves are not motivated to act. Beliefs alone are insufficient to motivate any action. We need to cite not only what the agent believes to explain what they do but also what they want or desire.

In explaining an action such as Fred's, we often use locutions that involve the term 'reason'. One might say that Fred's reason for boarding the London train was to get to the cricket. Here we can think of Fred's reason as the combination of psychological states that produces the relevant action, in this case his desire to see the cricket together with the beliefs about how to achieve that end. Let us call this sense of 'reason' a *motivating* reason. It is the combination of beliefs and desires that brings about the action. The Humean theory of motivating reasons is a theory that every such reason is a combination of beliefs and desires.

There is, however, another sense of 'reason' which is relevant to Humean theory, which turns not on explaining what one actually does, but in offering an account of what it is to provide a reason for one to act. That is, not what causes Fred's action but also an account of what he should do. Suppose Fred does not know that the train goes to London. I might say to him that he has a reason to catch this train because so doing is the means to satisfy his desire to watch the cricket. He has a reason to act because acting that way serves his desired end or goal. He *should* act that way, given his goal. In offering a reason for an action one is *justifying* that action. Hence, they are called 'justifying reasons' in contrast to motivating reasons. When Fred is asked, 'why did you board that train?', and he replies, 'because it was the best way to get to the cricket', he is expressing a reason which justifies what he is doing. His action makes sense in light of his desires.

We can assess whether reasons are better or worse in light of this model. Fred might say he caught that train via Birmingham to London to get to the cricket. However, if this takes him needlessly out of his way, we might say that he had better reason to catch the direct train to London. Second, we talk of 'practical reason', as opposed to theoretical reason, as a capacity to reflect upon and evaluate a course of action. When one engages one's practical reason, one considers and evaluates actions that serve one's desires or goals.

As one might imagine, the Humean theory I have just sketched is subject to immensely more complex and subtle refinement, but we have its essential outlines. Beliefs alone do not motivate action because beliefs alone do not set ends or goals. One can imagine someone having the same beliefs as another person, and one being motivated and the other not. Only desires or wants set ends. Beliefs are required in order to find the means to satisfy these ends. I also noted that the Humean theory is much discussed in connection with moral philosophy, so let us sketch its relevance before finally turning to Hume's text.

We begin with a distinction between *internalism* and *externalism* in moral judgment. Internalism is the thesis that when an agent judges something to be morally good, then, necessarily, they are motivated to act appropriately. Suppose Mabel claims that eating meat is wrong, and yet she continues to eat it. The natural response here is to think that Mabel is insincere in her claim that eating meat is wrong. If she *really* thought that eating meat is wrong, then she would not eat any. Moral judgments necessarily move us in some way and so the motivation is *internal* to the judgment. Externalism, by contrast, holds that one can sincerely judge that something is morally right or wrong, and yet remain unmotivated. On this view, Mabel sincerely judges that eating meat is wrong, but she remains unmoved by this judgment. She knows it is wrong but simply does not care and keeps eating meat. The motivation for acting in accordance with this judgment is *external* to that judgment: something else is required to move the agent other than the judgment that something is right or wrong.

Moral internalism is a plausible but controversial view. As one might imagine, like the Humean Theory of Motivation, it is subject to much refinement and sophistication. But let us now turn to the consequences of combining moral internalism with the theory of motivation. Beliefs alone do not motivate. What motivates an agent is a desire or similar state. Moral judgments are necessarily motivating. So moral judgments do not express beliefs but instead they express desires or motivating states. The moral claim, 'eating meat is wrong', cannot express a *belief* since beliefs do not motivate but must instead express some other state which motivates the agent such as disgust or dislike. When Mabel claims that eating meat is morally wrong, she is not expressing a belief but expressing her dislike or disgust at that practice. Hence a consequence of the combination of moral internalism and the Humean Theory of Motivation is that moral claims do not represent moral facts but instead simply express motivational states (or what philosophers call pro or con attitudes) to non-moral facts.

The term for this view is 'moral non-cognitivism' and it is a somewhat radical thesis. It is quite plausible to think that a version of non-cognitivism is true for judgments of gustatory tastes. Someone might say, 'Chocolate ice cream is good', or 'Chocolate ice cream is better than vanilla'. The form of words in these declarations may make them sound like claims to truth but the speaker is expressing not a belief that chocolate ice cream is good but simply her like of, or preference for, it. 'Chocolate ice cream is good' really means 'I like chocolate ice cream'. The claim that chocolate is good is therefore neither true nor false since it is not expressing a belief about the world but is instead simply the way in which someone expresses her like for chocolate. The radical thesis is that something like this picture is true of moral thought and talk. Claims such as 'murder is wrong' may appear on the surface to be fact stating, but instead express some attitude such as dislike to such actions. Explicit versions of this thesis emerged in the middle of the twentieth century, an early one of which was known as 'emotivism'. Morality is a matter of different emotional reactions to worldly actions. Mabel's claim that eating meat is wrong does not express a claim about the world but instead her fundamental dislike of the practice. 'Eating meat is wrong' should be understood as the way in which Mabel is expressing 'Boo to murder!'.

As one might imagine, many objections can be levelled against this idea and a good deal of metaethics in both this and the last century has been devoted to producing increasingly sophisticated versions of non-cognitivism. What is important for our concerns, however, is that even the most sophisticated versions of non-cognitivism find their roots in Hume in the combination of the Humean Theory of Motivation and texts where Hume seems to advance moral internalism. We will look at the texts which connect Hume with internalism in the next chapter, but here we focus on the Humean theory. As we shall see, it is far from clear that what Hume says in 'Of the influencing motives of the will' supports the Humean theory.

Hume begins the section by stating that there is in both common life and philosophy an assumption of the 'combat between reason and passion', and that passion should be subordinate to reason. The 'eternity, invariableness, and divine origin' of reason is emphasised, as is the 'blindness, unconstancy and deceitfulness' of passion. Hume's aim is to 'show the fallacy' of this view and he aims to do so by showing, first, 'that reason alone can never be a motive to any action' and, second, that reason 'can never oppose passion in the direction of the will' (T 2.3.3.1).

The first thing to note here is the supposed 'divine origin' of reason. Hume's target here is a form of non-naturalism, where reason is not a feature of the natural world but something the origins of which lie in the supernatural. The second thing is that Hume's claim that 'reason alone can never be a motive to any action' sounds superficially like a key component of the Humean Theory of Motivation, namely that beliefs alone are insufficient to motivate action. On the assumption that what Hume means by 'reason alone' is by 'beliefs alone', then what he says in the next two paragraphs of T 2.3.3 seems to fit neatly with the Humean theory. First, demonstrative or mathematical reasoning involves beliefs, but such reasoning cannot itself be a motive to action. What the object of any action is is something factual rather than an abstract relation of ideas, and for Hume that resolves itself to beliefs about causes and effects. Reason discovers connections of cause and effect, and hence beliefs about causes and effects. But that alone produces no 'impulse' or motive to action. The 'impulse arises not from reason but is only directed by it' (T 2.3.3.3). Without any such impulse or motive to action, reason alone cannot produce action. Thus:

> It can never in the least concern us to know, that such objects are causes, and such others effects, if both the causes and effects be indifferent to us. Where the objects themselves do not affect us, their connexion can never give them any influence; and 'tis plain, that as reason is nothing but the discovery of this connexion, it cannot be by its means that the objects are able to effect us.
>
> (T 2.3.3.3)

So 'reason alone' can sound like Hume means 'belief alone', and that beliefs alone do not motivate. What is further required are desires or conative states, or 'impulses', and this is presumably what Hume means by 'passions'. Hence what Hume has said so far can be understood as a statement of the Humean Theory of Motivation.

However, when we return to Book One and examine what Hume has to say about the influence of belief, matters are rather different. In T 1.2.10, 'Of the influence of belief', Hume tells us that nature has implanted in our mind 'a perception of good or evil, or in other words, of pain and pleasure, as the chief spring and moving of all its actions' (T 1.3.10.2). Sometimes this is simply a matter of being in a pleasurable state or being in pain, or, in other words, having an impression of pleasure or pain. These impressions do move us. All things being equal, we are drawn towards sources of pleasure and avoid sources of pain. We also have *ideas* of pleasures, pains, and the sources of those perceptions. With those ideas, we can imagine and think about such states and sources. Imagination and mere thought do not move us in any significant way. However, when embodied in states of *belief*, the ideas are enlivened and possess the 'power of actuating the will' (T 1.3.10.3). Thus:

> [although] an idle fiction has no efficacy, yet we find by experience, that the ideas of those objects, which we believe either are or will be existent, produce in a lesser degree the same effect with those impressions....The effect, then, of belief is to raise up a simple idea to an equality with our impressions and bestow on it a like influence on the passions.
>
> (T 1.3.10.3)

Beliefs about pleasure and pain themselves are motivating in the sense that they lead to action. It is true that such beliefs also produce passions, some of which include desire, but the 'impulse' mentioned above comes from the hedonic beliefs. As he puts it later, 'passions...are founded on pain and pleasure, and that in order to produce an affection of any kind, 'tis only requisite to present some good or evil' (T 2.3.9.1). Thus, when Hume tells us that 'reason alone' does not motivate action, he also tells us that it is 'from the prospect of pain or pleasure that the aversion or propensity arises towards any object' (T 2.3.3.3).

How then are we to understand 'reason alone'? We know from earlier in this book that reason is a faculty of comparison, and that reasoning is the discovery of relations. But that faculty alone is never going to produce any motivation to action if the objects it compares have no evaluative significance to us. In 'A dissertation on the passions', Hume puts matters like this:

> It seems evident, that reason, in a strict sense, as meaning the judgement of truth and falshood, can never, of itself, be any motive to the will, and can have no influence but so far as it touches some passion or affection. *Abstract relations* of ideas are the object of curiosity, not of volition. And *matters of fact, where they are not good and evil*, where they neither excite desire nor aversion, are totally indifferent; and whether known or unknown, whether mistaken or rightly apprehend, cannot be regarded as any motive to action.
>
> (D 5.1, my italics beginning 'matters...')

No amount of comparison and the discovery of relations will motivate any action if those relations are evaluatively indifferent. What is required, besides reason, are ideas of what is good and of what is evil. Ideas require impressions, and reason alone cannot provide impressions. This brings us to something I mentioned in the previous chapter, namely that value—good and evil—is tied up with pleasure and pain. An empiricist always seeks something in experience as the source of concepts, and a plausible candidate for what is good and evil in experience is the pair of pleasure and pain. This is why Hume uses the terms 'pleasure and pain' and 'good and evil' interchangeably. Michael Ayers, talking about John Locke, sums up matters very neatly thus:

> The question of how experience gives us ideas of good and evil was for [Locke] the question of what it is in our experience of things which makes anything matter to us, and which makes one thing preferable to another. Without something which constitutes a ground for preference there could be no evaluative concepts. The hedonist holds, not implausibly, that the only ingredients of experience which supply such

grounds are pleasure and pain....In that way, at least, it is tenable that hedonism explains how the words 'good' and 'bad' have meaning.[5]

Read this way, reason plus beliefs about pleasure and pain can motivate action. What then of Hume's second claim, namely that reason can never oppose a passion? Given that reason alone brings with it no evaluative contents, reason alone cannot oppose a passion:

> Nothing can oppose or retard the impulse of a passion, but a contrary impulse; and if this contrary impulse ever arises from reason, that latter faculty must have an original influence on the will....But if reason has no such influence, 'tis impossible it can withstand any principle which has such an efficacy....Thus it appears, that the principle, which opposes our passion, cannot be the same with reason, and is only call'd so in an improper sense.

(T 2.3.3.4)

This is again a matter of reason alone not itself providing evaluative content. When reason opposes passions 'in an improper sense', it does so by showing that some belief relevant to the motive is false, when either the belief is 'founded on the supposition of the existence of objects, which really do not exist' or when 'we choose means insufficient for the design'd end' (T 2.3.3.6). Of the former type, the belief about the object is tied to the pleasure or pain, good or evil. Thus 'I may desire any fruit as of an excellent relish; but whenever you convince me of my mistake, my longing ceases' (T 2.3.3.7), or, as he puts it later, a 'person may be affected with passion, by supposing a pain or pleasure to lie in an object, which has no tendency to produce either of these sensations, or which produces the contrary to what is imagin'd' (T 3.1.1.12). The 'moment we perceive the falshood of any supposition, or the insufficiency of any means our passions yield to our reason without any opposition' (T 2.3.3.7).

So far so good. But Hume also says something about the passions which has gained some notoriety. He writes:

> A passion is an original existence, or, if you will, modification of existence, and contains not any representative quality, which renders it a

> copy of any other existence or modification....'Tis impossible, therefore, that this passion can be oppos'd by, or be contradictory to truth and reason; since this contradiction consists in the disagreement of ideas, consider'd as copies, with those objects, which they represent.
>
> (T 2.3.3.5)

This passage is highly puzzling, as commentators have long noted.[6] First, how this is supposed to support the Humean Theory of Motivation is puzzling inasmuch as the connection between this claim and the theory is highly opaque.[7] Second, in aiming to show how passions cannot be 'contradictory to reason', Hume seems to commit himself to something very implausible. Passions are not copies of anything else, so it seems that we should regard them as impressions rather than ideas. Ideas manage to have intentionality—to be *about* something—in virtue, in part, of being a copy of another perception. If then we take this passage at face value, passions lack intentionality. They are not about anything. But this seems wrong. I am annoyed *about* losing my keys, delighted *about* England's cricket victory, or dismayed *at* the terrible weather. Treating passions as impressions and understanding intentionality as involving copies of impressions deprives passions of intentionality. So, what Hume says here must be wrong, and is another symptom of the rather limited conception of representation we mentioned in Chapter One of this book. But this passage does not support the Humean Theory of Motivation.

If Hume thinks that beliefs about good and evil, or pleasure and pain, can motivate action, then there is little in 'Of the motivating influences of the will' that supports the Humean Theory of Motivation. The question then is quite what it is that Hume is trying to establish in that section. I have suggested that Hume is saying that reason without impressions cannot produce or retard action. Why would that be of any interest? Hume brings up this topic when discussing morality at the beginning of Book Three of the *Treatise* and one of his key targets there shows the relevance of what we have been discussing. This view Hume describes as follows:

> Virtue is nothing but a conformity to reason; that there are eternal fitness and unfitnesses of things, which are the same to every rational

> being that considers them; that the immutable measures of right and wrong impose an obligation, not only on human creatures but on the Deity himself.
>
> (T 3.1.1.4)

Among those holding views along these lines include Samuel Clarke in his 1705 *A Discourse Concerning the Unchangeable Obligations of Natural Religion* and Nicholas Malebranche, whom Hume writes, 'was the first that stated this abstract theory of morals…[that] excludes all sentiment' (EPM, 3.34n). Moral facts are immutable relations among things, and we discern moral truths via reason by perceiving and discovering those relations. On this view, morality 'is discern'd merely by ideas, and by their juxtaposition and comparison' (T 3.1.1.4). Its epistemology involves only the faculty of reason. But this will not explain what above we called 'moral internalism', namely that any moral judgment involves being appropriately motivated. Hume certainly seems to subscribe to this idea, and since reason alone cannot motivate, he rejects the idea that morality is discerned by reason alone. Since morality has

> an influence on the actions and the affections, it follows, that they cannot be deriv'd from reason; and that because reason alone, as we have already prov'd can never have any such influence.
>
> (T 3.1.1.6)

CALM AND VIOLENT PASSIONS

We shall look at what Hume has to say about morality and reason in greater detail in the next chapter. Towards the end of 'Of the influencing motives of the will', there are two further things that we should register and discuss. First, whilst we have so far discussed beliefs about pleasure and pain as eliciting passions and hence being a motive to action, we should note that not all direct passions are caused by such beliefs. As well as those elicited by pleasure and pain, there are 'certain instincts originally implanted in our natures, such as benevolence and resentment, the love of life, and kindness to children' (T 2.3.3.8). So not all passions are produced by prior beliefs about good or evil, pleasure and pain. Second, in explaining why we sometimes think that reasoning is determining us to act, Hume notes that some passions operate with 'calmness and tranquillity' and, 'tho' they be real passions, produce little emotion, and are more known by their effects than by the immediate feeling and sensation' (T 2.3.3.8). These contrast with what he calls 'violent passions'. How are we to understand this contrast? Hume writes:

> When I receive an injury from another, I often feel a violent passion of resentment, which makes me desire his evil and punishment, independently of all considerations of pleasure and advantage to myself. When I am immediately threaten'd with any grievous ill, my fears, apprehensions, and aversions arise to a great height, and produce a sensible emotion.
>
> (T 2.3.3.9)

One difference then between the two is that calm passions have little in the way of raw feeling or phenomenology whereas violent passions do. Second, though not explicit in the passage, calm passions tend to be enduring whereas violent ones tend to be relatively fleeting. When Hume talks of advantage to oneself, he is alluding to the calm passion for one's own self-interest. In this case, the sudden violent passion might make one strike out against one's assailant and in doing so one acts against one's own long-term interest (one might get arrested, for example). Hence people sometimes 'act knowingly against their interest' (T 2.3.3.1) when they succumb to a violent passion which leads to actions contrary to their calm passions.

At first blush, the term 'violent' suggests a further difference between the two passions, namely that violent passions have greater causal influence than calm ones. However, some calm passions are such that there is a 'prevalence of the calm passions above the violent', and that those whose calm passions prevail over the violent possess what Hume calls 'strength of mind'. Nevertheless, this virtue is not perfect in the sense that, as a matter of fact, everyone on 'occasion yield[s] to the solicitations of passion and desire' (T 2.3.3.10).

In subsequent sections Hume discusses the influences that operate on passions which increase or decrease their violence and how certain passions can become calm and steady principles of action. A key feature here is habit and custom. A passion becomes calm and steady via habit and custom. Custom has two effects, first by 'bestowing a *facility* in the performance of any action' and, second, 'a *tendency* or *inclination* towards' the object of the passion (T 2.3.5.1). Facility is a kind of ease that is acquired through habit, making endeavour towards the object of the passion easier, which also brings a pleasure in the relative ease of performance. Second, it increases our tendency to pursue the object of the passion. It becomes 'a settled principle of action, and is the predominant inclination of the soul, [and] commonly produces no longer any sensible agitation' (T 2.3.4.1). The violence of any given passion depends on a number of different factors, which Hume calls 'circumstances and situations' (T 2.3.4.1). The violence of a passion can, for example, be a function of proximity: my desire for a bar of chocolate becomes more sensible when it is before my eyes. Passions related together can affect violence, and sometimes the 'predominant passion swallows up the inferior, and converts it into itself' (T 2.3.4.2). Thus, the minor jealousies and quarrels between two lovers increase the passion of love (T 2.3.4.3). Uncertainty can agitate the mind and increase passions such as fear. A change in circumstance can also change a calm passion into a violent one.

Hume offers quite a detailed discussion of the causes and effects of calm and violent passions, but the general lesson is that they 'are pretty variable, and depend, in great measure, on the peculiar temper and disposition' of each individual (T 2.3.9.13). This 'struggle of passion and of reason, as it is called'—the struggle between violent and calm passion—'diversifies human life, and makes men so different not only from each other, but from themselves in different times' (T 2.3.8.13).

DIRECT PASSIONS AND CURIOSITY

Hume offers a brief treatment of the direct passions before turning to the 'love of truth, which was the first source of all our enquiries' (T 2.3.10.1). Direct passions arise from good and evil, pleasure and pain, and the mind by an original 'instinct tends to unite itself with the good, and to avoid the evil, tho' they be conceiv'd merely in idea, and be consider'd as to exist in any future period of time' (T 2.3.9.2). As we mentioned above, there are a few passions which do not have good and evil and their ideas as their causes. These 'arise from a natural impulse or instinct, which is perfectly unaccountable', and include the desire for punishment, happiness for our friends, 'hunger, lust, and a few other bodily appetites' (T 2.3.9.8). In these cases, there is pleasure and pain, but they derived from their satisfaction. However, the majority of direct passions have objects that are related to good and evil.

Hume tells us that neither kind of direct passion 'seem[s] to merit our particular attention, except for hope and fear' (T 2.3.9.9). Beliefs about good and evil, when those beliefs are certain or highly probable, produce joy and grief or sorrow respectively. However, when uncertainty is involved, matters become more complex. Probability is diminished, and uncertainty results, when there are 'contrary chances or causes' such that the mind is left unable to decide between one or the other, and 'at one moment is determin'd to consider an object as existent, and at another moment the contrary' (T 2.3.9.10). These contrary judgments can produce contrary passions. In some cases, where the joy and grief have separate causes, these passions are themselves easily differentiated. Thus, to use Hume's example, one's sorrow at a lawsuit and one's joy at the birth of one's child are distinct and so the subsequent grief and joy are distinct. However, when the contrary passions have the same object and it is subject to uncertainty, a mixture of the two passions is produced, which is either hope or fear. These phenomena, Hume states, are 'of the same nature' as the experience of animals, again underscoring his naturalistic credentials. This should make us consider 'the additional force this bestows on the present system' (T 2.3.9.32).

Hume then turns to discuss the passion of the love of truth, or curiosity.[8] He had already raised the issue in the conclusion to the first book of the *Treatise* about just why he should continue the pursuit of philosophy and why he should be 'led a wandering into such dreary solitudes, and rough passages' (T 1.4.7.10). Rather than simply pursue every question in an unconstrained way, and to its bitter end, he resolved to follow his reason where it is natural and agreeable. He feels an 'ambition...of contributing to the instruction of mankind and of acquiring a name', and that if he does not do so, he would be 'a loser in point of pleasure; and this is the origin of [his] philosophy' (T 1.4.7.12). In that part of the *Treatise* there is an implicit rejection of the normative demand to follow the deliverances of reason no matter where they lead one. In this section, Hume seeks to explain why we are interested in truth in the first place.

Let us note some general features of this section before we turn to some detail.[9] This passion is, he says, 'an affection of so peculiar a kind' that it does not fall under the categories he has so far offered (T 2.3.10.1). First, the fact that it seems to be a peculiar passion might also suggest that Hume thinks that the passion for truth is peculiar to human beings. This would make him side with philosophers who think that this marks an absolute distinction between humans and other animals. Thomas Hobbes, for example, held that not only do animals differ from humans by not having reason, but also in not having the desire for knowledge and in particular knowledge of causes. As we shall see, however, the 'peculiarity' of the passion does not threaten Hume's attempt to account for the human in terms of the animal. Second, in the Christian tradition with which Hume and his readers were familiar there is a distinction to be drawn between a noble love of truth and mere curiosity which is a vice. The title of the section seems, somewhat provocatively, to run the two together, and yet in the discussion he distinguishes between 'the love of knowledge, as it displays itself in the sciences' and 'a certain curiosity implanted in human nature, which is a passion deriv'd from a quite different principle' (T 2.3.10.11). Does this mean that Hume agrees with the Christian-derived distinction? We shall see whether this is so below.

Our interest in truth does not emerge because truth has intrinsic value. It is not valuable 'in itself'. A different, but related way to put the point, is that we have no desire for truth considered independently of its consequences. Instead, Hume first suggests that we derive a certain pleasure in the exercise of 'genius and capacity' when the discovery of some truth involves effort and ingenuity. But this is not sufficient. As well as the difficulty involved the 'truth we discover must also be of some importance' (T 2.3.10.4). Without this further feature, there will be no 'considerable enjoyment' in such a discovery. But how does such 'importance' relate to the passion for truth? Hume approaches this question by observing that

> many philosophers have consum'd their time, have destroy'd their health, and neglected their fortune in the search of such truths, as they esteem'd important and useful to the world, tho' it appear'd from their whole conduct and behaviour, that they were not endow'd with any share of public spirit, nor had any concern for the interests of mankind.
>
> (T 2.3.10.4)

In response, Hume tells us that there are 'certain desires and inclinations, which go no farther than the imagination' which are 'rather the faint shadows and images of passions, than any real affections' (T 2.3.10.5). The idea of the utility of these philosophers' discoveries is the product of a very remote sympathy with human welfare, a 'faint shadow' which has little to no effect on the mind of the philosopher, and hence they behave in such a way that displays no concern for others. What really animates these ascetic types is the exercise of their own genius and capacity, together with a false image of the importance of the truths they seek.

In normal cases, however, a genuine sense of the importance of the particular truths is required as well as the pleasure derived from genius and capacity. But again, this is not sufficient to explain our passion for truth. What is required is *success* in this pursuit. It cannot simply be the pleasure of trying to find truths that one deems to be important, but there has to be some success in actually doing so. Hume then writes that:

> where the mind pursues any end with passion; tho' that passion be not deriv'd originally from the end, but merely from the action and pursuit; yet by the natural course of the affections, we acquire a

concern for the end itself, and are uneasy under any disappointment we meet with in the pursuit of it.

(T 2.3.10.7)

This 'general remark' is important because what Hume seems to be saying here is that we *do* acquire an interest in truth for its own sake, but its explanation lies not in having any such original desire or passion but rather an interest in pleasure and utility which leads to the pursuit of truth which then takes on a life of its own. The importance lies in the fact that it was quite widely held that truth does possess intrinsic value and because of that we have an interest in truth for its own sake. Hume recognises this but he does not see it as evidence of there being some innate or underived passion for it, divinely implanted, and marking some fundamental difference from the rest of the animals. Instead, it becomes explicable in terms of our pleasure in discovery, our success, and the utility of what we discover. Once, however, we get into the custom of seeking truth, we come to value the pursuit of truth for its own sake. To this end Hume compares the pursuit of truth with hunting. The hunter gets pleasure from 'the action of the mind and the body', the physical and mental exertion which could be gained by some other activity, together with the utility of the objects, the game that 'is fit for the table', and the success in achieving that aim. However, the entire activity of hunting becomes a pursuit in itself, something more than the sum of its parts. We take a pleasure in that activity itself rather than merely the exercise and the utility of its aim. However, all of this is readily intelligible in terms of the animal materials upon which Hume models human nature.

What though of curiosity in the sense of nosiness rather than the noble pursuit of truth, the 'insatiable desire of knowing the actions and circumstances of [one's] neighbours' (T 2.3.10.11)? Hume does not explicitly condemn this passion, and it is far from clear whether he does so implicitly. The origin of such nosiness lies not in the pleasure that the pursuit of truth involves but instead from uneasiness about possible sudden and dramatic changes in one's local environment. This leads to constant interest in what is presently happening in the locale, and to relying on others for information regarding it.

NOTES

1 Hume's views in the first *Enquiry* on this topic are somewhat different, but we shall not be discussing this here. For a clear and useful introduction, see Demeter (2018).
2 See Harris (2005), Chapter Three for an extremely useful discussion.
3 Russell (1995), p.98.
4 For what is still an excellent introduction to the issues surrounding the Humean Theory of Motivation, and its relation to moral internalism, see McNaughton (1988).
5 Ayers (1991), pp.197–198.
6 Fogelin says it is a 'disaster' (1985), p.113 and Baier 'a very silly paragraph' (1991), p.160.
7 See Bricke (1996), pp.21–22.
8 Hume also uses the term 'love of knowledge' interchangeably with 'love of truth', and I shall do the same here, even though the two are logically distinct.
9 I owe these insights to Watts (2019). See also his (2022).

FURTHER READING

Paul Russell (1995) covers a lot of the ground surveyed in this, and, indeed, the previous chapter, and presents an interestingly different conception of Hume's discussion of freedom. For a more introductory account, see Baillie (2000), Chapter Four. On freedom, see Harris (2005), Chapter Three, Russell (2015), and Pitson (2016). For different views on Hume's theory of motivation, consult the relevant chapters of Kail (2007a), Cohon (2008), and Radcliffe (2018). On curiosity, see Frasca-Spada (1998), pp.152ff, Gelfert (2013), and Watts (2022).

7
OF VIRTUE AND VICE IN GENERAL

INTRODUCTION

The short Part One of Book Three, 'Of vice and virtue in general', comprises two sections, 'Moral distinctions not deriv'd from reason' and 'Moral distinctions deriv'd from a moral sense'. The first section argues a negative thesis in the first, and the second section for a positive one.

T 3.1.1 MORAL DISTINCTIONS NOT DERIV'D FROM REASON

After some preliminaries, Hume asks, '[w]*hether 'tis by means of our* ideas *or* impressions *we distinguish betwixt vice and virtue, and pronounce an action blameworthy or praise-worthy?*' (T 3.1.1.3). Hume's answer will be impressions, and, as we shall see, these impressions are 'particular pains and pleasures' (T 3.1.2.3). But we first need to consider Hume's negative claim, that moral distinctions are not derived from reason.

Why is Hume interested in rejecting the claim that moral distinctions are derived from reason? To understand this claim we need a sight of his target, which was briefly mentioned in the previous chapter. He writes that there 'are those who affirm' that

> virtue is nothing but a conformity to reason; that there are eternal fitness and unfitnesses of things, which are the same to every rational being that considers them; that the immutable measures of right and wrong impose an obligation, not only on human creatures but on the Deity himself.
>
> (T 1.1.1.4)

This passage summarises an account of morality which is known as 'moral rationalism'. This view is an account of in what moral facts consist, namely that there are certain relations, of which 'fitness and unfitness' are instances. To modern ears it is an odd view and needs a little explanation. The first point that needs making turns on the remark that such relations also impose an obligation 'on the Deity himself'. This is made against the background of a discussion of a doctrine known as 'voluntarism', the thesis that moral facts depend solely on God's will and so are ultimately arbitrary in nature.[1] Rationalism is set against voluntarism, and models moral facts on something that is thought to be independent even of the will of God. The paradigm of that which is eternal, necessary, and independent of God's will is mathematics and such relations are the objects of demonstration.

In the *Enquiry Concerning the Principles of Morals*, Hume writes that Nicolas Malebranche 'was the first that stated this abstract theory of morals...[that] excludes all sentiment' (EPM 3.34n). Malebranche himself writes that:

> Since truth and order are relations of greatness and perfection, real immutable and necessary relations, relations comprehended in the substance of the divine word, he that sees these relations sees what God sees. He that regulates his love according to these relations observes a law which God invincible loves.[2]

Such relations are independent of even God's will. Samuel Clarke, another moral rationalist, is the one who talks of relations of fitness and unfitness in *A Discourse Concerning the Unchangeable Obligations of Natural Religion* (1704). One such relation is that of the superiority of the infinite over the finite, one of proportion. Thus, 'that God is infinitely superior to man is as clear as that infinity is larger than a point....And 'tis as certainly fit that men should honour and worship and imitate God'. Here we see not only the relation of proportion but also that it is fit that we should worship God. This is compared to the 'properties which flow from the essences of different mathematical figures'.³ The 'certainty and universality' of obligation

> is plainly confirmed [by reason] and the force of it particularly discovered and applied to every man by this; that in a like manner as no one, who is instructed in mathematics, can forbear giving his assent to every geometrical demonstration, of which he understands, but the terms.⁴

Moral truths are relations akin to mathematical relations which necessitate certain conclusions when discerned by reason.

This conception of moral facts fits with the view that morality is supposedly discerned by reason. Hume's immediate response is to remind the reader that reason alone is no motive to action and he seems to affirm moral internalism, saying that since 'morals...have an influence on the actions and affections, it follows, that they cannot be derived from reason; and that because reason alone...can never have any such influence' (T 3.1.1.6). This sounds like the position sketched in the last chapter where the combination of the Humean Theory of Motivation and moral internalism supports non-cognitivism. Beliefs alone do not motivate action. What is required is some other state, typically a desire, to move an agent. Internalism is the view that a sincere moral judgment is necessarily motivating. Since beliefs alone do not motivate, then moral judgments must express some other mental state, such as approval or revulsion. If we read 'Of the influencing motives of the will' as supporting the Humean Theory of Motivation, we can see this passage as supporting non-cognitivism about morality.

Hume's discussion here has been read this way and in a very sophisticated manner.⁵ However, we were sceptical of reading Hume as offering the so-called Humean theory. The point of 'Of the influencing motives of the will' is that the exercise of reason alone cannot motivate action if we are indifferent to the objects compared by reason. What is further required are impressions which provide evaluative contents which are sourced in pleasure and pain. In the light of this then, how do we understand Hume's critique of moral rationalism?

In brief, Hume argues that none of the relations suggested has any moral quality. As we saw in Chapter Three, he listed what he took to be all the philosophical relations. Those that comprise the objects of knowledge are resemblance, contrariety, degrees in quality, and proportion in quantity and number. None of these seems moral in character. His opponents might argue that there is some further relation which is moral in character, but Hume finds this mysterious (T 3.1.1.20). Furthermore, Hume argues that putative relations which we might hold to be candidates for moral relations also hold between inanimate objects which would, absurdly, mean those objects stand in moral relations. Thus, a child might kill her parent which we deem to be an immoral act. What then of a tree which grows and cuts off the light of another tree from which the tree sprang, and so is killing its parent? Thus, there is the destruction of the parent tree by its offspring (T 3.1.1.24). The fact that parricide might involve intention and will, in contrast to the death of the tree, Hume holds to be irrelevant since whatever its cause the relation—the death of a parent caused by its offspring—remains the same.

Hume concludes his discussion of why moral distinctions are not derived from reason by remarking that some authors draw an inference from statement of fact to a conclusion about what ought to be the case. Thus, as we saw, Clarke argued that God is infinitely superior to man. Ought we to therefore praise him? Hume is sceptical about drawing a conclusion about an ought from an is:

> ...as this *ought*, or *ought not*, expresses some new relation or affirmation, 'tis necessary that it shou'd be observed and explain'd; and at the same time that a reason shou'd be given, for what seems altogether inconceivable, how this new relation can be a deduction from others, which are entirely different from it. But as authors do not commonly use this precaution, I shall presume to recommend it to the reader; and am perswaded, that this small attention wou'd subvert all the

vulgar systems of morality; and let us see, that the distinction of vice and virtue is not founded merely on the relations of objects, nor is perceiv'd by reason.

(T 3.1.1.27)

This passage was often thought to state what was known as 'Hume's Law', namely that no normative conclusion can be derived from purely factual premises. If Hume were a non-cognitivist about evaluation, then his claim here could be read as an application of non-cognitivism. Moral judgments do not express truths so of course moral 'oughts' cannot be derived from factual premises. However, scholars are less confident that this is what lies behind what Hume is saying here. What else might it mean?

Much of Hume's criticism of moral rationalism and his subsequent favouring of a moral sense is drawn from the philosophy of Francis Hutcheson with whom he corresponded during the composition of the *Treatise*. A key work in this connection is the 1728 *Illustrations on the Moral Sense* which was appended to *An Essay Concerning the Nature and Conduct of the Passions*. In that work, Hutcheson attacks moral rationalism in a way similar to Hume's own and it is in the context of this attack that he raises a question about the intelligibility of the word 'ought'. It is a 'confused word',[6] and for clarification he refers us to his discussion of the meaning of 'obligation'. That is, Hutcheson is trying to explain the notion that Hume says other authors have not explained. For Hutcheson, there are many 'confused' accounts of this notion, but only two that are clear. The first concerns 'what action is necessary to obtain happiness to the agent, or avoid misery'.[7] Here the obligation is easy to explain. If some course of action is necessary to secure happiness or avoid misery, then the 'ought' becomes intelligible in light of the desire for happiness or the wish to avoid misery. If this course of action is required for your happiness, then you *ought* to perform it. Here Hutcheson says that the 'ought' depends on 'selfish affections'. That is, the 'ought' is made intelligible in light of the agent's own self-interest or self-concern. The second sense of 'obligation' Hutcheson spells out as follows. 'That every spectator, or he himself on reflection, must approve his action, and disapprove his omitting it, if he fuller considers all its circumstances'.[8] Here Hutcheson is talking of moral obligation, which we shall gloss as having a reason to act, not because it furthers our own interests, but because it is the *morally* right thing to do. The moral rationalists do not offer an explanation of this, but Hutcheson thinks that the moral sense does. Hume also tells us that moral distinctions are derived from a moral sense,[9] so presumably his answer is similar. But what is the moral sense? In the next section we examine Hume's view in light of Hutcheson's own in order to answer this question. It is important to do so, otherwise the sense of the moral sense can elude readers.

T 3.1.2 MORAL DISTINCTIONS DERIV'D FROM A MORAL SENSE

What is the moral sense? Hutcheson's key work in this connection is a two-volume work called *An Inquiry into the Original of Our Ideas of Beauty and Virtue* (1726). This comprises two treatises, the first 'concerning beauty, harmony, order and the design', the second 'concerning moral good and evil'. The two are intimately connected, not least because the moral sense is modelled on the sense of beauty that is the topic of the first treatise.

A sense is just 'the power to receive sensation' and an 'inner sense' is defined as 'a Determination of the Mind, to receive any Idea from the Presence of an Object which occurs to us, independent on our Will'.[10] The ideas that are produced are distinctive pleasures or pains, one aesthetic, the other moral, and the senses are 'inner' because these sensations are responsive to other ideas, namely ideas of external objects. When I look at a beautiful object, I have an idea of it and my aesthetic sense responds by producing a distinctive pleasure. There are three aspects of this of which we need to take note. First, the aesthetic response is *disinterested*. Second, it is responsive to something of which the subject has no immediate knowledge. Third, Hutcheson models this account on the function of animal sensation. Let us take these in turn.

Aesthetic experience is a form of evaluation that is disinterested in the sense that why we find some object valuable does not depend on the particular wants or desires of the observer. The sense of beauty is 'antecedent to and distinct from prospects of interest'.[11] Certain things I deem valuable because of some antecedent desire, either because I simply want something (a cup of coffee, say), or something as a means to something else (I value the fertiliser because it is conducive to growing the peppers in my garden). When I contemplate aesthetic beauty, however, I find it valuable irrespective of any antecedent want or desire I may have. I may of course come to desire the object once I perceive it. Thus, I see a picture in a gallery and decide to buy a print of it to hang in my house, but I come to desire it because it is beautiful rather than finding it beautiful because I desire it.

Second, the pleasure is a response to something of which the subject may have no immediate knowledge. What unites what we find beautiful is that everything beautiful possesses a formal property, namely uniformity amidst variety. What you are experiencing when you perceive a beautiful object is something that exhibits uniformity amidst variety though you may not know *that* the object exhibits that feature. You simply find the object beautiful without knowing just what it is you are finding beautiful.

This feature is linked to the third aspect of Hutcheson's treatment of aesthetic beauty, namely that it is modelled on the function of animal sensation. Animals seek out things that are beneficial to them and avoid things that are harmful without knowing that they are or why they are beneficial or harmful. Instead, what is beneficial to the animal is what the animal finds pleasant and what is potentially harmful is painful. The grass tastes good to the cow, and contains the nutrients that the cow requires, even though of course the cow has no idea of that fact. Conversely, the painful heat of the fire or the unpleasant smell of some rotten vegetable guides the cow away from what is potentially harmful. This allows animals to react appropriately to their environment in the absence of much knowledge of its nature. How though does this relate to the aesthetic sense? For Hutcheson, the pleasures of the aesthetic sense lead us to seek out and contemplate what exhibits uniformity amidst variety and it is this feature and our interest in it which helps us understand the world around us. To understand the universe is to seek explanation, and explanation involves understanding the complex in terms of the less complex, or to find uniformity amidst variety. Thus:

> ...as the AUTHOR of Nature has determin'd us to receive, by our *external Senses*, pleasant or disagreeable Ideas of Objects, according as they are useful or hurtful to our Bodys:...[we] receive from *uniform Objects* the Pleasures of *Beauty* and *Harmony*, to excite us to the Pursuit of Knowledge and reward us for it.[12]

How then does this provide the model for the moral sense? The disinterested aesthetic response provides a model for *moral* evaluation which stands in opposition to what was known as the 'selfish theory', a position associated with Thomas Hobbes and Bernard Mandeville. Very roughly, Hobbes and Mandeville offered explanations of moral language and behaviour that ultimately rest on the self-interest of individuals. Seemingly selfless or generous action is ultimately grounded in a particular individual's views of how conforming to such behaviour forwards his or her private interests. Hutcheson, by contrast, uses the aesthetic model to show that moral evaluation can be perfectly disinterested. We can find something morally laudable quite independently of any private interests or wants. And, as the aesthetic sense is responsive to uniformity amidst variety, the moral sense is responsive to something. The 'general foundation' of morality for Hutcheson is benevolence. Acts of benevolence, which stem from the general trait to perform such acts, tend to be conducive to the wellbeing of society as a whole or 'the external good of every one'.[13] So, while bodily pleasure is tied to that which is conducive to bodily wellbeing, the moral sense is responsive to benevolence, which is conducive to societal wellbeing.

So, we find that we feel pleasure when encountering 'some apparent species of benevolence',[14] even if we do not recognise it is *that* to which we are responding. At the most basic level we just find *something* morally admirable even if we cannot quite specify what that might be. But this is merely the most basic form of moral responsiveness and it is liable to error. Through experience and reflection, we come to correct and refine the responses of the moral sense. We come to recognise that we have only 'partial representations of the tendencys of actions',[15] and so we should not 'stupidly follow the first Appearance of publick good'.[16]

Now that we have some grasp of the moral sense, let us return to Hume. Hume tells us that morality is discovered by impressions and that these impressions are a particular impression of pleasure which is the impression of virtue, and that of pain in the case of vice (T 3.1.2.4). These particular sensations differ from, and are distinct from, any other pleasures and pains and so are the impressions which make *moral* goodness and vice distinct from natural good and evil, the pleasures and pains we discussed when talking about the passions. For both Hutcheson and Hume, this emphasis on the distinctness of the concepts of moral good and ill is an important element in responding to Hobbes and Mandeville. Both Hutcheson and Hume think that the attempt to explain moral practice simply in terms of calculated self-interest cannot explain why we have moral concepts. Hume, later in the *Treatise*, puts the point this way:

> Any artifice of politicians may assist nature in the producing of these sentiments...but 'tis impossible it should be the sole case of the distinction we make betwixt vice and virtue. For if nature did not aid us in this particular, 'twould be in vain to talk of *honourable* or *dishonourable*, *praiseworthy* or *blameable*. These words wou'd be perfectly unintelligible...The utmost politicians can perform, is, to extend the natural sentiments beyond their original bounds; but still nature must furnish the materials, and give us some notion of moral distinctions.
>
> (T 3.2.2.25)

These pleasures and pains of the moral sense also produce the indirect passions, pride, humility, love, and hatred. When we feel the moral sentiment when contemplating another person, it produces love, and hatred when that contemplation produces the pain of vice. When one contemplates one's own virtues, pride is produced, and humility when one contemplates one's own vices.

This brings us to the causes of the moral sentiments. We noted that in Hutcheson the pleasures of the moral sense are elicited by the trait of benevolence. Hume's position, by contrast, is rather more complicated. Having introduced the moral sense, Hume turns to ask from 'what principles is it deriv'd, and whence does it arise in the human mind?' (T 3.1.2.6) and makes two points in this connection. First, he holds that it is too implausible to suggest that 'in every particular instance' the sentiments are produced by an *'original* quality and *primary* constitution' (T 3.1.2.6). Very roughly, Hume thinks that the production of the moral sentiments in many cases is not instinctual in the way that Hutcheson holds. Our original sentiments in many cases require the cooperation of other principles of the mind, notably sympathy, and we shall be looking at these later. But this complication is further reflected in the fact that, whilst Hutcheson picks out a single character trait, namely benevolence, as the object of the moral sense, Hume recognises a whole range of virtues, including prudence, wit, greatness of mind, industry, and a whole host of others. What unites virtues is, to use the language of the *Enquiry Concerning the Principles of Morals*, the disjunction of qualities that are useful or agreeable to one's self or others. Wit is agreeable to others, tranquillity agreeable to one's self. Both traits are valuable because they produce a pleasing state of mind. Other qualities are admired because they are useful. Thus, prudence is useful to one's self, and benevolence is useful to others.

Second, Hume asks whether we should look for the causes of the sentiments in nature or in the artifice of humanity? This question foreshadows a distinction Hume makes between what he calls the *natural* and *artificial* virtues. At a first approximation, natural virtues are as follows. What is approved by the moral sense is a character trait which is a tendency to a certain end which is distinct from any moral motive. A father cares for his child not because he holds that it is the right thing to do but because he naturally loves and cares for his child. We find such a tendency to be morally praiseworthy and so it is approved by the moral sense. However, there are some moral virtues for which there seems to be no motive independent of moral rightness. When someone acts justly, they do so from a sense of its being the right thing to do rather than having some other motive of which the moral sense approves. Hume thinks he has an explanation of how these 'artificial virtues' are possible, and this is the topic of the next chapter.

NOTES

1. This worry ultimately stems from Plato's *Euthyphro*. For a superb discussion of the issue in connection with Hume and moral rationalism see Schneewind (2000).
2. Malebranche, *Treatise on Ethics*, p.48.
3. Clarke, *A Discourse Concerning the Unchangeable Obligations of Natural Religion, and the Truth and Certainty of the Christian Religion*, p.37. Hereafter *Discourse*.
4. Clarke, *Discourse*, pp.52–53.
5. For two such readings, see Bricke (1996) and Radcliffe (2018).
6. Hutcheson, *Illustrations on the Moral Sense*, p.155. Hereafter *Illustrations*.
7. Hutcheson, *Illustrations*, p.156.
8. Hutcheson, *Illustrations*, p.156.
9. Many commentators, for a number of reasons, tend to be very sceptical of Hume's sincerity, and see no role for a moral sense in Hume's theory. See e.g. Wright (2009), Turco (2003) and (2007), and, in the context of the *Enquiry Concerning the Principles of Morals*, Abramson (2000). This scepticism partly owes itself to a more general scepticism about the influence of Hutcheson on Hume, the most extreme of which is encapsulated in Moore's claim that 'Hume's moral philosophy is not at all Hutchesonian in its origin or inspiration' (1994), p.54. Here is not the place to discuss this controversy, but see Kail (2007a), Chapters Seven to Nine and (2020).
10. Hutcheson, *Inquiry*, p.90.
11. Hutcheson, *Inquiry*, p.25.
12. Hutcheson, *Inquiry*, p.75.
13. Hutcheson, *Inquiry*, p.197.
14. Hutcheson, *Inquiry*, p.137.
15. Hutcheson, *Inquiry*, p.137.
16. Hutcheson, *Inquiry*, p.141.

FURTHER READING

Discussions of the moral sense cannot be adequately addressed without discussion of the general point of view, which we shall address in Chapter Nine. However, good introductory starting points are Wright (2009), Chapter Eight, and Baillie (2000), Chapter Five. For more advanced discussion, see Bricke (1996), Kail (2007a), Chapters Seven to Nine, Cohon (2008), Part One, and Radcliffe (2018).

8

OF JUSTICE AND INJUSTICE

INTRODUCTION

Book Three, Part Two of the *Treatise* is titled 'Of justice and injustice'. To some extent the title is misleading. First, because Hume discusses things that we might think of as distinct from what we might take to be the sphere of justice, such as political allegiance and sexual modesty. Second, and differently, where he does talk of justice, he seems to focus on something rather narrower than what we ordinarily take to be the sphere of justice, namely our relation to property. What unites the topics of Part Two, however, is something introduced at the end of the previous chapter, namely that the virtues discussed in this part constitute what he calls the 'artificial' virtues. In what follows, we shall explore this notion by following the general course of Hume's text.

NATURAL OR ARTIFICIAL?

As I mentioned at the beginning of this chapter, Hume's conception of justice is generally taken to be rather narrow in character. Hume restricts justice to property rights and our respect for them. Thus, for example, he orients the subject around the question

DOI: 10.4324/9781315667874-9

of 'wherein consists this honesty and justice, which you find in restoring a loan and, abstaining from the property of others' (T 3.2.1.9). But justice, arguably, concerns more, including fairness, equity, the criminal law, the protection of individuals and families, as well as the protection of rights and impartial adjudication when they might conflict. Why Hume's view is so narrow, and the extent to which it is, is not something we shall pursue here, but it is something which we must be aware of as we proceed.[1]

Let us revisit the distinction between natural and artificial virtues. Hume writes:

> all virtuous actions derive their merit only from virtuous motives, and are consider'd merely as signs of those motives. From this principle I conclude, that the first virtuous motive, which bestows a merit on any action, can never be a regard to the virtue of that action, but must be some other natural motive or principle.
>
> (T 3.2.1.4)

Suppose we see a parent caring for their child by making sure they are well tucked in and warm at bedtime. We take this action to be a sign of an enduring disposition to act in ways that result in the care of the child. Of course, this act might be a one-off, say that of a baby-sitter who is paid to look after the child whilst you are at a concert, but equally the action can express the stable disposition to care for the child. These abiding dispositions to action are what Hume calls virtues and, as we noted in Chapter Five, it is these which produce the moral sentiment of approval in the spectator, and, in turn, the indirect passion of love. This notion of natural virtue will be discussed more extensively in the next chapter. The important point here is that the motives for action in natural virtues are not those of our sense of moral rightness or requiredness of those actions. We must have some motive distinct from our 'regard to its virtue'. 'To suppose', Hume writes, 'that the mere regard to virtue of the action, may be the first motive, which produc'd the action, and render'd it virtuous, is to reason in a circle' (T 3.2.1.4).

This, for obvious reasons, has become known as Hume's 'Circle Argument', but scholars are not entirely in agreement of quite how the argument is supposed to work.[2] But what seems to on the cards is the thought that, when we morally approve of something, we must be able to specify and recognise *what* it is we are approving of. So, when I approve of the caring father, I can specify that which I am approving of, namely his love and care for his child. But if the motive which I approve of is simply that of acting out of a sense that the action is the morally right one, I would be at a loss to say what it is that *makes* that particular motive morally praiseworthy. What is needed is to identity some motive in the agent independent of the sense of moral rightness of which I can approve. None of this precludes cases of natural virtues where, nevertheless, actions are performed out of a sense of rightness or duty. As Hume notes, someone may lack some natural motive and 'may perform the action without the motive, from a certain sense of duty' (T 3.2.1.8). Someone might have no natural sense of gratitude but might nevertheless perform actions expressive of gratitude because he recognises that it is morally right so to do.

When it comes to justice, however, there is no natural motive to perform just actions distinct from the sense of the rightness of such actions. Hume considers, and rejects, some possible motives to respect property rights, or to act justly. One is that we are motivated to comply with the rules of justice by self-interest. But this is not only a motive which we disapprove of but is also one inimical to justice. It is the motive that 'is the source of all injustice and violence; nor can a man ever correct those vices, without correcting and restraining those *natural* movements of that appetite' (T 3.2.1.10). So perhaps the natural motive to comply with justice is a general affection for the public good. But Hume thinks, quite plausibly, there is no such passion as a general concern for the public good as such. The object of this putative passion would be 'too remote and too sublime' to affect us (T 3.2.1.11). Concern for others, whilst real, is limited to one's local circle and is facilitated by sympathy (T 3.2.1.12). Nor can this local concern of benevolence be the motive of justice. One may owe someone even if they are someone whom one dislikes personally.

So, there is no natural motive to justice. Nevertheless, there *is* a virtue of justice. How is that possible? Hume offers an ingenious explanation of how certain practices emerge from natural motives, limited benevolence, and how these practices become conventions that form the basis of the rules of justice. Our *original* or natural motives that lead to the establishment become transformed into a *moral* motive to comply with those rules.

Part of Hume's ingenuity lies in his response to the 'selfish' theory, the rough idea that moral behaviour is underpinned by self-interest. My acting (apparently) generously toward another person can be understood as expressing my calculation that doing so will ultimately benefit myself. On a larger scale, the conventions that govern property can be seen as emerging through awareness that such conventions serve the self-interest of all those involved. If I do not take what you have, and I pay my debts, my own interest is served. Crucially, furthermore, my justifying reason to adhere to such conventions is my recognition that doing so benefits me. The theory provides, therefore, an explanation of how such conventions arise and an account of what reasons there are to follow them. As should be evident, this is a very crude version of the theory, and it is capable of being developed into a rather more sophisticated one. The major point in its favour is that it is able to *explain* how respect for property came into being, why people comply with it, and why there are reasons to respect the conventions governing it. The theory does not rest on some instinct to respect property, an implausible concern for the wellbeing of society, or something metaphysically baroque.

Hume recognises the importance of offering an explanation and sees the attraction of the selfish theory. Nevertheless, the key difference between his account and the selfish account lies in the following. Self-interest plays a crucial role in the *origin* of the conventions which govern property, but when such conventions are established the motives that lead to compliance change. Once the conventions are established out of self-interest, we come to appreciate them independently of the motives that lead to their establishment. That is, we come to see them in distinctly moral lights. So, a key sense in which justice is an *artificial* virtue is that the motivation distinctive of justice is the product of the conventions. This is different from the selfish theory which appeals to self-interest not merely to explain how the conventions are established but also why people comply and why they have a reason to comply. Let us now turn to Hume's explanation of the emergence of justice to get a better sense of his position and its relation to the selfish theory.

HUME'S GENEALOGY OF JUSTICE

Hume presents his account of the origin of justice in T 3.2.2. The account he offers is what a near-contemporary of Hume, Dugald Stewart, called 'a conjectural history'.[3] The origins of the practice of justice stretch further back than historical documentation can attest, so we need to offer a theory of the origins of justice in the absence of historical evidence. As Stewart puts it, when 'we are unable to ascertain how men have actually conducted themselves upon particular occasions, [we consider] in what manner they are likely to have proceeded, from the principles of their nature, and the circumstances of their external situation'.[4] The explanation proceeds with a hypothesis of what kinds of situations human beings prior to the invention of justice found themselves in, what kinds of psychology they had, and how the combination of the two would lead to the emergence of justice.[5] With regard to circumstances, Hume begins by noting that we are animals to whom the environment has not been particularly kind. Humanity has 'numberless wants and necessities' and 'slender means' to meet them (T 3.2.2.2), needing shelter, labour to produce food, and other inconveniences. The labour of a solitary person lacks three features Hume calls force, ability, and security. Acting alone, one's requirements outstrip one's time and effort or force. Furthermore, there is a great variety of different tasks, so it is not possible to become sufficiently practiced and skilled in each. Finally, even one's best efforts can fail, and to a ruinous and possibly fatal extent.

What solves this problem is 'society' which, at this rudimentary stage, is best conceived of as co-operative behaviour between human beings. Hume emphasises that society could not emerge if humans were ever really in some 'savage and solitary state' (T 3.2.22) even though it is true that society solves the problems engendered were they in such a state. This is because the supposed individuals need to come to realise that co-operation would be beneficial. They need to 'be sensible of its advantages; and 'tis impossible, in their wild uncultivated state, that by study and reflection alone, they shou'd ever be able to attain such knowledge' (T 3.2.2.4). This remark is significant since it marks a key difference between Hume's account and that of Thomas Hobbes.[6] Hobbes's account of the emergence of human society famously envisages human beings outside of society—the state of nature—as radically solitary and antagonistic. Life for pre-social humans, Hobbes tells us, would have been 'solitary, nasty, brutish, and short'. Hume thinks that if that were really the case, society could never arise and so the 'very first state and situation [of humanity] may justly be esteemed social' (T 3.2.2.14). One needs to bear in mind that Hume holds that the state of nature Hobbes describes is an impossible one. The 'suppos'd *state of nature*,...[should be allowed] as a mere philosophical fiction, which never had, and never cou'd have any reality' (T 3.2.2.14). Some commentators have taken this to mean that *Hume* holds that his own account of the emergence of justice is a fiction,[7] but what he is referring to here is Hobbes's position, one that is 'describ'd as full of war, violence and injustice' (T 3.2.2.15).

Given that people need to be sensible of the advantages of society in order to form it, how then does Hume envisage the situation prior to the formation of justice? Hume thinks that humans live together because 'the natural appetite betwixt the sexes' initially brings people together and the relationship is supplemented with a 'a new tye' which is 'their concern for common offspring'. This yields 'a principle of union betwixt the parents and offspring, and forms a more numerous society' (T 3.2.2.4). In other words, prior to justice, humans lived in families, and in such a group the benefits of co-operation are easily observable.

So, humans naturally form small social groups. For such groups, nevertheless, there are 'incommodious' circumstances which involve 'natural temper' and 'outward' circumstances which prevent the larger social co-operation necessary for justice. By 'natural temper' Hume means that human beings are by nature generous as well as naturally selfish, but this generosity is limited. It tends to extend only to one's immediate circle. So 'instead of fitting men for large societies', limited generosity is almost as contrary to such societies 'as the most narrow selfishness' (T 3.2.2.6). The 'outward circumstances' concern the instability of goods. Hume distinguishes three kinds of goods, internal satisfaction of the mind, external advantages of the body, and 'the enjoyment of such possessions as we have acquir'd by our industry and good fortune' (T 3.2.2.7). The first, Hume thinks, is 'perfectly secure', and the second can be damaged by others, but to no direct advantage to those doing the injury. It is only the third type of goods that can be taken away from us.

This instability of possessions is what is key to the establishment of justice. As Hume emphasises more in the second *Enquiry*,[8] the instability of possessions is compounded by their *scarcity*. If we lived in a world with unlimited goods and resources, there would be no need for justice in Hume's sense. The limited extent of our generosity (our 'partial affections'), together with the instability and scarcity generate problems (the 'temptations arising from our circumstances') to which justice is a solution. But, of course, the idea of justice does not suddenly spring into the minds of the human animal. Instead, the remedy to the problems involves the gradual creation of an 'artifice', or 'more properly speaking, nature provides a remedy in the judgment and understanding' (T 3.2.2.9). Having perceived the benefits of co-operation within the family group, a convention emerges to 'bestow stability on the possession of those external goods, and leave everyone in the peaceable enjoyment' (T 3.2.2.9) of their own goods. The convention emerges not out of some explicit promise (we shall turn to what Hume says about promises later) but instead 'gradually', and 'acquires force by slow progression, and by our repeated experience of the inconveniences of transgressing it', just as 'two men, who pull the oars of a boat, do it by an agreement or convention, tho' they have never given promises to each other' (T 3.2.2.10).

Though one can become aware of the advantages of adhering to such conventions, there is a separate but related question of which passion motivates such adherence. The convention is supposed, among other things, to constrain the temptations of our natural selfishness. It is our natural selfishness, however, that in the end motivates our adherence. As Hume says, '[t]here is no passion...capable of controuling the interested affection, but the very affection itself, by an alteration of its direction' (T 3.2.2.13). When one reflects, we realise we 'make much greater advances in the acquiring possessions than by running into the solitary and forlorn condition, which must follow upon violence and an universal licence' (T 3.2.2.13).

Thus, we have an explanation of the emergence of the *stability* of property—of refraining from taking that of others—together with an account of the passion which underlies our adherence to that convention. As Hume puts it, it is 'only from the selfishness and confin'd generosity of man, along with the scanty provision nature has made for his wants, that justice derives its origin' (T 3.2.2.18). Given also what we have mentioned about interest being that passion which motivates compliance with the convention, it might seem that Hume's position does not differ in relevant ways from other variants of the 'selfish theory'. But what is important to note is that his account does not stop here. For, he says, although '*self-interest* is the original motive to the *establishment* of justice [it is]...a *sympathy* with *public* interest [that] is the source of the *moral* approbation, which attends that virtue' (T 3.2.2.24). Human beings become motivated to comply with justice by the moral sense rather than self-interest. How so?

A first thing to consider is that, as Hume notes, although the convention is established by the passion of interest, the relation between interest and the convention is 'somewhat singular' (T 3.2.2.22). A single act of justice can be contrary to the interest of some individual. Thus, someone might impoverish themselves and therefore have 'reason to wish...the laws of justice were for a moment suspended' (T 3.2.2.22). Second, a single act of justice can also be contrary to public interest. A generous and caring person might restore a huge sum of money to a miser and so the money fails to do the good it might have, were the generous person to give it to charity instead. What this shows, according to Hume, is that the object of our regard with respect to justice is the convention itself or 'the whole plan or scheme', and a recognition that it is 'highly conducive...to the support of society, and the well-being of every individual' (T 3.2.2.22). Furthermore, we recognise that each individual must 'find himself a gainer, on ballancing the account', because without that convention humans would return to the 'savage and solitary' condition (T 3.2.2.22).

This, however, does not explain why we come to approve morally of just agents. As society grows larger, the connection between our own interests and the observance and violation of the conventions can become remote. We can lose sight of how a particular violation of them by ourselves can have deleterious effects on society. However, sympathy allows us to engage with the feelings of others who are the victims of injustice. Sympathising with the injury to another's interest distances us from our own interests and brings with it an impartiality. Even when 'the injustice is so distant from us, as no way to affect our interest, it still displeases us' (T 3.2.2.24). This explains how the moral sense comes into the picture and makes us evaluate morally acts of justice. But what of justice as a *virtue*? Recall that one key feature of a virtue is that it is a steady motive to action. And, as Hume notes, sympathy might produce moral sentiments, although it is 'too weak to controul our passions' (T 3.2.2.24). The virtue is acquired by 'private education and instruction'. Parents instil in children the 'principles of probity, and teach them to regard the observance of those rules, by which society is maintain'd, as worthy and honourable'. We take on as second nature 'sentiments of honour' (T 3.2.2.26) that 'acquire such firmness and solidity, that they may fall little short of those principles, which are the most essential to our natures, and the most deeply radicated in our internal constitution' (T 3.2.2.24). So, although the conventions of justice are products of artifice, they become the objects of moral appropriation which in turn leads to the inculcation of a character trait or disposition to respect justice.[9] This is the disposition that can be itself the object of moral approbation. The disposition is reinforced by another interest, namely an interest we have in our own reputations. Here Hume is picking up on what Mandeville took to be the origins of honour itself, namely a form of 'self-liking' which is reinforced by the opinions of others directed towards us. Honourable behaviour, very roughly, is motivated by a desire for the approval of others.[10] Hume, however, takes our reputation, the view of ourselves in the eyes of others, as reinforcing the independent disposition inculcated by education rather than as constituting it.

RULES, PROPERTY, AND THE INTELLIGIBILITY OF PROMISING

The establishment of a convention changes the natural relation of *possession* to the moral relation of *property*. But Hume recognises that his discussion of the convention thus far is a highly abstract one, and as such, 'it can never serve to any purpose, while it remains in such general terms' (T 3.2.3.1). At the beginning of the convention, Hume takes it that the natural relation of possession is the starting point, and that 'everyone continue[s] to enjoy what he is at present possess'd of' (T 3.2.3.4). After this there are issues that need to be settled by appeal to more determinate rules, namely occupation, prescription, accession, and succession.

The rule of occupation is essentially the same as first possession, but, Hume notes, this brings difficulties including, for example, the extent of possession. One might claim the right to an unoccupied small desert island but the first person landing on a land mass 'as large as *Great Britain*, extends his property no farther than his immediate possession' (T 3.2.3.8). More importantly, it is difficult to determine first possession since how long ago it was first possessed is often obscure, so the next thing to appeal to in adjudicating disputes is *prescription* or 'long possession' (T 3.2.3.9). Goods that are 'connected in an intimate manner' with one's property become one's property by *accession*. Thus, to use Hume's own example, the fruits of a tree that you own are your property by accession (T 3.2.3.10). Property is also determined by *succession*, which is a matter of property bequeathed to those 'who are dearest to them' (T 3.2.3.11).

These rules tend to focus on the stability of possession, but of course property can be transferred and traded. Hume notes that such a transference can sometimes take on a solemn and symbolic character where, for example, the giving of a key to a granary represents the transference of the corn within it. This, he says, is a 'kind of superstitious practice...resembling the *Roman Catholic* superstitions' (T 3.2.4.2), though in the second *Enquiry* he emphasises that, whereas the ceremonies of religion are 'frivolous, useless, and burdensome', those of justice have great utility (EPM 3.38).

Hume then turns to discuss the nature of promises. He argues that promises would be unintelligible before the advent of human conventions and that, even if they were so intelligible, they could not morally obligate. Suppose there were no conventions of the kind we have already discussed. How then would we understand a promise? Hume considers and rejects some possible candidates which centre on the idea that promises have the status they do in virtue of some kind of 'act of the mind'. The first candidate he considers is that promising consists in some *resolution*. I might resolve to mow the lawn this weekend but not carry through that resolution. This would not be considered a moral failing in a way that breaking a promise would be, so promising is not a matter of a mere resolution. Nor can it be a *desire* to perform some action, not least because often promises bind us to things that we do not want to do. The act of *willing* to do something will not do the trick either. Willing only produces immediate actions whereas promises concern future actions. But perhaps one could say that a promise is a matter of willing an *obligation*. However, the moral status of something is determined by the sentiments so to will an obligation is to will into existence a particular sentiment. But we cannot, by a simple act of will, bring into existence any sentiment, let alone a moral one. Finally, Hume reiterates the considerations that led him to view justice as an artificial virtue to support the view that the disposition to keep promises is equally artificial. The motivation to keep promises is, like justice, simply that of the rightness of promise keeping. That is, there is no independent motive of which we approve, as there is in the case of parental care.

If then, we cannot make sense of promising independently of convention, how do conventions make them intelligible? The point of justice was to ensure the stability of possessions, and the original motive for the establishment of that convention was self-interest. But as well as stability of possession, we can also mutually benefit by exchange of possessions. This was already touched upon when Hume discusses the transference of property by consent, but there the exchange is an immediate swap. What, though, if I offer to give you something at a later date in exchange for something now? Suppose I am growing chilli peppers that will not be ready until the summer, but you have garlic presently, so I offer you chillis in the future in exchange for garlic now. Now, I might do this out of affection for the other party, but what Hume is considering are exchanges between persons who share no such affection for each other. These arrangements have an obvious weak point. I could take your garlic now but not hold up my side of the bargain. Nevertheless, the overall utility of such patterns of behaviour where the agreement is fulfilled is an obvious one. What is needed is some way to secure future compliance. To that end:

> there is a *certain form of words* invented...by which we bind ourselves to the performance of any action. This form of words constitutes what we call a *promise*, which is the sanction of the interested commerce of mankind. When a man says *he promises any thing*, he in effect expresses a resolution of performing it; and along with that, by making use of this *form of words*, subjects himself to the penalty of never being trusted again in the case of failure.
>
> (T 3.2.5.10)

The key thing here is the penalty of not being trusted again in case of failure. What one is doing when promising is putting one's reputation at stake. The resolution itself is secondary, since, even if the resolution were weak or even absent, the making of the promise—the speech act—puts one's reputation on the line.

Let us expand upon two aspects of this account. The first turns on the notion of credit. Hume's account of the emergence of this phenomenon is centred on the exchange of property, and notice that the person promising to repay what is owed at a later date is one who is in credit. During the eighteenth century, the notions of credit, trust, and honour were bound tightly together.[11] The etymology of 'credit' comes from the Latin for trust (credere), and in Samuel Johnson's dictionary, the second definition of 'credit' is 'honour, reputation', and the third 'esteem and good opinion'. Hume here is bringing the notions together in the explanation of the phenomenon of promising. Second, it is clear that the practice—the 'faithful fulfilling of engagements'—emerges from a 'sense of interest' (T 3.2.5.11), but like our disposition to act justly, Hume thinks that practice moves beyond that 'sense of interest'. He calls this sense of interest 'the first obligation to justice', but fidelity to promises itself then acquires the distinctly moral character which 'becomes a new obligation upon mankind' (T 3.2.5.12). Remember that an artificial virtue is distinct from a natural virtue in a number of respects, one of which is that the former actions are motivated solely by a sense of the moral rightness of the actions. Like the case of justice, this does not preclude the idea that some people respect the property of others or keep their promises solely because of their own self-interest. But it does provide an account of how, despite its artificiality, humans can be motivated to keep promises in virtue of its being morally right so to do.

GOVERNMENT AND ALLEGIANCE

After some further reflections on justice, Hume turns to the origin of government. We have noted how self-interest plays a role in the origin of justice, but at the beginning of his discussion of government, Hume notes that our imagination and passions tend to extend only to what is local to us in space and time (T 3.2.7.2), and so remote breaches of justice tend to affect us very little. What is needed is a way to correct this weakness and constrain action so that temptations are curbed, and that in turn requires a view from some position which is independent from my narrow one. This is a position that can be occupied by very few, the persons 'whom we call civil magistrates, kings, and their ministers, our governors and rulers...have no interest...in any act of injustice...[and] have an immediate interest in every execution of justice, which is so necessary to the upholding of society' (T 3.2.7.6). Government not merely further stabilises justice but also enables co-ordinated planning for larger projects that further our interests (T 3.2.7.7).

What though of our allegiance to such a state or government? Again, Hume appeals to self-interest in the establishment of a political state, but in a way that differs from those of the 'selfish' theory. Thomas Hobbes saw the state of nature—the one without political society—as a state of perpetual war between solitary individuals, and the formation of a political society as a way of providing an end to the miserable state. Whilst Hume sees government as offering a solution to problems that would emerge without it, he does not think that there could be no society without government. He thinks that the problems are different ones and that the starting points are different, writing that

> ...so far am I from thinking with some philosophers, that men are utterly incapable of society without govern, that I assert the first

rudiments of government to arise from quarrels, not among men of the same society, but among those of different societies.

(T 3.2.8.1)

Hume thinks that smaller societies would be led to a notion of government from conflict and war between those societies. During these periods a unifying authority is required, which initially is a temporary arrangement, dispensed with when peace is secured, but through its existence the society becomes aware of its advantages, not only in securing relations between those small societies but also within such societies.

As societies grow, so does the tendency of internal tensions. Humans comprising societies are still prone to the temptations of self-interest as well as an inability to appreciate long-term over short-term self-interest, and when more desirable goods are produced by co-operation, the greater the temptations. The establishment of some kind of authority is therefore necessary. Whilst the martial leaders are the obvious candidates in times of war, when it comes to issues of justice in peacetime, we would select persons to be magistrates and 'determine their power, and *promise* them obedience' (T 3.2.8.3). Now, those 'magistrates' can be martial leaders, declared to be kings, and the like, but the important point in calling them 'magistrates' is their role in administering justice. We offer our consent to such persons, and presumably incentivise them in some way to play that role.

Hume though is very clear that his position differs from a social contract account of our obligation to any state. He describes this view as follows:

> All men...are born free and equal: Government and superiority can only be establish'd by consent: The consent of men, in establishing government, imposes on them a new obligation, unknown to the laws of nature. Men, therefore, are bound to obey their magistrates, only because they promise it; and if they had not given their word, either expressly or tacitly, to preserve allegiance, it wou'd never have become a part of their moral duty.
>
> (T 3.2.8.3, italics removed)

This view, very crudely, is that the legitimacy of any state is given by the consent of its constituents. This may be explicit but what is doing the bulk of the work is that of tacit consent. If you live within the state and share in the benefits it provides, then you are tacitly consenting to its legitimacy. Hume, however, thinks this confuses the causes that bring about the establishment of the state and its present source of authority. Instead, although the duty of allegiance was 'at first grafted onto the obligation of promises' (T 3.2.8.3), it is subsequently the advantages of government that provide an obligation. And as in the cases of justice and promises, the concern with self-interest is then transformed to moral rightness by the moral sense (T 3.2.8.7).

OF CHASTITY AND MODESTY

Hume closes his account of the artificial virtues with a discussion of female chastity and that 'exterior modesty, which we require in the expressions, and dress, and behaviour of the fair sex' (T 3.2.12.2). As one might expect given the placement of the discussion in the *Treatise*, Hume views this as an artificial virtue. His main interest is the explanation of its presence and so, Lorne Falkenstein notes, it is an exercise in social psychology.[12]

Two things are worth noting before we discuss Hume's explanation. The first is that Hume takes sexual appetite and child-rearing as powerful forces in human nature. As we noted, he takes human beings to be social prior to the creation of justice and this owes itself to sexual appetite and affection for one's offspring. Second, as noted by Christopher Berry, Hume's contemporaries, including Mandeville and Rousseau, tended to think that women were naturally chaste and modest in behaviour.[13]

What animates this view, Hume thinks, is that appeal to social utility cannot explain the presence of such dispositions (T 3.2.12.1). Hume seeks to show that it can. He begins with the observation that human infancy is protracted and that infants require a great deal of care. This is another way in which humans experience an 'unnatural conjunction of infirmity, and of necessity' (T 3.2.2.2). The concern for childcare leads to a relationship between the parents, again something Hume refers to in his account of pre-justice societies. It is a 'new tye' in addition to the sexual one which 'takes place in their concern for their common offspring' (T 3.2.2.4). But, Hume notes, there is a 'trivial and anatomical' difference which produces difference in behaviour (T 3.2.12.3). Whilst mothers can be sure that the offspring is theirs, fathers cannot. So, fathers need some way to ensure that their parental concern is not, as Hume puts it, 'directed to the wrong object', and so there needs to be something that secures conjugal fidelity (T 3.2.12.3).

Hume considers views he associates with 'speculative philosophers' to secure some fidelity. First, the idea that transgression from the conjugal bed be punished either legally or by impugning the woman's reputation. Hume's speculative philosopher reasons that any legal case would be impossible to prove and that furthermore, the temptation might be too much to outweigh the fear of reputational damage. So, there must be some way of even extinguishing the temptation by 'some preceding backwardness or dread' (T 3.2.12.5).

This, however, is a position Hume rejects. If the speculative philosopher had

> not a perfect knowledge of human nature, he would be apt to regard [this view] as...chimerical....For what means, wou'd he say, of perswading mankind, that the transgressions of conjugal duty are more infamous than any other kind of injustice, when 'tis evident they are more excusable, upon account of the greatness of the temptation? And what possibility of giving a backwardness to the approaches of a pleasure, to which nature has inspir'd so strong a propensity; and a propensity that 'tis absolutely requisite in the end to comply with, for the support of the species?
> (T 3.2.12.6)

Hume thinks that this explanation makes relationships rather too contractual and cynical. Instead, he offers an altogether more straightforward explanation:

> Those who have an interest in the fidelity of women, naturally disapprove of their infidelity, and all the approaches to it. Those, who have no interest, are carry'd along with the stream, and are also apt to be affected with sympathy for the general interests of society.
> (T 3.2.12.7)

Instead of the sanctions of the reputational threat, Hume holds that a general rule of fidelity is simply instilled during education. But Hume also recognises a double-standard. He says that men 'bear nearly the same proportion to the obligations of women', and that it is contrary to the interest of society that men should have 'an *entire* liberty of indulging their appetites' (T 3.2.12.9). Nevertheless, the obligation for men measured in terms of disapproval for such infidelity is much less, as testified by the 'practice and sentiments of all nations and ages' (T 3.2.12.9).

NOTES

1. Cohon (2008), Chapter Six refers not to justice when discussing the relevant sections of the *Treatise*, preferring instead to talk of the virtue of 'honesty with respect to property'. For a historical explanation of Hume's view of justice, see Harris (2019). For a discussion of just how narrow or not Hume's account might be, see Cruise (2020).
2. See, for example, Garret (2007) and Cohon (2008), Chapter Six.
3. Stewart, *An Account of the Life of Adam Smith*.
4. Stewart, *An Account of the Life of Adam Smith*, p.32.
5. Conjectural histories are forms of inference to the best explanation. For discussion in connection with Hume, see Evnine (1993) and Santos Castro (2017).
6. I owe this observation to Alessio Vaccari.
7. See Williams (2002), p.29, and Queloz (2021), Chapter Four. For criticisms see Kail (2025).
8. See *An Enquiry Concerning the Principles of Morals*, 4.2–3.
9. Hume's justice can be seen as what is known as a 'negative virtue', that is a disposition to refrain from certain actions.
10. For an informative discussion of Mandeville's views, and Hume's relation to them, see Watts (2019), Chapter Two.
11. For discussion, see Pearsall (2008), Chapter Four.
12. Falkenstein (2015), p.146.
13. Berry (2003)

FURTHER READING

Useful introductions to this part of the *Treatise* are Baillie (2000), Chapter Six, and Wright (2009), Chapter Nine. For different accounts of the artificial virtues, see Cohon (2008), Part Two, Baier (2010), and Magri (2015). For a general study of Hume's political thought, see Stewart (1992). On chastity and modesty, see Baier (1979), Berry (2003) and Falkenstein (2015).

9
OF THE OTHER VIRTUES AND VICES

INTRODUCTION

Part Three of Book Three of the *Treatise* contains Hume's discussion of the natural virtues. We touched briefly on what those are in the previous chapter but here we look at them in more detail. We begin by discussing the interplay of sympathy and the moral sense in the epistemology of the natural virtues. We then discuss greatness of mind, benevolence, and Hume's provocative views on natural abilities. Finally, we discuss Hume's conclusion to Book Three.

T 3.3.1 OF THE ORIGIN OF THE NATURAL VIRTUES AND VICES

T 3.3.1 begins by outlining in general Hume's theory of the natural virtues. He reminds us of his thesis that the 'chief spring or actuating principle of the human mind' (T 3.3.1.2) is pleasure and pain, the perceptions of good and evil which then produce motivation. This is coupled with the claim that moral distinctions 'depend entirely on certain peculiar sentiments of pain and pleasure' (T 3.3.1.3), the perceptions of the moral sense we discussed in Chapter Seven. Virtues are the durable character traits that produce actions, and actions are 'a sign of some quality… which extend over the whole conduct, and enter into the personal character' (T 3.3.1.4). Our awareness of virtue causes the moral pleasure, vice the moral pain, and these perceptions in turn produce the indirect passions. If I am sensing my own virtue, I will feel pride, or humility when sensing my vices. When sensing the virtue of others, I feel love or, in the case of vice, hatred.

As I mentioned in Chapter Seven, the natural virtues fall into four different kinds: qualities or character traits that are (1) useful to their possessors, (2) useful to others, (3) immediately agreeable to oneself, and (4) agreeable to others. Thus, working backwards from this list, that which is agreeable to others includes '[w]it, and a certain easy and disengaged behaviour' (T 3.3.1.27). Those which are agreeable to ourselves, Hume discusses at length in EPM 7, and include cheerfulness, dignity of character, tranquility, and benevolence. This last example shows how some virtues can have two directions. Benevolence is immediately agreeable to the benevolent person, but it is also useful to others. This brings us to the virtues useful to others which include 'beneficence, charity, generosity' (T 3.3.1.11), and many others. Finally, qualities useful to ourselves include 'prudence, temperance, frugality, industry' (T 3.3.1.24) and, again, many others.

This departs from Hutcheson's view that the moral sense picks out a single character trait, namely that of benevolence. Hume's disjunctive account of virtue is empirically grounded, a survey of the qualities which humans call virtues and vices. As we saw in Chapter Seven, the pleasures and pains of the moral sense in Hutcheson's account constituted a form of sensitivity to benevolence, modelled on the function of bodily sensation which makes salient to creatures that which is conducive to their bodily wellbeing. The moral sense makes salient to human beings that which is conducive to societal wellbeing. We also saw that the relation between the perceptions of pleasure and pain and the character traits is not at all straightforward, that the perceptions need to be corrected by reason and reflection, but that nevertheless the general sensitivity is a natural one. Let us now apply that to Hume.

Hume writes that virtues must 'be allowed to have a natural beauty and amiableness, which, at first, antecedent to all precept or education, recommend them to the esteem of uninstructed mankind, and engages their affections' (EPM 5.4), but, like Hutcheson, he holds that the sensitivity of the moral sense is complicated. Some virtues, like wit, immediately produce moral sentiments, but in other cases the mechanism of sympathy is required.

Hume begins his discussion of the role of sympathy at T 3.3.1.7 by 'considering anew the nature and force' of sympathy. When a passion in the mind of someone causes an action, our perception of that action brings to our mind the passion that causes the action. Sympathy, Hume reminds us, is also important in the explanation of our moral approval of justice. It is our extensive sympathy with others which leads us to feel the moral sentiment of disapproval for actions that pain others. He notes that the qualities that are useful to others, those with the 'tendency to public advantage' (T 3.3.1.11), operate similarly by sympathy. The difference between the two is that the natural virtues always produce good, whereas a particular act prescribed by justice might sometimes go against the good, such as a judge taking 'from a poor man to give to the rich' (T 3.3.1.12).

Often, then, moral sense is triggered by our sympathetic response to others and their interests. But it is very important to note that sympathy is a highly variable mechanism. That is to say, our sympathetic responses are affected by a number of different factors which we can nevertheless bring under the umbrella term of 'closeness'. The closer a person is to us the more powerful the sympathetic response, the further away the less powerful its effect. First, we can think of this in terms of spatial contiguity. My sympathetic response to someone hitting their head next to me is far more powerful than learning of the same thing happening miles away. Similarly, distance in time affects sympathy. Hearing of a fatal accident that happened yesterday tends to elicit a stronger response than to one that happened 100 years ago. Furthermore, closeness can be understood in familial and cultural terms. I sympathise more readily with my family and friends, and I sympathise more with those culturally more similar to me than others. But if sympathy is thus variable, this appears to pose a problem for

Hume. For judgments about the virtue of character do not vary even though sympathy, and hence the liveliness of sentiments, does. We judge someone to be virtuous whether they are next door or 100 miles away, living today or a century ago. As Hume puts it:

> sentiments...must vary according to the distance or contiguity of the objects; nor can I feel the same lively pleasure from the virtues of a person, who liv'd in *Greece* two thousand years ago, that I feel from the virtues of a familiar friend and acquaintance. Yet I do not say that I esteem the one more than the other.
>
> (T 3.3.1.15)

How is this possible? Hume's answer begins with the observation that our 'situation, with regard to both persons and things, is in continual fluctuation' (T 3.3.1.15). Our relation to people changes and with it there is a constant shift in our sympathetic responses. Furthermore, each of us occupies our peculiar positions with the concomitant sympathetic fluctuation. Because of this, it is 'impossible we cou'd ever converse together on any reasonable terms, were each of us to consider characters and persons, only as they appear from his peculiar point of view' (T 3.3.1.15). Thus:

> to prevent those continual *contradictions*, and arrive at a more *stable* judgment of things, we fix on some *steady* and *general* point of view; and always, in our thoughts, place ourselves in them, whatever may be our present situation. In like manner, external beauty is determin'd merely by pleasure; and 'tis evident, a beautiful countenance cannot give so much pleasure, when seen at the distance of twenty paces, as when it is brought nearer us.
>
> (T 3.3.1.15)

There are two aspects of this feature of Hume's discussion that we should note. The first is the method of correction. Correction occurs not because we recognise that our sympathetic responses are out of line with the virtues and vices. It is rather that, unless we are responsive to possible mistakes and our partial views, interpersonal communication would not be possible. The words we use need standards of use, and with that, our recognition that we might be wrong. Hence, we converge on a point of view which corrects our peculiar situations. It would be 'impossible we cou'd ever make use of language, or communicate our sentiments to one another, did we not correct the momentary appearances of things' (T 3.3.1.16). What, however, this correction converges on is precisely those character dispositions that comprise the virtues.

The second point concerns the fact that the variability of sympathy relates to the different degrees of force and liveliness of the sentiments. The issue, as we have seen, is that the liveliness of sentiments is greater the closer we are to the object of sympathy. This is what the general point of view aims to correct. At one point, in this connection, Hume writes the following:

> We blame equally a bad action, which we read of in history, with one perform'd in our neighbourhood the other day: The meaning of which is, that we know from reflection, that the former action wou'd excite as strong sentiments of disapproval as the latter, were it plac'd in the same position.
>
> (T 3.3.1.18)

This seems straightforward, but it raises an issue.[1] Hume has told us that moral judgments involve sentiments essentially, partly based on the considerations related to moral internalism which we have discussed previously. Passages such as these, however, seem to go back on that claim. It seems to allow that moral judgments do not involve actual sentiments but involve instead beliefs about what sentiments we would have, were we to be in the appropriate circumstances. From what Hume tells us it appears there is an inconsistency between Hume telling us that moral sentiments are essential to moral judgments on the one hand, and, on the other, the nature of a moral judgment made from the moral point of view.

There is a problem for Hume here, but not the one that commentators identify. That problem is the apparent inconsistency between the claim that moral judgments must involve sentiments with the claim that corrected moral judgment only requires beliefs about sentiments we would have in certain circumstances. Instead, the real problem lies in Hume's general account of *belief*. Recall what we said about the role of sentiments and the nature of belief. *Ideas* of pleasures and pains, ideas of sentiments, are themselves nothing but faint copies of those sentiments which figure in the contents of belief. Sentiments are present in every thought and judgment, even merely hypothetical ones, because they are constituents of the contents of such thoughts and judgements. The claim that there are no sentiments involved, merely thoughts about hypothetical ones in the general point of view is mistaken since it does not take into account Hume's views on ideas and content. When there are beliefs there *are* sentiments because beliefs involve lively ideas. There is, therefore, no inconsistency of the kind described. However, there is a problem for Hume's account of belief. The state of belief for Hume is one where those ideas or sentiments are forceful and lively, and the *degree* of belief is a matter of the degree of force and liveliness of the idea. But the degree of force and liveliness of any idea, and hence belief, also varies with sympathy in the manner we have described which, absurdly, would appear to imply that we believe to a higher degree in the virtue of a present person than one in the past. 'Yet I do not say', Hume says, 'that I esteem the one more than the other' (T 3.3.1.15). So, the variation of sympathy seems to imply a variation of the degree of belief which is inconsistent with the fact that we do not vary the degree of belief across distance.

Hume notes a second feature, or 'remarkable circumstance' (T 3.3.1.19) in our approval of the natural virtues. We have talked of character traits, and these are tendencies towards different actions. To say someone is generous is to say that they tend to act in a certain way in the relevant circumstances. To put this differently, a generous person is *disposed* to act in certain ways under certain circumstances. Philosophers often illustrate the notion of a disposition with the example of fragility. To say a glass is fragile is to say that under certain circumstances the glass would break (e.g. were I to drop it on concrete or hurl it against the wall). The glass remains fragile even if it never breaks, which is to say it is disposed to break even though that disposition is never *manifested* when the glass is never dropped or hurled against the wall. That is, the circumstances of its breaking are never realised. But there is a further complication to add to the notion of a disposition. Suppose I wrap the glass in bubble wrap. The glass is still disposed to break, even though, when it is hurled against the wall or dropped on the concrete, it does not break. That is because the bubble wrap *masks* the disposition: the circumstances for its breaking are met, but something gets in the way, preventing its manifestation.

With this in mind, we now turn to Hume's second 'remarkable circumstance'. Character traits are dispositions and what Hume means by those qualities useful to others include, among other things, their disposition to produce useful ends. But what happens in cases when people act in certain ways that would tend to be useful, but something prevents those actions from producing useful ends? Hume puts the point like this:

> Where a person is possess'ed of a character...we esteem him virtuous, and are delighted with the view of his character, even tho' particular accidents prevent its operation, and incapacitate him from being serviceable to his friends and country.
>
> (T 3.3.1.19)

Such a situation Hume dubs 'virtue in rags', and it raises what might seem to be a problem. Hume has told us that we come to know the character dispositions of another person through her actions, actions that constitute the manifestations of that character. But when the virtue is in rags, the actions do not produce good, and yet we do still esteem that character trait. How then is this possible?

Hume responds by noting that we can distinguish between the general tendency of a thing and the circumstances with which it interacts, or the 'external circumstances...[which] render it altogether effectual' (T 3.3.1.2). We might esteem a house good when it provides 'all the commodities of life' though it is unoccupied. Here it is disposed to produce certain effects but the circumstances for its manifestation are not met. Analogously, a generous person alone in a desert has no opportunity to express her generosity. Furthermore, a generous person might be presented with the opportunity to help a needy person, but prevented from doing so because the road between the two persons is blocked, hence masking the disposition. We respond to the general tendency of the disposition despite the complications of the particular circumstances.

GREATNESS AND GOODNESS

Having discussed the epistemology of natural virtues, Hume then discusses some particular instances. We noted in Chapter Five that Hume giving a central role to pride in human nature can be seen as part of his campaign against a Christian interpretation of human nature, hence his claim 'that the world naturally esteems a well-regulated pride, which secretly animates our conduct' (T 3.3.2.13). This claim is made in the section entitled 'Of greatness of mind' which we discuss in this section, before turning to Hume's observations in T 3.3.3, 'Of goodness and benevolence'.

The topic considered in 'Of greatness of mind' is pride and humility and the 'vice or virtue that lies in their [i.e. pride's and humility's] excesses or just proportion' (T 3.3.2.1). Pride is a virtue when it is in 'just proportion' and, as such, resembles what Aristotle called 'magnanimity' which, literally translated, means 'great souled'. This is a complicated notion but for Aristotle it is a conception of one's self as worthy of great things, and, in particular, honour. A magnanimous person in this sense possesses virtues but is also proudly aware that one is such a person, an awareness that is itself a virtue. This would be pride in just proportion, whereas an 'over-weaning conceit' (T 3.3.2.1) is a vice and an excess.

Hume begins by describing the psychology which leads us to conceive of over-weaning conceit as a vice. There are two relevant principles, sympathy and comparison. Sympathy is of course something we have discussed, and we touched upon comparison in Chapter Five. The key point is encapsulated in the following:

> We judge more of objects by comparison, than by their intrinsic worth and value; and regard every thing as mean, when set in opposition to what is superior of the same kind.

(T 3.3.2.4)

This seems fairly straightforward. I might have, for example, two extremely good shirts but because one is better than the other, I tend to underestimate the value of the lesser shirt. This phenomenon is particularly pertinent when we compare ourselves with others. Our sense of our self can fluctuate depending on whom we are comparing ourselves with. But, Hume says, sympathy and comparison seem directly contrary to each other in operation. In straightforward sympathy, my sentiments become like your own. However, where comparison is operative, I come to feel the opposite sensation. Hume examines this phenomenon through variants of an example. First, I might find myself safely on land and imagine the miserable condition of some sailors in the midst of some storm. I may think on their misery to reinforce my happiness, but to little or no effect. It does not have the psychological force that actually being on the beach and witnessing the ship being tossed by the waves has. The ideas, and hence their effects, are more lively in this case. If, however, I am much closer to the sailors, and see the fear on their faces, my sense of my own safety and happiness, fostered by comparison, becomes overwhelmed by sympathy, and I share in the fear and distress of the sailors. From this, Hume concludes that, if the distance between two persons (in the different senses of distance we noted in the previous section) is very great, then comparison has little to no effect on us, and if we are very close to that person, sympathy overwhelms us. It is when matters lie in the middle that comparison operates (T 3.3.2.5).

What does this have to do with pride and greatness of mind? Often when we are in the presence of a superior person, comparison leads to our relative downgrading of ourselves, which is sometimes expressed in envy, but more often in terms of respect and esteem. Here sympathy operates. When we idly imagine someone vastly superior to us, the comparison has little effect on us. But when we are in the 'medium', comparison leads to a condemnation of 'over-weaning conceit'. By this, Hume means someone whom we judge to be inferior but who vastly overestimates themselves. On the one hand, their own overestimation makes us think less of ourselves in comparison, but at the same time, we know this not to be true of the person, so we come to disapprove of them. Hence our condemnation of false pride.

However, Hume generally thinks that pride is a good thing, something which is both useful and agreeable to the possessor. The agreeability does not require much comment: pride itself is a pleasure. But what about its usefulness? Unlike the other virtues, pride is not itself a direct source of motivation. So, if pride is not motivating, how could it be useful? Hume writes that whatever 'capacity any one may be endow'd with, 'tis entirely useless to him, if he not be acquainted with it, and form not designs suitable to it' (T 3.3.2.8). Why pride, therefore, may not only be 'allowable, but requisite in a character' (T 3.3.2.1) is because it constitutes a form of self-awareness that gives us a sense of our own capacities that encourages their expression. It is useful because it gives us a sense of ourselves which motivates us.

Indeed, Hume thinks, a little over-estimation of one's character is welcome (T 3.3.2.8). The 'rules of good breeding', nevertheless, require a mutual deference which has 'the appearance of modesty' (T 3.3.2.10). This leads to a telling observation about humility:

> I believe no one, who has any practice of the world, and can penetrate into the inward sentiments of men, will assert, that the humility, which good-breeding and decency require of us, goes beyond the outside, or that a thorough sincerity in this particular is esteem'd a real part of our duty. On the contrary, we may observe, that a genuine and hearty pride...if well-conceal'd and well-founded, is essential to the character of a man of honour.
>
> (T 3.3.2.11)

Humility, it seems, is not really a virtue in itself but instead is simply an interpretation of the rules of good breeding. This is significantly different from a Christian conception of humility where humility is an appropriate attitude to one's self when considering our dependence on God and our immeasurable inferiority to Him.

Pride is also the source of what Hume calls the 'heroic virtues', which include courage, intrepidity, ambition, love of glory, magnanimity, and 'all the other shining virtues of that kind' (T 3.3.2.13), and it is here that he contrasts his view with the Christian valorisation of humility which would take such virtues as 'pagan' rather than as genuine virtues. But he notes one further issue with pride, namely that, whilst heroic and military glory is 'much admir'd by the generality of mankind', a more nuanced judgment would be less sanguine in its praise, given the danger and bloodshed wrought by those embodying it. Nevertheless, there is something 'so dazzling' in such characters that we 'cannot refuse it our admiration' (T 3.3.2.15).

T 3.3.3 is entitled 'Of goodness and benevolence', and concerns virtues such as generosity, humanity, compassion, gratitude, friendship, fidelity and others. Such virtues fall under the category of being useful to others, but also stem from love which is immediately agreeable to the possessor. They therefore constitute an intersection of those useful to others and those immediately agreeable to their possessors. In terms of being useful to others, the utility tends not to extend beyond the possessor's immediate circle 'or, at most, beyond [the possessor's] native country' (T 3.3.3.2). So, as far as our moral approval is concerned, what we must take into account is how that character affects those in their immediate circle which requires adopting the common point of view described in the previous section. Hume also makes a number of observations in connection with these virtues, two of which are worth noting. First, he notes that anger, though always disagreeable, is not always vicious. Anger is sometimes an appropriate response to a situation, and its absence can sometimes show a failure to appreciate a situation, or 'imbecility' as Hume puts it. When, however, it issues in cruelty, it is the 'most detested of all vices' (T 3.3.3.7). Second, Hume mentions the 'ultimate test of merit or virtue' in this context: if I were to consider someone's character and 'if there be no relation in life, in which I cou'd not wish to stand to a particular person, his character must so far be allow'd to be perfect' (T 3.3.3.9).

NATURAL ABILITIES

We have noted during the discussion that Hume intimates that his conception of moral virtue is rather different from the versions of Christianity with which he was familiar. Indeed, he writes in a letter to Hutcheson, 'I desire to take my catalogue of virtues from Cicero's *Offices* rather than *The Whole Duty of Man*',[2] the latter being a rather dour Calvinist tract of the seventeenth century. What Hume says about natural abilities was also seen as provocative and he thinks again that there is a misunderstanding of human nature and virtue that is fostered by religious interpretation which his philosophy uncovers. This is a point that he makes more explicit in the comparable section of the *Enquiry Concerning the Principles of Morals*, an appendix he added in 1764 entitled 'Of some verbal disputes'. Theology, when united with ethics, he says, 'bends every branch of knowledge to its own purpose, without much regard to the phenomena of nature, or the unbiassed sentiments of the mind' (EPM AP 4.21).

As I mentioned, what Hume says about natural abilities was seen as provocative.[3] James Balfour, for example, writes that Hume

> has paved the way to enrich mankind with the possession of a thousand virtues that were never once dremt of before. For every minster of pleasure, even of the lowest kind, may put in his claim for virtue, and rise in his demands in proportion as he can increase our sensual gratifications. Strange morality indeed![4]

In addition to Balfour, Hume's view was attacked by James Beattie, John Leland, and anonymous publications. What then is controversial about what Hume is saying?

Balfour's complaint obviously gives us a hint of what Hume's position might be. Hume argues that the supposed distinction between natural abilities and moral virtues is mostly a verbal one, and whilst they 'are not altogether of the same kind, yet they agree in most material circumstances' (T 3.3.4.1). Hume agrees that natural abilities are 'suppos'd to have no merit or moral worth annex'd to them'(T 3.3.4.1), but he thinks there is no interesting differences between them and moral virtues. Among the natural abilities are sagacity, penetration, apprehension, charm (a 'certain *je-ne-sais-quoi* of agreeable and handsome' (T 3.3.4.11)), decorum, and memory. Some of these are straightforwardly intellectual capacities, and some, like charm and decorum, are social abilities. They are standing mental dispositions which, like the traditional virtues, produce pleasure, and have an 'equal tendency to procure the love and esteem of mankind' (T 3.3.4.1).

Hume's first move in questioning the distinction is to note that, as well as being the objects of love and esteem, some natural abilities add a 'new lustre to other virtues' (T 3.3.4.2). Thus, intellectual sensitivity adds to our view of a person's virtue. As he rhetorically asks in the *Enquiry Concerning the Principles of Morals*, who 'did ever say, except by way of irony, that such a one was a man of great virtue, but an egregious blockhead?' (EPM AP 4.21). However, his main contention is that the distinction is based on a faulty assumption that natural abilities are entirely involuntary and hence have no 'merit attending them' (T 3.3.4.3), whereas virtues are voluntary. Hume makes three replies to this claim. First, some virtues, especially those in pagan philosophy, are also involuntary, including fortitude and constancy, and so involuntariness is no bar to being a virtue. Second, the mark of being virtuous consists in the tendency to produce the moral sentiments, and this does not seem to depend on whether something is voluntary or not. Third, Hume notes that as 'to free-will, we have shown that it has no place with regard to actions' (T 3.3.4.3). Let us examine these responses, beginning with the third.

We must assume that the notion of free will mentioned here must be the liberty of indifference we discussed in Chapter Six. Hume rejected that and so here 'it has no place with regard to actions'. This means further that the voluntary and involuntary distinction at play in this discussion must be that resting on the liberty of indifference, whereby 'voluntary' must involve the capacity to have acted or chosen otherwise than one did. Of course, we might think that liberty of indifference is a mistaken notion but still draw the distinction between voluntary and involuntary, though in a different way. We might think that voluntary acts are those that are not coerced or caused by something that is in the relevant sense external to us. But here Hume is clearly thinking of voluntariness in the liberty of indifference sense.

Hume's second point, namely that we receive the moral sentiments from both, irrespective of whether the actions are voluntary or not, might lead us to question whether this is really the case. Do we really have the same sentiments from moral virtue as we do from a view of someone's intelligence? Let us, however, put this to one side and focus on his first response, which is the most interesting. He is objecting to the view that the distinction between a moral virtue and a natural ability might be thought to turn on the idea that we cannot blame or praise someone for something that is beyond their control. Hence, when something is subject to one's control, it is subject to moral appraisal and not when it is not. We might therefore think that this does mark a distinction, and that therefore Hume is wrong. Consider the following. One might say that an act that stems from a generous character is voluntary in the less metaphysically demanding sense than liberty of indifference. That is, the act is voluntary when it is not coerced or caused by something that is external to us. Hume might reply that the key point turns not on the act but the virtue itself. One cannot voluntarily choose to be generous or kind, nor change one's virtues. This being equally true of natural abilities means that there is no distinction between virtues and abilities. One might reply that there is some merit attached to the fact that one is capable of the *cultivation* of one's disposition to act generously. One is responsible in the sense that one should act in ways that try to make that disposition habitual. However, the key point to make here is to say on Hume's behalf that natural abilities can also be thus cultivated. My intellectual skill might be subject to cultivation by exercise or practice just as the supposedly moral one. So, there is no genuine difference here.

Hume takes matters even further in T 3.3.5, 'Some farther reflections concerning the natural virtues'. Thus far we have been talking about the approval of mental qualities, and Hume's scepticism that there is a difference between qualities that are moral as opposed to natural. Here he shifts to discuss qualities of body or fortune, again insinuating that the distinction between the admiration we have for someone's moral virtues, on the one hand, and their physical beauty, sexual attractiveness, and their wealth and estate on the other hand, is not as great as we might think.

There is something, depending on one's temperament, attractive about Hume's view. He takes a view of the evaluation of human beings in a rounded sense rather than focusing on the narrow sense of the moral. However, there is a way of marking the difference between moral virtues and natural abilities that seems plausible which Hume does not consider. One can use natural abilities to aim at vicious ends, but not so moral virtues. For example, a conman uses his intelligence and charm to exploit and manipulate people for his nefarious ends. An act of generosity necessarily aims at producing some good, and whilst it might unintentionally cause harm (I might give money to someone who uses it to fund crime), it is not the aim of the virtue. Moral virtues necessarily aim at the good, whereas natural abilities do not.

T 3.3.6 CONCLUSION OF THIS BOOK

Book One of the *Treatise* ended in a very dramatic conclusion as we discussed in Chapter Four. There we saw Hume exercised by the fact that reflection seems to destroy confidence and belief. In the conclusion to this book, Hume writes in such a way that suggests that reflection has the opposite effect, namely that it leads to the endorsement of the object of reflection. Let me quote at length.

> All lovers of virtue (and such we all are in speculation, however we may degenerate in practice) must certainly be pleas'd to see moral distinctions deriv'd from so noble a source, which gives us a just notion both of the *generosity* and *capacity* of our nature. It requires but very little knowledge of human affairs to perceive, that a sense of morals is a principle inherent in the soul, and one of the most powerful that enters into the composition. But this sense must certainly acquire new force, when reflecting on itself, it approves of those principles, from whence it is deriv'd, and finds nothing but what is great and good in its rise and origin. Those who resolve the sense of morals into original instincts of the human mind, may defend the cause of virtue with sufficient authority; but want the advantage, which those possess, who account for that sense by an extensive sympathy with mankind.
>
> (T 3.3.6.3)

Before we turn to the role of reflection, we should note that the last sentence of this paragraph reflects an exchange Hume had with Hutcheson whilst the two were corresponding about the draft of the *Treatise*. Hutcheson complained that the writing therein 'wants a certain warmth in the cause of virtue', and Hume replies by contrasting the roles of the painter and the anatomist of morality, identifying himself with the latter, someone interested to 'discover its secret springs and principles', rather than to 'describe the grace and beauty of its actions'.[5] Here Hume is both announcing that his philosophy both warmly recommends virtue and discovers its secret springs.

But what of the idea that the moral sense approves of itself when it reflects upon its origins? Some commentators here have taken this to be an account of normativity. We have thoughts of things being better or worse, right or wrong, good or bad, all of which require standards. But whence the source of such standards? Here the thought is that these standards owe themselves to reflection. There are different versions of this idea. Annette Baier, for example, reads the entire *Treatise* as embodying this view of normativity, writing that the 'whole of the *Treatise* searches for mental operations that can bear their own survey'.[6] Christine Korsgaard, on the other hand, works out a theory of normativity in terms of reflection independently, but nevertheless applies it to the passage quoted above. 'A faculty's verdicts are normative', she writes, 'when the faculty takes itself and its own operations for its objects, it gives a positive verdict'.[7]

Space prevents a thorough discussion of these views, but there are grounds to be sceptical that Hume is engaged in an overall project of accounting for normativity by reflection.[8] There is, however, a different way of understanding what Hume is driving at here. Recall that Hume is offering a naturalistic explanation of human phenomena, including morality, and, of course, part of this is offering an account of morality that does not appeal to a supernatural source. For those of a different and less secular view, such a project is not a welcome one, and, as we have seen, Hume's philosophy was not welcomed by those who saw—or wanted—a link between religion and morality. Hume's account might be seen to debunk morality itself, but he does not see it that way, and indeed he takes some religious practices to be positively inimical to morality. Hume's naturalistic explanation will not give religious interpretations of the claims of morality everything they require. However, what it does offer is an explanation that does not imply, as his critics might fear, that without God there is nothing recognisable as morality. It is in this connection that we need to recognise that Hume's claim that our moral distinctions have a 'noble' source and that there is 'nothing but what is great and good in its rise and origin' is made in a context where his secular naturalist interlocutors, such as Hobbes and Mandeville, do not believe that moral distinctions have a noble source, or good origin. Hume's theoretical account of the practice of morality 'discovers' something that Mandeville and Hobbes deny. Mandeville's explanation of the emergence of the co-operative practices Hume considers turns on the idea that vanity is the key determinant inasmuch as it is the 'glory' of the public recognition of one's overcoming one's tendency to immediate gratification, reinforced by the rhetoric of politicians, that underwrites seemingly co-operative behaviour, and Hobbes takes morality to be sustained by self-interest. But if one were to acknowledge the account of what explains that practice (its rise and origin) as correct, one cannot maintain with any confidence our ordinary view that moral motivation is *more* than motivation from self-interest (or vainglory). This version of naturalism might *explain* but it does not *vindicate*. It involves at some level a mismatch between the content of the motivations (I am acting for others) and the fact that it emerges is vainglory. So, it might seem that a naturalistic account could destabilise what it explains. But as we have seen, that is not Hume's position. He can explain our moral practice and allow that morality is how we think it is. Hence our moral sense can approve of itself.

NOTES

1 See e.g. Radcliffe (1994), Bricke (1996), pp.156ff, and Cohon (1997) for different views of this issue.
2 HL, I, pp.33–34.
3 For a survey of the reactions to Hume's 'wide view of the virtues', see Feiser (1998).
4 From *A delineation of the nature and obligation of morality*, quoted in Feiser (1998), p.300.
5 HL, I, p.32. For a discussion of the anatomist and the painter, see Abramson (2007).
6 Baier (1991), p.97.

7 Korsgaard (1996), p.60.
8 See Gill (1996) for critical discussion.

FURTHER READING

For a rather different take on the natural virtues, see Abramson (2015). For more discussion on the natural abilities see Attfield (1971), Fieser (1998) and Russell (1995), pp.125–127. On the general point of view—which connects to the moral sense—see Sayre-McCord (1994), Radcliffe (1994), and Cohon (1997). On reflective endorsement, see Baier (1991), Chapter Twelve, Gill (1996), and Cohon (1997), Chapter Twelve.

BIBLIOGRAPHY OF SECONDARY LITERATURE

Abramson, K., 2000, 'Sympathy and the Project of Hume's Second *Enquiry*', *Archiv für Geschichte der Philosophie*, 83:1, pp.45–80.
Abramson, K., 2007, 'Hume's Distinction between Philosophical Anatomy and Painting', *Philosophy Compass*, 2:5, pp.680–698.
Abramson, K., 2015, 'What's so "Natural" about Hume's Natural Virtues?', in D. C. Ainslie and A. Butler (eds), *The Cambridge Companion to Hume's* Treatise, Cambridge: Cambridge University Press.
van Ackeren, M. and Queloz, M. (eds), 2025, *Bernard Williams on Philosophy and History*, Oxford: Oxford University Press.
Ainslie, D. C., 1999, 'Scepticism about Persons in Book II of Hume's *Treatise*', *Journal for the History of Philosophy*, 37:3, pp.469–492.
Ainslie, D. C., 2005, 'Sympathy, and the Unity of Hume's Idea of the Self', in J. Jenkins, J. Whiting, and C. Williams (eds), *Persons and Passions: Essays in Honor of Annette Baier*, Notre Dame: University of Notre Dame Press.
Ainslie, D. C., 2015, *Hume's True Scepticism*, Oxford: Oxford University Press.
Ainslie, D. C. and Butler, A. (eds), 2015, *The Cambridge Companion to Hume's* Treatise, Cambridge: Cambridge University Press.
Alanen, L, 2006, 'The Powers and Mechanisms of the Passions', in S. Traiger (ed.), *The Blackwell Guide to Hume's* Treatise, Oxford: Blackwell.
Árdal, P., 1989, *Passion and Value in Hume's* Treatise, 2nd edition, Edinburgh: Edinburgh University Press.
Attfield, R., 1971, 'Talents, Abilities, Virtues', *Philosophy*, 46:177, pp.255–258.
Ayers. M., 1991, *Locke*, London and New York: Routledge.
Baier, A., 1979, 'Good Men's Women: Hume on Trust and Chastity', *Hume Studies*, 5:1, pp.1–19.
Baier, A., 1991, *A Progress of Sentiments: Reflections on Hume's* Treatise, Cambridge MA: Harvard University Press.

Baier, A., 2010, *The Cautious Jealous Virtue*, Cambridge MA: Harvard University Press.

Baillie, J., 2000, *Hume on Morality*, London: Routledge.

Barfoot, M., 1990, 'Hume and the Culture of Science in the Early Eighteenth Century', in M. A. Stewart (ed.), *Studies in the Philosophy of the Scottish Enlightenment*, Oxford: Clarendon Press.

Baxter, D., 2008, *Hume's Difficulty: Time and Identity in the* Treatise, London: Routledge.

Baxter, D., 2016, 'Hume on Space and Time', in P. Russell (ed.) *The Oxford Handbook of Hume*, Oxford: Oxford University Press.

Beebee, H., 2006, *Hume on Causation*, London: Routledge.

Beebee, H., 2011, 'Hume's Two Definitions: The Procedural Interpretation', *Hume Studies*, 37:2, pp.243–274.

Bell, M., 2002, 'Belief and Instinct in Hume's First *Enquiry*', in P. Millican (ed.) *Reading Hume on Human Understanding*, Oxford: Clarendon Press.

Berry, C., 2003, 'Lusty Women and Loose Imagination: Hume's Philosophical Anthropology of Chastity', *History of Political Thought*, 24:3, pp.415–433.

Boehm, M., 2014, 'Hume's Definitions of "Cause": Without Idealizations, within the Bounds of Science', *Synthese*, 191:16, pp.3803–3819.

Boehm, M., 2018, 'Causality and Hume's Foundational Project', in A. Coventry and A. Sager (eds) *The Humean Mind*, London: Routledge.

Boyd, C., 2014, 'Pride and Humility: Tempering the Desire for Excellence', in K. Timpe and C. Boyd (eds) *Virtues and their Vices,* Oxford: Oxford University Press.

Bricke, J., 1996, *Mind and Morality: An Examination of Hume's Moral Psychology*, Oxford: Oxford University Press.

Bridges, J., Kolodny, N. and Wong, H. (eds), 2011, *The Possibility of Philosophical Understanding: Reflections on the Thought of Barry Stroud*, Oxford: Oxford University Press.

Broadie, A. (ed.), 2003, *The Cambridge Companion to the Scottish Enlightenment*, Cambridge: Cambridge University Press.

Buckle, S., 2001, *Hume's Enlightenment Tract: The Unity and Purpose of* An Enquiry concerning Human Understanding, Oxford: Clarendon Press.

Butler, A., 2015, 'Hume's Doubt's about Personal Identity', in D. C. Ainslie and A. Butler (eds), *The Cambridge Companion to Hume's* Treatise, Cambridge: Cambridge University Press.

Cohon, R., 1997, 'The Common Point of View in Hume's Ethics', *Philosophy and Phenomenological Research*, 57:4, pp.827–850.

Cohon, R., 2008, *Hume's Morality*. New York/Oxford: Oxford University Press.

Coventry, A. and Sager, A. (eds), 2018, *The Humean Mind*, London: Routledge.

Craig, E. J., 1987, *The Mind of God and the Works of Man*, Oxford: Clarendon Press.

Cruise, I., 2020, 'Hume's Account of the Scope of Justice', *Hume Studies*, 46:1, pp.101–119.

Demeter, T., 2018, 'Hume on Moral Responsibility and Free Will', in A. Coventry and A. Sager (eds) *The Humean Mind*, London: Routledge.

Des Chene, D., 2006, '*Animal* as Category: Bayle's *Rorarius*', in J. Smith (ed.), *The Problem of Animal Generation in Early Modern Philosophy*, Cambridge: Cambridge University Press.

Evnine, S., 1993, 'Hume, Conjectural History, and the Uniformity of Human Nature', *Journal of the History of Philosophy*, 31:4, pp.589–606.

Falkenstein, L., 1997, 'Hume on Manners of Disposition and the Ideas of Space and Time', *Archiv für Geschichte der Philosophie*, 79:2, pp.179–201.

Falkenstein, L., 2009, 'The Ideas of Space and Time and Spatial and Temporal Ideas in *Treatise* 1.2', in D. Fate Norton and J. Taylor (eds), *The Cambridge Companion to Hume*, 2nd edition, Cambridge: Cambridge University Press.

Falkenstein, L., 2015, 'Without Gallantry and Without Jealousy: The Development of Hume's Account of Sexual Virtues and Vices', *Hume Studies*, 41:2, pp.137–170.

Fieser, J., 1998, 'Hume's Wide View of the Virtues: An Analysis of his Early Critics', *Hume Studies*, 24:2, pp.295–311.

Flew, A., 1986, *David Hume: Philosopher of Moral Science*, Oxford: Basil Blackwell.

Fodor, J., 2003, *Hume Variations*, Oxford: Oxford University Press.

Fogelin, R. J., 1985, *Hume's Scepticism in the* Treatise of Human Nature, London: Routledge and Kegan Paul.

Fogelin, R. J., 2009, *Hume's Skeptical Crisis*, Oxford: Oxford University Press.

Fosl, P., 2020, *Hume's Scepticism: Pyrrhonian and Academic*, Edinburgh: Edinburgh University Press.

Frasca-Spada, M., 1998, *Space and the Self in Hume's* Treatise, Cambridge: Cambridge University Press.

Frasca-Spada, M. and Kail, P. J. E. (eds), 2005, *Impressions of Hume*, Oxford: Clarendon Press.

Garrett, D., 1997, *Cognition and Commitment in Hume's Philosophy*, Oxford and New York: Oxford University Press.

Garrett, D., 2006, 'Hume's Naturalistic Theory of Representation', *Synthese*, 152:3, pp.301–319.

Garrett, D., 2007, 'The First Motive to Justice: Hume's Circle Argument Squared', *Hume Studies*, 33:2, pp.257–288.

Garrett, D., 2011, 'Rethinking Hume's Second Thoughts about Personal Identity', in J. Bridges, N. Kolodny, and H. Wong (eds), 2011, *The Possibility of Philosophical Understanding: Reflections on the Thought of Barry Stroud*, Oxford: Oxford University Press.

Garrett, D., 2015, *Hume*, London and New York: Routledge.

Gelfert, A., 2013, 'Hume on Curiosity', *British Journal for the History of Philosophy*, 21:4, pp.711–732.

Gill, M., 1996, 'A Philosopher in His Closet: Reflexivity and Justification in Hume's Moral Theory', *Canadian Journal of Philosophy*, 26:2, pp.231–255.

Gorman, M., 1993, 'Hume's Theory of Belief', *Hume Studies,* 19:1, pp.89–101.

Hankins, T., 1967, 'The Influence of Malebranche on the Science of Mechanics During the Eighteenth Century', *Journal of the History of Ideas*, 28:2, pp.193–210.

Hanley, R., 2019, 'Magnanimity and Modernity: Greatness of Soul and Greatness of Mind in the Enlightenment', in S. Vasalou (ed.) *The Measure of Greatness: Philosophers on Magnanimity*, Oxford: Oxford University Press.

Harcourt, E. (ed.), 2000, *Morality, Reflection, and Ideology,* Oxford: Oxford University Press.

Harris, J., 2005, *Of Liberty and Necessity: The Free Will Debate in Eighteenth-Century British Philosophy*, Oxford: Oxford University Press.

Harris, J., 2015, *Hume: An Intellectual Biography*, Cambridge: Cambridge University Press.

Harris, J., 2019 'Hume's Peculiar Definition of Justice', in I. Hunter and R. Whatmore (eds), *Philosophy, Rights and Natural Law: Essays in Honour of Knud Haakonssen*, Edinburgh: Edinburgh University Press.

Hunter, I. and Whatmore, R. (eds), 2019, *Philosophy, Rights and Natural Law: Essays in Honour of Knud Haakonssen*, Edinburgh: Edinburgh University Press.

Inoue, H., 2003, 'The Origin of the Indirect Passions in Hume's *Treatise*', *Hume Studies,* 29:2, pp.205–221.

Jacquette, D., 2001, *David Hume's Critique of Infinity*, Leiden: Brill.

James, S., 2005, 'Sympathy and Comparison: Two Principles of Human Nature', in M. Frasca-Spada and P. J. E. Kail (eds), *Impressions of Hume*, Oxford: Clarendon Press.

Jenkins, J., Whiting, J., and Williams, C. (eds), 2005, *Persons and Passions: Essays in Honor of Annette Baier*, Notre Dame: University of Notre Dame Press.

Kail, P. J. E., 2003, 'Conceivability and Modality in Hume', *Hume Studies*, 29:1, pp.43–61.

Kail, P. J. E., 2005, 'Hume's Ethical Conclusion', in M. Frasca-Spada and P. J. E. Kail (eds), *Impressions of Hume*, Oxford: Clarendon Press.

Kail, P. J. E., 2007a, *Projection and Realism in Hume's Philosophy*, Oxford: Oxford University Press.

Kail, P. J. E., 2007b, 'Leibniz's Dog and Humean Reason', *Rivista di Storia della Filosophia*, 62:3, pp. 65–80.

Kail, P. J. E., 2012, 'The Sceptical Beast in the Beastly Sceptic: Human Nature in Hume', *Royal Institute of Philosophy Supplement*, 70, pp.219–231.

Kail, P. J. E., 2014a, *Berkeley's* A Treatise Concerning the Principles of Human Knowledge: *An Introduction*, Cambridge: Cambridge University Press.

Kail, P. J. E., 2014b, 'Hume on Efficient Causation', in T. Schmaltz (ed.), *Efficient Causation: A History*, Oxford: Oxford University Press.

Kail, P. J. E., 2016, 'Hume's "Manifest Contradictions"', *Royal Institute of Philosophy Supplement*, 78, pp.147–160.

Kail, P. J. E., 2019, 'Hume and "Reason as a Kind of Cause"', in D. Perler and S. Bender (eds), *Causation and Cognition in Early Modern Philosophy*, London: Routledge.

Kail, P. J. E., 2020, '"Concerning Moral Sentiment": The Moral Sense in the *Enquiry Concerning the Principles of Morals*', in J. Taylor (ed.), *Reading Hume on the Principles of Morals*, Oxford: Oxford University Press.

Kail, P. J. E., 2025, 'Genealogy: Williams, Hume, and Nietzsche', in M. van Ackeren and M. Queloz (eds), *Bernard Williams on Philosophy and History*, Oxford: Oxford University Press.

Kemp, C., 2007, 'Contrariety in Hume', *Rivista di Storia della Filosofia*, 62:3 suppl., pp.55–64.

Korsgaard, C., 1996, *The Sources of Normativity*, Cambridge: Cambridge University Press.

Landy, D., 2006, 'Hume's Impression/Idea Distinction', *Hume Studies*, 32:1, pp.119–139.

Landy, D., 2017, 'Recent Scholarship on Hume's Theory of Representation', *European Journal of Philosophy*, 26:1, pp.333–347.

Livingston, D., 1998, *Philosophical Melancholy and Delirium: Hume's Pathology of Philosophy*, Chicago: University of Chicago Press.

Loeb, L. E., 2002, *Stability and Justification in Hume's* Treatise, New York: Oxford University Press.

Loeb, L. E., 2008, 'Inductive Inference in Hume's Philosophy', in E. S. Radcliffe (ed.), *A Companion to Hume*, Oxford: Blackwell.

Magri, T., 2015, 'Hume's Justice', in D. C. Ainslie and A. Butler (eds), *The Cambridge Companion to Hume's* Treatise, Cambridge: Cambridge University Press.

McIntyre, J., 1989, 'Personal Identity and the Passions', *Journal for the History of Philosophy*, 27:4, pp.545–557.

McNaughton, D., 1988, *Moral Vision*, Oxford: Basil Blackwell.

Marušić, J., 2010, 'Does Hume Hold a Dispositional Account of Belief?', *Canadian Journal of Philosophy*, 40:2, pp.155–183.

Mazza, E. and Ronchetti, E. (eds), 2007, *New Essays on David Hume*, Milan: FrancoAngeli.

Meeker, K., 2013, *Hume's Radical Scepticism and the Fate of Naturalized Epistemology*, Basingstoke: Palgrave Macmillan.

Mercer, P., 1972, *Sympathy and Ethics,* Oxford: Oxford University Press.

Millican, P. (ed.), 2002a, *Reading Hume on Human Understanding*, Oxford: Clarendon Press.

Millican, P., 2002b, 'Hume's Sceptical Doubts about Induction', in P. Millican (ed.) *Reading Hume on Human Understanding*, Oxford: Clarendon Press.

Millican, P., 2009, 'Hume, Causal Realism, and Causal Science', *Mind*, 118, pp.647–712.

Moore, J., 1994, 'Hume and Hutcheson', in M. A. Stewart and J. P. Wright (eds), *Hume and Hume's Connexions*, Edinburgh: Edinburgh University Press.

Noonan, H. W., 1999, *Hume on Knowledge*, London and New York: Routledge.

Norton, D. F. (ed.), 1993, *The Cambridge Companion to Hume*, 1st edition, Cambridge: Cambridge University Press.

Norton, D. F. and Taylor, J. (eds), 2009, *The Cambridge Companion to Hume*, 2nd edition, Cambridge: Cambridge University Press.

Owen, D., 2000, *Hume's Reason*, Oxford: Oxford University Press.

Pears, D., 1990, *Hume's System*, Oxford: Oxford University Press.

Pearsall, S. M. S., 2008, *Atlantic Families: Lives and Letters in the Later Eighteenth Century*, Oxford: Oxford University Press.

Penelhum, T., 2000, 'The Self of Book I and the Selves of Book II', in *Themes from Hume: The Self, the Will, Religion*, Oxford: Clarendon Press.

Penelhum, T., 2015, 'The Indirect Passions, Myself, and Others', in D. C. Ainslie and A. Butler (eds), *The Cambridge Companion to Hume's* Treatise, Cambridge: Cambridge University Press.

Perler, D. and Bender, S. (eds), 2019, *Causation and Cognition in Early Modern Philosophy*, London: Routledge.

Pickavé, M. and Shapiro, L. (eds), 2012, *Emotion and Cognitive Life in Medieval and Early Modern Philosophy*, Oxford: Oxford University Press.

Pitson, A., 2016, 'Hume, Free Will, and Moral Responsibility', in P. Russell (ed.) *The Oxford Handbook of Hume*, Oxford: Oxford University Press.

Price, H., 2011, *Naturalism without Mirrors*, Oxford: Oxford University Press.

Qu, H., 2020, *Hume's Epistemological Evolution*, Oxford: Oxford University Press.

Queloz, M., 2021, *The Practical Origins of Ideas: Genealogy as Conceptual Reverse-Engineering*, Oxford: Oxford University Press.

Radcliffe, E. S., 1994, 'Hume on Motivating Sentiments, the General Point of View, and the Inculcation of "Morality"', *Hume Studies*, 20:1, pp.37–58.

Radcliffe, E. S. (ed.), 2008, *A Companion to Hume*, Oxford: Blackwell.

Radcliffe, E. S., 2018, *Hume, Passion, and Action*, Oxford: Oxford University Press.

Richman, K. and Read, R., 2007, *The New Hume Debate*, revised edition, London: Routledge.

Ridge, M., 2003, 'Epistemology Moralized: David Hume's Practical Epistemology', *Hume Studies*, 29:2, pp.165–204.

Rorty, A., 1990, '"Pride Produces the Idea of Self": Hume on Moral Agency', *The Australasian Journal of Philosophy*, 68:3, pp.255–269.

Rocknak, S., 2018, 'Hume and the External World', in A. Coventry and A. Sager (eds) *The Humean Mind*, London: Routledge.

Rosenberg, A., 1993, 'Hume and the Philosophy of Science', in D. Fate Norton (ed.), *The Cambridge Companion to Hume*, 1st edition, Cambridge: Cambridge University Press.

Russell, B., 1979, *A History of Western Philosophy*, 2nd edition, London: Unwin.

Russell, P., 1995, *Freedom and Moral Sentiment*, Oxford: Clarendon Press.

Russell, P., 2008, *The Riddle of Hume's* Treatise*: Skepticism, Naturalism, and Irreligion*, Oxford: Oxford University Press.

Russell, P., 2015, '"Hume's Lengthy Digression": Free Will in the *Treatise*', in D. C. Ainslie and A. Butler (eds), *The Cambridge Companion to Hume's* Treatise, Cambridge: Cambridge University Press.

Russell, P. (ed.), 2016, *The Oxford Handbook of Hume*, Oxford: Oxford University Press.

Santos Castro, J., 2017, 'Hume and Conjectural History', *Journal of Scottish Philosophy*, 15:2, pp.157–174.

Sayre-McCord, G., 1994, 'On Why Hume's "General Point of View" Isn't Ideal – and Shouldn't Be', *Social Philosophy and Policy*, 11:1, pp.202–228.

Schafer, K., 2013, 'Hume's Unified Theory of Mental Representation', *European Journal of Philosophy*, 23:4, pp.978–1005.

Schmaltz, T. (ed.), 2014, *Efficient Causation: A History*, Oxford: Oxford University Press.

Schmitt, F. F., 2014, *Hume's Epistemology in the* Treatise: *A Veritistic Interpretation*, Oxford: Oxford University Press.

Schmitt, F. F., 2019, 'Hume on Induction and Probability', in A. Coventry and A. Sager (eds) *The Humean Mind*, London: Routledge.

Schmitter, A., 2012, 'Family Trees: Sympathy, Comparison, and the Proliferation of the Passions in Hume and his Predecessors', in M. Pickavé and L. Shapiro (eds), *Emotion and Cognitive Life in Medieval and Early Modern Philosophy*, Oxford: Oxford University Press.

Schneewind, J., 2000, 'Hume and the Religious Significance of Moral Rationalism', *Hume Studies*, 26:2, pp.211–224.

Smith, J. (ed.), 2006, *The Problem of Animal Generation in Early Modern Philosophy*, Cambridge: Cambridge University Press.

Smith, N. K., 1905a, 'The Naturalism of Hume', *Mind*, 14:54, pp.149–173.

Smith, N. K., 1905b, 'The Naturalism of Hume', *Mind*, 14:55, pp.335–347.

Smith, N. K., 1941, *The Philosophy of David Hume*, London: Macmillan.

Slavov, M., 2016, 'Empiricism and Relationism Intertwined: Hume and Einstein's Special Theory of Relativity', *Theoria: An International Journal for Theory, History and Foundations of Science*, 31:2, pp.247–263.

Stewart, J. B., 1992, *Opinion and Reform in Hume's Political Philosophy*, Princeton: Princeton University Press.

Stewart, M. A. (ed.), 1990, *Studies in the Philosophy of the Scottish Enlightenment*, Oxford: Clarendon Press.

Stewart, M. A., 2005, 'Hume's Intellectual Development', in M. Frasca-Spada and P. J. E. Kail (eds), *Impressions of Hume*, Oxford: Clarendon Press.

Stewart, M. A. and Wright, J. P. (eds), 1994, *Hume and Hume's Connexions*, Edinburgh: Edinburgh University Press.

Strawson, G., 1989, *The Secret Connexion: Causation, Realism and David Hume*, Oxford: Oxford University Press.

Strawson, G., 2011, *The Evident Connexion: Hume on Personal Identity*, Oxford: Oxford University Press.

Stroud, B., 1977, *Hume*, London: Routledge and Kegan Paul.

Taylor, J., 2015, *Reflecting Subjects: Passion, Sympathy, and Society in Hume's Philosophy*, Oxford: Oxford University Press.

Taylor, J., 2016, 'Hume on Pride and Other Direct Passions', in P. Russell (ed.) *The Oxford Handbook of Hume*, Oxford: Oxford University Press.

Taylor, J. (ed.), 2020, *Reading Hume on the Principles of Morals*, Oxford: Oxford University Press.

Timpe, K. and Boyd, C. (eds), 2014, *Virtues and their Vices,* Oxford: Oxford University Press.

Traiger, S. (ed.), 2006, *The Blackwell Guide to Hume's* Treatise, Oxford: Blackwell.

Turco, L., 2003, 'Moral Sense and the Foundation of Morals', in A. Broadie (ed.), *The Cambridge Companion to the Scottish Enlightenment*, Cambridge: Cambridge University Press.

Turco, L., 2007, 'Hutcheson and Hume in a Recent Polemic', in E. Mazza and E. Ronchetti (eds), *New Essays on David Hume*, Milan: FrancoAngeli.

Vasalou, S. (ed.), 2019, *The Measure of Greatness: Philosophers on Magnanimity*, Oxford: Oxford University Press.

Vitz, R., 2016, 'The Nature and Functions of Sympathy in Hume's Philosophy', in P. Russell (ed.) *The Oxford Handbook of Hume*, Oxford: Oxford University Press.

Waldow, A., 2009, *David Hume and the Problem of Other Minds*, London: Continuum.

Watts, G., 2019, *A Study of Hume's Philosophy of the Passions in Book Two of* A Treatise of Human Nature, Oxford D.Phil. thesis.

Watts, G., 2022, 'A Peculiar Mix: On the Place of Curiosity within Hume's *Treatise*', *Hume Studies*, 47:2, pp.261–283.

Waxman, W., 1994, *Hume's Theory of Consciousness*, Cambridge: Cambridge University Press.

Williams, B., 2000, 'Naturalism and Genealogy', in E. Harcourt (ed.), *Morality, Reflection, and Ideology,* Oxford: Oxford University Press.

Williams, B., 2002, *Truth and Truthfulness: An Essay in Genealogy*, Princeton: Princeton University Press.

Winkler, K., 2016, 'Hume's Skeptical Logic of Induction', in P. Russell (ed.) *The Oxford Handbook of Hume*, Oxford: Oxford University Press.

Wright, J. P., 1983, *The Sceptical Realism of David Hume*, Minneapolis: University of Minnesota Press.

Wright, J. P., 2009, *Hume's* A Treatise of Human Nature*: An Introduction*, Cambridge: Cambridge University Press.

Yolton, J., 1983, *Thinking Matter: Materialism in Eighteenth-Century Britain*, Minneapolis: University of Minnesota Press.

INDEX

Note: Page numbers followed by "n" denote endnotes.

abilities (natural) 216–18
abstract ideas 38–41, 49; of space and time 49
An Abstract of a Book Lately Published; Entituled A Treatise of Human Nature, &c. 4, 34–5, 79
Academic (mitigated) scepticism 18–20
actions: free vs. unfree 158; moral necessity of 155–6; motives for 158; and passions 158, 165, 179–80; and responsibility 158–9; right (or good) thing to do 155
adequate ideas 46–8
aesthetic experience (beauty) 182–4
Ainslie, Donald 140–1
amorous love 149–50
anger 215
animal nature: animal inference 15, 36, 69; association of ideas 35–6; external behaviour 97; vs. human nature 12–17, 37, 96–7, 173; love and hatred 150; pride and humility 145; reason 13–16, 55–6, 97
Annandale, Marquess of 3

antecedent scepticism 18
Appendix 47, 79, 124–5
Árdal, Páll 145
Aristotle 29, 212
artificial virtues *see* virtues
association of ideas 14–16, 34–42, 45; as cause of passions 136–7; physiological basis 51
association of impressions 136
associative inferences 74–5
Assurance Norm 101–3, 128
atheism 13
attitudes (propositional) 82
authority *see* government
awareness (of bodies and objects) 108–9
Ayers, Michael 166–7

Bacon, Francis 9
Baier, Annette 220
Baillie, James 150
Balfour, James 216
Bayle, Pierre 117
Beattie, James 4, 7, 216

beauty 135–6, 139, 150, 182–4, 208
behaviour 31, 37; from experience 14–15; forceful impressions 80–1; *see also* actions; animal nature
beliefs 80–1; in body 104–10; vs. conception 79, 82; conscious 82–3; in continuous existence (of objects) 105–15, 123; vs. fiction 83–4; formation of 81–2, 111–12; functionalism 81–3; vs. knowledge 76–7; in moral judgments 209; as motivation 160–7; vs. perceptions 79; pleasure (and pain) 165–7; and sentiments 83, 209–10; total extinction of 100–3, 114, 128; uncertainty of 172
benevolence 150, 184–6, 206
Berkeley, George 38–40, 109, 119, 131
bodily appetite 150
body: awareness of 108–9; belief in 104–10; existence of 103; primary/ secondary qualities 116–18; qualities of 218; relation to self 140–1; vulgar vs. philosophical view of 105–14
Book One (Of the Understanding) (1739) 2, 4, 140
Book Three ('Of Morals') (1740) 4, 6
Book Two (Of the Passions) (1739) 2, 4, 32, 37, 133
Boufflers, Comtesse de 3
Boyd, Craig 134
Burke, Edmund 95

calm passions 170–1
causal inference *see* cause and effect
causal maxim 66–7
causal power 65, 87–8, 90–1, 93
causal questions 72
causal reason 63, 115
causal relation 64–5, 90
causation 64–5, 84–5, 95–6, 143; components of 88–9; and contiguity 64, 84–5, 88–9, 139; and determinism 155–6; 'Humean theory of causation' 84–5, 121; metaphysics of 156–7; vs. moral necessity 155–7; and personal identity (self) 123–4
cause and effect 62, 64–5; causal inference 64, 68–70, 74, 86, 90–2; constant conjunction 65, 71–3, 89, 92, 121, 154; distinction of 67; experience 71; impressions vs. ideas 31; judging (8 rules) 96; natural relation of 34, 62–3; sceptical view 68–71; temporal priority of 64–5, 89
cause (definitions) 84–95
Chambers, Ephraim: *Cyclopedia* 32
character traits (natural virtues) 206, 210–15
chastity 202–4
childcare *see* parental concern
Christianity 12–13, 17, 134–5, 215–16
Circle Argument 189–90
Clarke, Samuel 67, 169, 180; *A Discourse Concerning the Unchangeable Obligations of Natural Religion* 178
closeness 137, 143, 207–8, 213
co-operation (benefits of) 192–4, 221
cognition (animal vs. human) 16–17
coherence 106, 108, 115
College of Edinburgh *see* Edinburgh University
colour 29, 39, 116–17
comparison 212–13; of objects 63, 72, 147; and passions 147–9; principle of parallel direction 148
compassion (pity) 147
compatibilism 153–4, 157
complex perceptions 25, 28
conceit (over-weaning) 212–13
conceivability (substance vs. mode) 120
conception (vs. belief) 79, 82
concepts (implications of) 60–1
conceptual empiricism 7–8, 26
conjunction (constant) 65, 71–3, 89, 92, 121, 154
connection (necessary) 65, 90–3, 154–5
consequent scepticism 18
constancy 106–8

INDEX 233

constant conjunction 65, 71–3, 89, 92, 121, 154
constant relations 56–7
contempt 149
contiguity: and causation 64, 84–5, 88–9, 139; natural relation of 34, 139, 143
contrariety 57
contrary sentiment 104, 111–12
Copy Principle *see* First Principle of Human Nature (Copy Principle)
correction (sympathetic responses) 208–9
criticism 6
Cudworth, Ralph 87
curiosity 172–5
custom 171

darkness (utter) 50
deduction (vs. demonstration) 58–9
deductive reason 58–9
definition (meaning of) 95
demonstration: of causal maxim 66–7; vs. deduction 58–9; falsity of conclusion 59–60; implications of concepts 60–1
demonstrative reason 58, 164
Descartes, René 10, 18, 87, 116–20
Des Chene, Denis 12
desires 160–2, 182–4, 198
determinism 153–5
diachronic identity (identity through time) 122
Dialogues Concerning Natural Religion 3, 13, 124
direct passions 133–4, 171–2
'Disease of the Learned' 2
dispositions *see* character traits (natural virtues)
'Dissertation on the Passions' 5
distance (two kinds of) 50
distinctions: moral 172–86, 181, 185, 219, 221; of reason 61
distinctness: existences 126; notion of 104–5, 110; perceptions 120, 126
divisibility 45–6

doctrine of double existence *see* philosophical view (of belief in bodies)
dogmatism 19
double associative relation 139–41
durable features (of mind) 158

Edinburgh 3
Edinburgh University 1, 3
Einstein, Albert 44
emotions (as perceptions) 24
emotivism 163
empiricism 7–8, 26, 166
empiricist (Hume as) 7–8, 26, 28–9, 42
An Enquiry Concerning Human Understanding 3–5, 18, 19; causal inference 70, 75, 92–3, 95–6; ideas vs. impressions 27; metaphysics of causation 156–7; nature of reason 78; notion of existence 52; scepticism 131
An Enquiry Concerning the Principles of Morals (1751) 3–5, 169, 178, 186, 194; appendix 216–17
envy 147–8
epistemological perspectives 100–3
errors *see* mistakes
essence (of substance) 119–20
evil (vs. good) 166, 172
excessive scepticism *see* Pyrrhonian (excessive) scepticism
existence 81–2; of body 103; continuous (belief in) 105–15, 123; distinct 126; external 52–3; independent (belief in) 105, 120; notion of 51–2, 71; of objects 104
experience: becomes behaviour 14–15; and causal inference 71; ownership of 125
extension: of ideas 46–7; of perceptions 121
external causes (of impressions) 32–3
external existence 52–3
externalism (epistemic) 76–8
externalism (moral judgment) 162
external objects 104, 110, 114

facility 171
Falkenstein, Lorne 202
families (vs. society) 193–4
feeling 29–33
fiction (vs. beliefs) 83–4
fidelity 203–4
First Principle of Human Nature (Copy Principle) 26–9, 42, 122
force 31, 33
'founded' (notion of) 73
Four Dissertations (1757) 3
France 2, 3
freedom 153–4, 157–8
free will 153–8, 217
functionalism 81–3

general ideas 41–2; *see also* abstract ideas
generosity 193–5
genius 173–4
geometry 48–9, 61–2
God: active power of 87; image of 13; and moral facts 178; as substance 119; superiority over man 178–80; voluntarism 178
good (moral) 185
good (vs. evil) 166, 172, 185; *see also* pleasure (and pain)
goods (scarcity of) 193–5
government (origin of) 200–2
Green, T. H. 7

habit 171
hatred 145–6
hedonism 166–7
heroic virtues 214
History of England 3
Hobbes, Thomas 14–16, 35, 67, 184, 193, 200
Home, Henry (Lord Kames) 6
human nature: vs. animal nature 12–17, 37, 96–7; Christian interpretation of 12–13; *see also* naturalism
Humean theory of causation 84–5

Humean theory of motivation 160–5, 168, 179
Hume, David 1–3
Hume's Law 181
humility 134–5, 137, 149; causes of 138–9; influence of sympathy 144–5; and self 141; as virtue 214
Hutcheson, Francis 206–7, 215, 219–20; *Illustrations on the Moral Sense* (1728) 181; *An Inquiry into the Original of Our Ideas of Beauty and Virtue* (1726) 182–6
hypotheses 10–11

ideas: abstract 38–41, 49; adequate 46–8; association of 14–15, 35–42, 45, 51, 136–7; expressing 8; extended 46–7; force/vivacity of 80–1, 83–4, 131; vs. impressions 15, 25–33; infinite divisibility of 45; original vs. secondary 133; particular 40; relative 53; of space and time 45–8
identity: diachronic (through time) 122; numerical 106–8, 122–3; personal 123–5, 140; through change 123
images (ideas as) 30, 34
imagination 30; association of ideas 34–8; belief in continuous existence 106; principles of 114–15; substance 113–14; trayne of the imagination 15, 35
impressions: as adequate representations 48; association of 136; causal inference 71–2, 80; coherence 106, 108; constancy 106–8; effects on the mind 116–17; force/vivacity of 80–1; vs. ideas 15, 25–33; as instances of feelings 31–2; and morality 185; of necessary connection 91–2; original vs. secondary 133–4; of physical objects 116–17; of pleasure and pain 185; of reflection vs. sensation 31–2, 49
incompatibilism 155

inconstant relations 56–7
independence (substance vs. mode) 120
indifference, liberty of 155, 157–8, 217–18
indirect passions 133–4, 136, 206
indirect realism 109
induction (problem of) 69, 73, 160
inductive inferences 72
inference: animal 15, 36, 69; associative 74–5; Assurance Norm 101, 128–9; causation of 72–4; of cause and effect 68–70; inductive 72; just 70–1, 77; vs. reason 14–15, 63, 72; Uniformity Principle (UP) 69, 72–8
infidelity 203
injustice 195
intellectual abilities 216–19
intentionality (of passions) 168
interest (passion of) 195, 199
internalism 77, 162–3, 169, 179
intuition (of relations) 57
iterative reflection 130–1

judgment (of reasoning) 100–3
justice 188–200
justifying reasons 161

Kemp Smith, Norman 8, 10
knowledge: vs. belief 76–7; objects of 57; *a priori* 10–12, 61–2; and probability 101
Korsgaard, Christine 220

language *see* linguistic meaning
Leibniz, Gottfried Wilhelm 13–14, 119; association of ideas 35–7, 74; *Monadology* 15; *New Essays on Human Understanding* 15; potency of ideas 80; on reason 55–6, 74–5
Leland, John 216
A Letter from a Gentleman to his Friend in Edinburgh 2, 7
liberty of indifference 155, 157–8, 217–18

liberty of spontaneity 157
linguistic meaning 8, 16
liveliness 30, 80, 130
Locke, John 28, 47–8, 67, 116–17, 166–7; abstract ideas 38, 40; *Essay Concerning Human Understanding* 36; indirect realism 109; and personal identity (self) 124
logic (as subject) 6
Longman, Thomas 2
love 145–6, 149–50, 216–17

magnanimity 212
Malebranche, Nicolas 11, 21n23, 87, 117; animal inference 36; communication of the passions 145; on morality 169, 178; *The Search After Truth* 33; on substance 119
malice 147
Mandeville, Bernard 145, 184, 196, 221
manifest contradictions 128–30
materialism 119
material substance 119–20
mathematics 61–2, 178–9
matter (vs. thought) 121
meaning (acquiring) 8
melancholy (of Hume) 127–9
memory 14, 124
methodological naturalism 9–12
mind 120, 141; as bundle of perceptions 118, 121, 124–7, 140; durable features of 158; true idea of 140
minima sensibilia 46
mistakes (resemblance) 50–1
mitigated scepticism *see* Academic (mitigated) scepticism
mode (vs. substance) 28, 120–2
modus ponens 58–9
de Montaigne, Michel 17
moral distinctions 181, 185, 219, 221; deriv'd from a moral sense 182–6; not deriv'd from reason 177–82
moral facts 178–9
moral good (and ill) 185

morality 13, 169; emotivism 163; and impressions 185; and reason 169, 177, 179–80; and religion 220–1
moral judgment 162–3, 169, 179, 209
moral necessity (of actions) 155–6
moral non-cognitivism 163, 179, 181
moral obligations 181–2
moral quality (of relations) 180
moral rationalism 178
morals (as subject) 6
moral sense 182, 184–6, 206–7, 221
moral sentiments 186, 189–90, 196, 207–9
moral subjects 9
moral truths 179
moral virtues *see* virtues
motivating reasons 161
motivation 221; and beliefs 160–7; Humean theory of 160–5, 168, 179; moral internalism 162–3; moral judgment 162–3; pride as 214
motives (for actions) 158, 179–80
'*My Own Life*' 2

natural (vs. non-natural) 87–8
natural abilities 216
naturalisation project 13, 16
naturalism 8–9, 88, 145; inference of cause and effect 68, 88; methodological 9–12; object vs. subject 88, 90; ontological 12, 88; and religion 220–1; subject naturalism 87
natural philosophy 9
natural relations 34, 37, 42
natural religion 13
natural temper 193
natural virtues *see* virtues
natural world (conceptions of) 87
nature 12, 119
necessary connection 65, 90–3, 154–5
necessity 155–8; moral vs. causal 155–7
Newton, Sir Isaac 10–12
non-cognitivism (moral) 163, 179, 181

Noon, John 2
normativity 220
nosiness (vs. curiosity) 175
numerical identity 106–8, 122–3

object naturalism 88
objects: appearances 47–8; comparison 63, 72; continuous 49–50, 109–10, 123; external 104, 110, 114; impossible 39–40; of knowledge 57; perceptions of 25, 53–4, 105–6, 109; primary/secondary qualities 116–18; relative idea of 53
obligation (sense of) 181–2, 198–9, 201–2
occupation (vs. possession) 197
'Of miracles' 13
'Of the Dignity or Meanness of Human Nature' 17
ontological naturalism 12, 88
ought (vs. is) 180–1
outward circumstances (instability of goods) 193–8

pain (and pleasure) *see* pleasure (and pain)
parental concern 202–3
Paris 3
particular ideas 40
passions: calm vs. violent 170–1; causes of 135–9, 142, 169–70; curiosity 172–3; direct and indirect 133–4, 136, 171–2, 206; durability of 138; external advantages and disadvantages 139, 141; habit and custom 171; intentionality of 168; limitations (refinements) 137–8, 144; motivation for actions 158, 165; principle of parallel direction 148; vs. reason 164–8; as secondary (reflective) impressions 134, 142, 147; subject/object vs. quality 135–6, 139; *see also* beliefs; pleasure (and pain)

perceptions 23–4, 139–40; awareness of 109; vs. beliefs 79; constancy 107; distinctness 120, 126; double relation of 136; emotions as 24; (non-)extended 120–1; faint 26, 32; impressions vs. ideas 15, 25–33, 53; of objects and things 25, 53–4, 105–6, 109–10; of sensation vs. reflection 24–5; simple vs. complex 25–8, 30; substance vs. mode 120–2
personal identity 123–7, 140
philosophers (ancient) 113–14
Philosophical Essays in Human Understanding see An Enquiry Concerning Human Understanding
philosophical relations 34, 56–7, 84, 88–9
philosophical view (of belief in bodies) 105–12, 114
pity *see* compassion (pity)
pleasure (and pain) 139, 165–7, 169, 172, 185
Political Discourses (1752) 3
politics (as subject) 6
positivism 8
possession 196–8; *see also* goods (scarcity of)
power 113, 139–40; *see also* causal power
practical reasons 161
prescription (long possession) 197
Price, Huw 87
pride 134–7, 145, 149; causes of 138–9; influence of sympathy 144–5; as motivation 214; and self 137–9, 141; subject/object vs. quality 135–6, 139; as virtue 212, 214–15; *see also* conceit (over-weaning)
principle of parallel direction (of passions) 148
principles of association 123–7; *see also* association of ideas
a priori knowledge 10–12, 61–2
priority (temporal) 64–5, 89

probable reason 62–4, 73–4, 79, 97, 101–3
promises 197–200
property (rules of) 197–8
property rights (respect for) 190, 191, 195
proportion (relation of) 178–9
propositional attitudes 82
prudence 15–16, 186
pseudo-reason 74
psychology 108
psychology of religion 13
Pyrrhonian (excessive) scepticism 16, 18–19

quality (degree in) 57
Quine, W. V. O. 86

rationalism (moral) 178
rational reflection 128–9
realism (indirect) 109
reason (reasoning): Assurance Norm 101–3, 128–9; belief in continuous existence 105, 131; deductive 58–9; demonstrative 58, 164; distinction of 61; divine origin of 164; faculty of 63, 75; fallibility of 101; humans vs. animals 13–16, 37, 55–6; vs. inference 14–15, 63, 72; internalist vs. externalist view 76–8, 179; judgment of 100–3; vs. memory 14; and morality 169, 177, 179–80; vs. passions 164–8; probable 62–4, 73–4, 79, 97, 101; pseudo-reason 74; rules and norms 101; shadow of reason 74; Title Principle 130–1
reason alone 164–6
reasons (motive to action) 161, 164–8
reflection 99–100, 219; iterative 130–1; motivation for 130; normativity 220; perceptions of 24–5; rational 128–9
regularity theory 85
Reid, Thomas 4, 7

relations 34; causal 64–5; close 137, 139, 143; double associative relation 136, 139–41; of fitness and unfitness 178–9; intuition of 57; moral quality of 180; natural 34, 37, 42; objects of knowledge 57; philosophical 56, 84, 88–9; pride and self 137–9; of proportion 178–9
relative idea (of objects) 53
reliabilism 75–6
religion: Hume as atheist 13; and morality 220–1; moral virtues 215–16; 'natural' religion 13; psychology of 13; *see also* Christianity
representations 27, 48
reputation 196, 199
resemblance (natural relation of) 34, 37, 41, 57, 136; and memory 124; mistakes 50–1; and personal identity (self) 123–4; sympathy 143
resolution (of promise) 198
respect 149
responsibility (for actions) 158–9
riches (as cause of pride) 139–40
Rorty, Amelia 138
Rousseau, Jean-Jacques 3
Russell, Bertrand 7
Russell, Paul 158

sameness (numerical and qualitative) 106
scepticism 103; Academic (mitigated) 18–20; antecedent vs. consequent 18; of Hume 7, 8, 16–17, 33, 129–30; inference of cause and effect 68–71; internalism 77; problem of induction 69; Pyrrhonian (excessive) 16, 18–19; Title Principle 130–1
science 9–12
self: as bundle of perceptions 122–7; as cause of passions 135–6, 139; enduring 124, 142; features of 141; notion of 122–5, 140–3; pride and humility 137–9, 141, 212; relation to body 140–1; as substance 122–3; and sympathy 142–3; *see also* soul
self-consciousness 141
self-interest 191, 195, 201–2, 221
selfishness (natural) 194–5
selfish theory 184, 191–2
sensation 24–5, 31–2
sense (moral) *see* moral sense
sense experience 8, 15, 26
senses 24–5, 29–30, 105–6; *see also* moral sense
sentiments 142–3, 186; and beliefs 83, 209–10; contrary sentiment 104, 111–12; *see also* moral sentiments
separability principle 60–1
sexual appetite 202
simple perceptions 25–7, 30
Smith, Adam 150
social abilities 216
society (emergence of) 192–5, 200
Socrates 9
solidity 118
soul 118–21, 123, 124
space 50
space and time 45–9
spectator (perspective of) 157–8
Spinoza, Baruch 47–8, 119
spontaneity, liberty of 157
Stanhope, Lord 44
Stewart, Dugald 192
Strahan, William 44
Strawson, Galen 95
strict identity 123
subject naturalism 87, 88, 90
substance 119–23
succession (and time) 49–50
sympathy 137, 142–4, 147–50, 195–6; degrees of 149; extensive vs. limited 149; influence on pride and humility 144–5, 212–13; and moral sense 207–8; and sense of self 142–3; variability of 207–9

temper (natural) 193
theology 216
theoretical reasons 161
things *see* objects
thinking (vs. feeling) 29–33
thought 121, 125
time 49–50
time and space 45–9
Title Principle 130–1
traits (character) 206
truth 172–5, 179

uncertainty (of beliefs) 172
Uniformity Principle (UP) 69, 72–8
utter darkness 50

vacuum 50
valuable (meaning of) 136
value (of truth) 175
vanity 221
vice (impression of) 185

violent passions 170–1
virtue, conception of 13
virtues 168–9, 178, 186; artificial 189–91, 199–202; heroic 214; impression of 185; of justice 190–1, 196; moral 186, 216–19; natural 205–15; vs. natural abilities 216–19; natural vs. artificial 186, 189, 199–200; in rags 211; useful (to others) 215; (in)voluntary 217–18
vivacity 30, 33, 80, 131
voluntarism 178
vulgar view (of belief in bodies) 105–10, 114

wants 206
wellbeing 206
will (free) *see* free will
willing (act of) 198
women 202–3
words (and linguistic meaning) 8, 16

For Product Safety Concerns and Information please contact our EU
representative GPSR@taylorandfrancis.com
Taylor & Francis Verlag GmbH, Kaufingerstraße 24, 80331 München, Germany

www.ingramcontent.com/pod-product-compliance
Lightning Source LLC
Chambersburg PA
CBHW070314240426
43661CB00057B/2643